WHERE ID WAS

Disseminations: Psychoanalysis in Contexts

Series Editor: Anthony Molino

Reason and Unreason: Psychoanalysis, Science and Politics Michael Rustin

Ecstasy Michael Eigen

Dreams and Drama: Art and Psychoanalytic Criticism Alan Roland

The Vitality of Objects: Exploring the Work of Christopher Bollas edited by Joseph Scalia

Culture, Subject, Psyche: Anthropology, Social Theory and Psychoanalysis Anthony Molino and Wesley Shumar

WHERE ID WAS

Challenging Normalization in Psychoanalysis

Edited by

Anthony Molino and Christine Ware

CONTINUUM
London and New York

CONTINUUM

The Tower Building, 11 York Road, London SE1 7NX
370 Lexington Avenue, New York, NY 10017-6503
www.continuumbooks.com

First published 2001

British Library Cataloguing-in-Publication Data
A catalogue record for this book is available from the British Library.

ISBN 0 8264 5580 8 (paperback)
     0 8264 5579 4 (hardback)

Designed and typeset by Acorn Bookwork, Salisbury, Wiltshire
Printed and bound in Great Britain by Biddles Ltd, Guildford and King's Lynn

Contents

In memory of Marie Coleman Nelson and Donald Ware

The standard translation of Freud's, 'Wo Es war, soll Ich werden' is 'Where id was, ego will be.' Lacan speaks against a warrior psyche, where ego dislodges id. His version is more like, 'I will go where it is. I will go where you are. I will follow you. I will go with you-it. I'll return to the place of dreams, to the place dreams come from, through the dream navel.' Another formulation might be, 'My home is in the field of the unconscious, the unrealized-unrealizable. My home is Mystery.'

(Michael Eigen, *Ecstasy*)

Acknowledgements

'Psychoanalysis as a surrogate for life experience' (La psicoanalisi come surrogato della vita) by Simona Argentieri originally appeared (in Italian) in *Micromega* 3/98. Translated and reprinted by permission of the author.

'Cutting', from *Being a Character: Psychoanalysis and Self Experience* (pp. 137–43) by Christopher Bollas. Copyright © 1992 by Christopher Bollas. Reprinted by permission of the author, in conjunction with Hill & Wang, a division of Farrar, Strauss and Giroux, LLC; and with Routledge, London.

An earlier version of 'Sexuality, psychoanalysis, and social changes' by Juliet Mitchell originally appeared in The Institute of Psycho-Analysis Newsletter, Summer 1998. Reprinted by permission of the author, in conjunction with Stephen Grosz, editor of the *Institute of Psycho-Analysis News & Events*.

'Psychoanalysis: a rendezvous with disappointment' by Chris Oakley originally appeared in *The Irish Forum for Psychoanalysis*, vol. 4, no. 2. Reprinted by permission of the author.

'The possibilities of pleasure: a conversation with Adam Phillips' from *Freely Associated: Encounters in Psychoanalysis with Christopher Bollas, Joyce McDougall, Michael Eigen, Adam Phillips, and Nina Coltart*, edited by Anthony Molino, Free Association Books, 1997. Reprinted by permission of Free Association Books.

An earlier version of 'Freud-baiting' by Paul Williams originally appeared in *The Sunday Times*, 26 June 1994. Copyright © Paul Williams/Times Newspapers Limited, 1994. Reprinted by permission of the author, in conjunction with the Syndication Department of Times Newspapers Limited.

'Analysis: growth or cure?' (Psicoanalisi: Guarigione o Crescita?) by Luigi Zoja originally appeared (in Italian) in *Coltivare l'anima* (Moretti & Vitali, 1999). Translated and reprinted by permission of the author.

'Delirium, or the sway of desire' by Anthony Molino originally appeared in *JPCS: Journal for the Psychoanalysis of Culture and Society*, vol. 6, no. 1 (Spring 2001). Copyright 2001 The Ohio State University. All rights reserved.

Notes on Contributors

Pina Antinucci-Mark (translator) is a full member of the British Psycho-Analytical Society. She works in London, in both private practice and at the Anna Freud Centre.

Simona Argentieri is a training and supervising analyst with the Italian Association for Psychoanalysis (Associazione Italiana di Psicoanalisi). Based in Rome, she is also a full member of the International Psychoanalytical Association and co-author of the psychoanalytic classic, *The Babel of the Unconscious*.

David M. Black took a first-class degree in Philosophy at Edinburgh University and an MA in Eastern Religions at Lancaster. A founder member of the Institute of Psychotherapy and Counselling, since 1974 he has been on the staff of the Westminster Pastoral Foundation, London. After training as a psychoanalyst with the British Psycho-Analytical Society, he now works mainly in private practice.

Christopher Bollas earned his BA in History at the University of California and his PhD in Literature at the State University of New York at Buffalo. He began clinical work with autistic children in 1967 and alongside his clinical career has taught English at the University of Massachusetts while he was Director of Education of the Austen Riggs Center. His latest book is *Hysteria*. He practises in London and lives in London and North Dakota.

Vincent Crapanzano is Distinguished Professor of Anthropology and Comparative Literature at the Graduate Center of the City University of New York. Among his many works are the celebrated ethnography *Tuhami: Portrait of a Moroccan*, as well as the essays collected in *Hermes' Dilemma and Hamlet's Desire: On the Epistemology of Interpretation*. His most recent book is *Serving the World: Literalism in America from the Pulpit to the Bench*.

Patricia Gherovici is a Lacanian analyst in private practice in Philadelphia and a founding member of the Philadelphia Lacan Seminar. She has published in numerous journals and collections internationally and has most recently contributed to *The Subject of Lacan* and *Lacan in America*. Former clinical director of a Latino mental health clinic in Philadelphia's *barrio*, she is currently completing *Puerto Rican Syndrome: Freud, Lacan, and the Barrio's Hysteria*, forthcoming from Other Press.

James Hillman is a former director of studies at the Jung Institute in Zurich and a Founding Fellow of the Dallas Institute of Humanities. Dr Hillman has written more than 20 books on archetypal psychology, ecopsychology, and the human condition. His *Revisioning Psychology* was nominated for a Pulitzer Prize in 1975. His most recent books are *The Soul's Code: In Search of Character and Calling*, *The Force of Character*, *Politica della Bellezza* and a new edition of *Pan and the Nightmare*.

Suzanne R. Kirschner is Assistant Professor of Psychology at the College of the Holy Cross in Worcester, Massachusetts. She received her doctorate from Harvard University, where she was a Lecturer in the Committee on Degrees in Social Studies and a Research Fellow in the Department of Social Medicine at Harvard Medical School. She has published a number of articles on the philosophy and history of psychology and psychoanalysis, as well as a book, *The Religious and Romantic Origins of Psychoanalysis*. Recent publications include the entry on Postmodern Psychology in the Oxford *Encyclopaedia of Psychology*.

Dorinne Kondo is Director of Asian American Studies and Professor of Anthropology and American Studies and Ethnicity at the University of Southern California. The author of *Crafting Selves: Power, Gender, and Discourses of Identity in a Japanese Workplace*, and *About Face: Performing Race in Fashion and Theater*, she is the recipient of fellowships from both the Getty Foundation and the National Endowment for the Humanities for her forthcoming *Re(visions) of Race*, a book on cross-racial performances and new racial formations.

Robert Jay Lifton is Distinguished Professor of Psychiatry and Psychology at John Jay College and the Graduate Center of the City University of New York, and at the Mt Sinai School of Medicine. He is also the Director of the Center on Violence and Human Survival.

Among his many celebrated books are: *The Broken Connection: On Death and the Continuity of Life, Death in Life: Survivors of Hiroshima* (winner of the 1967 National Book Award), and *The Protean Self: Human Resilience in an Age of Fragmentation*. He is also co-editor with M.T. Singer and J. Lalich of *Cults in Our Midst*.

David Marriott is a lecturer in English at the University of London. His publications include *On Black Men*, as well as numerous articles on psychoanalysis and race. He is currently working on a collection of essays on psychoanalysis, race and modernism.

Juliet Mitchell is a full member of the Institute of Psychoanalysis, London and the International Psychoanalytic Association. Her most recent book, *Mad Men and Medusas*, was published by Allen Lane, Penguin Press. She is a lecturer on Gender and Society at Cambridge University where she is a Fellow of Jesus College.

Anthony Molino is a psychoanalyst and literary translator. Based in Italy, he is the *Disseminations* Series Editor and counts among his works: *Freely Associated: Encounters in Psychoanalysis*; *The Couch and the Tree: Dialogues in Psychoanalysis and Buddhism* (ed.); and *Squiggles and Spaces: Revisiting the Work of D.W. Winnicott* (co-editor). With Wesley Shumar he is co-author of the forthcoming *Culture, Subject, Psyche: Anthropology, Social Theory and Psychoanalysis*.

Chris Oakley is a psychoanalyst working with the Site for Contemporary Psychoanalysis in London. His most recent publications are as a contributor to *Returns of the 'French Freud': Freud, Lacan and Beyond* (edited by Todd Dufresne), and as editor of *What is a Group? A Fresh Look at Theory in Practice*.

Haya Oakley has been a psychoanalyst in private practice in London for over 30 years. She is the Chair of the Site for Contemporary Psychoanalysis and a member of the Guild of Psychotherapists. A contributor to a number of books on psychotherapy, she is currently editing a book on psychosis.

Noreen O'Connor is co-author, with Joanna Ryan, of *Wild Desires and Mistaken Identities: Lesbianism and Psychoanalysis* and a contributor to *Disorienting Sexuality: Psychoanalytic Reappraisals of Sexual Identities*

(Thomas Domenici and Ronnie C. Lesser, eds). She works in full-time private practice in London.

Adam Phillips is a child psychotherapist in London, and General Editor for Penguin's new collection of the works of Sigmund Freud. His most recent works are *Promises, Promises: Essays on Psychoanalysis and Literature* and *Houdini's Box*.

Jeffrey B. Rubin practises psychoanalysis and psychoanalytically oriented psychotherapy in New York City and Bedford Hills, New York. He has taught at the Postgraduate Center for Mental Health, the Object Relations Institute, the C.G. Jung Foundation of New York, and Yeshiva University. He is the author of *Psychotherapy and Buddhism: Toward an Integration*; *A Psychoanalysis for Our Time: Exploring the Blindness of the Seeing I*; and the forthcoming *Psychoanalysis and the Good Life: Reflections on Love, Ethics, Creativity, and Spirituality* and *The Art of Living*.

Wesley Shumar holds a Master's degree in Cinema Studies and a PhD in Cultural Anthropology. He is an Assistant Professor of Anthropology in the Culture and Communication Department at Drexel University in Philadelphia. With Anthony Molino he is co-author of the forthcoming *Culture, Subject, Psyche: Anthropology, Social Theory and Psychoanalysis*.

M. Guy Thompson trained with R.D. Laing at the Philadelphia Association in London. He received his PhD in Clinical Psychology from the Wright Institute, Berkeley, and is Founder and Director of Free Association, Inc. in San Francisco. Dr Thompson is author of *The Death of Desire: A Study in Psychopathology*; *The Truth About Freud's Technique: The Encounter with the Real*; and the forthcoming *The Enigma of Honesty: The Fundamental Rule of Psychoanalysis*.

Christine Ware is a graduate of the University of Pennsylvania and Temple University, Philadelphia. She received her analytic training at the Philadelphia School of Psychoanalysis. A practising psychotherapist in Philadelphia for more than ten years, Ms Ware now earns her living as a computer programmer.

Paul Williams is a member of both the British Psycho-Analytical Society and the Royal Anthropological Institute. A Professor at Anglia Polytechnic University, Dr Williams is Deputy Editor of the *Inter-*

national Journal of Psychoanalysis. His published works include *Unimaginable Storms: A Search for Meaning in Psychosis* (with Murray Jackson); and *A Language for Psychosis* (ed.).

Polly Young-Eisendrath is a psychologist and Jungian psychoanalyst practising in Burlington, Vermont. Clinical Associate Professor of Psychiatry at the University of Vermont Medical College, she has published ten books, many chapters and articles, and lectures on resilience, women's development, couple relationship, and the interface of psychoanalysis and spirituality. Her most recent books are *Women and Desire: Beyond Wanting to be Wanted: Being Human* and *The Psychology of Mature Spirituality: Integrity, Wisdom, Transcendence* (edited with Melvin Miller).

Luigi Zoja, former President of CIPA (Italian Centre for Analytical Psychology), has served in recent years as both Vice-President and President of the International Association of Analytical Psychology. The author of several volumes in Italian, his translated works include *Drugs, Addiction and Initiation: The Secret Search for Ritual* and *Growth and Guilt: Psychology and the Limits of Development*. His most recent title, *The Father*, looks at the history of fatherhood as a social construction.

Introduction

Wo Es war, soll Ich werden. Freud's dictum of 1933 has, in many ways, come to define the psychoanalytic project throughout most of the discipline's first century. This project, however, is not a monolithic one – as is readily attested by two of the better-known English translations of Freud's celebrated phrase. In point of fact, entirely different philosophical and, ultimately, ideological claims are staked, depending on whether one identifies in those words the cornerstone of American ego psychology ('where id was, there ego shall be') or the hymn to subjectivity that is the manifesto of a Lacanian psychoanalysis ('where id was, there I shall become'). Whatever the case, it remains true that the psychoanalytic project, in its many visions and versions, takes as its starting point the notion of a metaphorical space, of a 'place' in the psyche understood as a locus of dynamism and change. 'Where id was' suggests, in fact, a movement: a displacement of something altogether amorphous, unruly, and indeed tumultuous, dislodged from that space in favour of a greater value. Of an outcome arguably privileged not only as the end result of a psychoanalysis, but of the project of a human life as well.

But the problem of value is not a negligible one. Robert Pirsig, in his justly praised *Zen and the Art of Motorcycle Maintenance*,[1] makes this point as cogently and sharply as anyone. For the problem of value evokes dimensions of experience traditionally and all too frequently seen as alien to the psychoanalytic project: we refer here to the dimensions of ethics, civics, aesthetics, even politics. Issues of value bear inevitably on the idea of the kind of society one wishes to live in, and of the quality of human relations that might define or govern such a society. Again, we realize that such concerns have long been regarded as tangential to the more immediate concerns of a clinical psychoanalysis. But this, we would argue, is true only to the extent that adherents, proponents and practitioners of psychoanalysis ignore the discipline's own conception as a metapsychology, and indeed a *Weltanschauung*, and not simply as a therapeutics; this, we argue, is true only if we fail to recognize how the dominant values of a given society come, through our own personal

efforts, to inform, suffuse and even shape cultural praxes like psychoanalysis. Such a failure betrays, at best, an 'unconscious' or acritical assent
to the influence of such values, while it inspires – at worst – attitudes
ranging from resigned submission to open acceptance and celebration of
those values. In today's globalized consumer culture, one such insidious
and unquestioned value – which, applied to the psychoanalytic project,
has in some instances come to occupy the 'spaces' of 'where id was' – is
that of *normalization.*

Among the many 'returns to Freud' of recent years, the recovery of the
first psychoanalyst's radical challenge to the dominant culture of his day
has yet to be fully propounded. And yet, in a time when values of
conformity and adaptation, or what we call normalization, pervade not
only our society but the consulting rooms and mindsets of increasing
numbers of psychoanalysts, it is important to sift through the ossifica-
tions of Freudian theory to recapture the early, political spirit of Freud's
discoveries. Many psychoanalysts, some prominent, others lesser known,
are doing just that, in an attempt to focus attention on the inherently
political dimensions both of human existence and of psychoanalytic
culture. To date, however, the work of these thinkers, writers and clinicians has not been collected in a representative volume that would
highlight both their individual concerns as well as the broad spectrum of
social realities from which their concerns spring. This is a gap that the
'challenges' of *Where Id Was* intend to fill.

Where id was, there shall normalization be? In the preface to his 1983
*The Repression of Psychoanalysis: Otto Fenichel and the Political
Freudians*,[2] social historian Russell Jacoby writes:

> The specter of psychoanalysis continues to haunt society; few,
> however, are frightened. Over the years the ghost has become a
> ghost of itself. It traded a threatening, sometimes revolutionary,
> mien for an affable comportment ... Once incorporated into
> medical schools, psychoanalysis came to attract those who find
> security in conformity and propriety.

Jacoby ends his book with reflections on what he calls 'The Americaniza-
tion of Psychoanalysis', and with an overview of the life and times of a
psychoanalyst best known, perhaps, for the title of a book later adopted
for a film. *Rebel Without a Cause* was not, however, the sum total of
Robert Lindner's legacy.[3] A fierce critic of medicalization (or what has

since become known as the dominant 'medical model' of psychoanalysis), Lindner, over forty years ago, was already writing: 'Today, in the struggle between man and Society over the issue of conformity, Society is winning.' According to Jacoby, 'Lindner signified a final and eloquent protest against the impoverishment of American psychoanalysis.'

Where Id Was takes as its starting point not only the idea, but the historical fact, that a political element persists in both American and continental psychoanalysis. In order, however, to build on Jacoby's work and not to see Lindner's own as the swansong of the political conscience of psychoanalysis, it is important to understand the broadened scope and definition of what now constitutes 'the political' in a postmodern society such as our own. From a 1996 pamphlet of London's 'Rolling Parliament', a grass-roots organization working to challenge and extend England's political agenda, comes an echo of this 'new politics' (and of the values it encodes): 'Unless and until politics includes much more fully the dimensions of psychology, ethics, ecology and religion, we are faced with catastrophic breakdown.' It is the internalization and recognition of similar concerns and related perspectives within psychoanalysis that have inspired this collection, intended as a testament to that radicalizing presence within the profession that insists on challenging mainstream processes of conformity, adjustment and 'normalization'.

'Since psychoanalysis is my home,' wrote Robert Stoller, 'I feel free not to treat it politely. It needs constant upkeep and can always use renewal.'[4] This attitude is shared by the authors in this volume. While greatly respectful of psychoanalysis, they all challenge the domestications of established theory and practice. They also challenge the growing cultural, political and economic prejudice against psychoanalysis, both as a philosophy and a treatment method. (See, for example, British analyst Paul Williams' chapter in response to the assaults on Freud and his theories by Frederick Crewes and others.) For while those who would defend Freud locate his legacy at the intersections of art and science, and see it as perhaps the most thorough and systematic attempt to explore and understand the human condition, there are those who would denounce that legacy as a misguided pseudoscience. Indeed, the passion and violence with which the debate over Freud has been waged highlight the love–hate relationship that society maintains with the founder of psychoanalysis and, perhaps more significantly, with his ideas. In our view, these passionate exchanges mark a place where the potential for explosive growth exists alongside the possibility of gratuitous debasement. And yet the adoption of a Manichaean position which privileges Freud as either god or guru is, while tempting, an arid one. For such a position, from either side, opens the door to normalizing forces which invariably demand submission and preclude the freedom and curiosity essential to creativity and innovation. Such tensions, and the resulting temptations of authoritarianism, were not unknown to Freud. Our hope, in fact, is that this book will reflect something of the curiosity and creativity that enabled Freud's own original inquiry, and helped steer it clear of the pitfalls of self-serving dogmatism. For it is no secret that, despite his shortcomings and blind spots, Freud's basic attitude was a genuinely critical one, forever intent on rethinking and refining the intuitions and discoveries that first gave birth to psychoanalysis.

Against such a backdrop, the structure of this book attempts to illustrate some of the tensions that exist within psychoanalysis today. There must be structure of some kind to fathom these tensions and yet, in many ways, the content of the book is constantly subverting the structure. Parts bleed into and feed off each other; chapters at once fall into different categories. Thus were we reminded, when mapping out this volume, of T.S. Eliot's admonition:

> Words strain,
> Crack and sometimes break, under the burden,
> Under the tension, slip, slide, perish,
> Decay with imprecision, will not stay in place,
> Will not stay still.[5]

So too these chapters, these challenges to normalization, will not stay still in places like 'Reappraisals', 'At the Boundaries of Theory and Practice', 'Self and Culture', and 'Challenging Normalization in Psychoanalysis'. Such designations are at the same time both purposeful and arbitrary, a door in and a door out. In many ways, ours is an interdisciplinary project, dedicated to exploring the relationship between psychoanalysis and contemporary culture. To this end, and as we have already suggested, it is a project that involves the production of a critique from within psychoanalysis that is little invested in the preservation of psychoanalysis as a master discourse. To the contrary: it is through the deployment of strategies concerned with reflexivity, representation, narrativity, and literary and feminist discourses that psychoanalysis now situates its basic insights on the nature of consciousness and the construction of the self within a world that is increasingly multiple and fragmented – a world which, precisely because of these centrifugal tendencies, is faced as never before with the reactive pressures of normalization. In this context, we see psychoanalysis in the throes of a fertile crisis of 'identity' and redefinition which by necessity calls into question its relationship with other disciplines.

The thresholds between psychoanalysis and other fields are interesting, fertile and sometimes disorienting places. So while the chapters in *Where Id Was* reflect, on the one hand, the capacity of psychoanalysis to rethink and examine itself critically from within, they also seek out genuine interdisciplinary encounters, instances of diverse energies capable of infusing each other with new insights and findings. Consider, for example, anthropologist Vincent Crapanzano's reflections on other cultures' challenging conceptualizations and constructs of self. Crapanzano's explorations of the blurred borders of so-called 'reality' and personal experience – suggesting how one culture's psychosis is another's demonic possession – remind us of the cultural specificities of psychoanalysis and of the dangerous ethnocentrism of its universalist claims. It is precisely such 'moments of the self', those liminal spaces investigated by the likes of Crapanzano, Dorinne Kondo, and others in this volume, that help chart new courses for the future of psychoanalysis.

There are, of course, also such spaces or thresholds within psychoanalysis, between its own competing traditions and truth claims. As with any collection, restrictions of space and the privileges accorded to the editors of such a volume necessarily reflect personal biases and aims. But to ignore in this context the expanding 'political' voice of analysts from the Jungian tradition would amount, today, to a gross act of negligence. From Luigi Zoja's inquiry into the epistemology of psychoanalysis to James Hillman's revisitation of its failures and promise to Polly Young-Eisendrath's denunciation of the ideology of 'biobabble', these authors do more than illustrate important developments within an increasingly diversified Jungian community. It is, in fact, our impression that they also embody a radical presence which attests to a growing and welcome critique of the essentialism inherent in much traditional Jungian thought.

The theme of this book is normalization. It is a phenomenon, an attitude, a value, that sneaks into treatment rooms and wafts through musty, historic halls. It exerts pressure on contemporary analytic theorizing as well as on psychoanalytic institutes, regardless of theoretical persuasion. It pushes for similarity and uniformity, in an attempt to mould the singularities and idiosyncrasies of human experience into decipherable and reliable diagnostic categories. Normalization, like it or not, is everywhere. And it has, for a long time, been a silent partner in psychoanalysis. Perhaps it is time to reveal its presence, and expose its workings. This is our aim, in an attempt to dislodge its influence from the spaces of where id was.

We would like to express our gratitude to each and every one of the contributors to this book, for their creativity, courage and generosity. This includes those colleagues whose work, intended for inclusion in earlier conceptions of *Where Id Was*, is not represented in this final incarnation. In this *chiaroscuro*, our thanks also go to three editors who, at different stages over the course of five long years, worked to help this book materialize: to Gill Davies, Nancy Peters, and, especially, Continuum's Tristan Palmer, who stayed with the project long enough to have it inaugurate the Disseminations series. From a distance, and in ways probably unknown to them, both Christopher Bollas and Cesare Viviani helped inspire this volume. Wesley Shumar and Pina Antinucci-Mark deserve special mention for incarnating the essences of friendship and collegiality, as does Mike Eigen, who kindly let us quote from his book *Ecstasy*. Finally, our heartfelt appreciation to Jan Middeldorf, Franco De Masi, Fred Chase, Henry Beck, Linda Hopkins and Elmer Miller for their support and encouragement, and to Lucinda Mitchell and Jeffrey Ware for their occasional but precious assistance.

Anthony Molino and Christine Ware

NOTES

1.   Robert M. Pirsig, *Zen and the Art of Motorcycle Maintenance*. New York: Morrow & Co., 1974.
2.   Russell Jacoby, *The Repression of Psychoanalysis: Otto Fenichel and the Political Freudians*. New York: Basic Books, 1983.
3.   Robert Lindner, *Rebel Without a Cause*. New York: Grove Press, 1994.
4.   Robert Stoller, *Observing the Erotic Imagination*. New Haven, CT: Yale University Press, 1985, p. 209.
5.   T.S. Eliot, 'Burnt Norton'. *The Four Quartets*. New York: Harcourt, Brace Jovanovich, 1943, p. 19.

PART I

Reappraisals

1

Normalization and its Discontents

Suzanne R. Kirschner

There are two broad perspectives on the social meanings and functions of psychotherapy and psychoanalysis. One perspective emphasizes the ways in which therapy and analysis 'free'[1] the subject, for better or for worse. The other orientation highlights the constrained character of 'psychological man', and aims to unmask the alleged illusion that analysis and therapy make the subject more free.

According to the first perspective, therapeutic discourse and practices have enabled the self to achieve a form of emancipation not previously available. This freeing of the subject is seen to possess both felicitous and problematic aspects. On the positive side, it is affirmed that the subject endowed with a strengthened ego is more rational, more autonomous, more self-controlled, and hence more able to appraise, choose and resist. Such a self possesses the capacity for a more flexible and empowered relationship with its own wishes and desires and with society's conventions. From a liberal-individualist point of view, the promotion of this type of self can be viewed as good for society too (at least in principle), since like the ideal modern citizen, the strong ego is sceptical of arbitrary authority and is able in a controlled and civilized manner to appraise how much it should follow convention and tradition and how much it need not do so. (Of course, Freud himself did not believe analysis would necessarily make us better citizens; nor was this, for him, its intended purpose. Furthermore, he believed that only a minority of people could attain this level of autonomy and rationality.)

A number of analysts of social life have emphasized the problematic aspects of such liberation. Thus Philip Rieff wrote with some irony of the 'triumph of the therapeutic'.[2] That triumph in contemporary life was seen by him to entail, concomitant to the ascendance of 'psychological man', the decline of an inherited moral order that was not being replaced in kind. And Robert Bellah and his colleagues, in *Habits of the Heart*,[3] criticized even more sharply (and with less ambivalence than Rieff) the loss of shared visions and values, of communal practices and sanctions that they hold to be essential components of a good society. The 'expressive individualism' promoted by the therapeutic ethos is an impoverishment not only for society, argued Bellah, but for the self as well. A corollary of this more communitarian position is that the healing effected by classical psychoanalysis and conventional psychotherapies is not adequate unless it also includes the fostering of an attunement on the part of the patient to the larger social world and cultural values – a harmonization with, and integration into, communal order.[4]

Liberal individualist and communitarian-interpretivist perspectives on psychological healing are usually presented with an emphasis upon their differences, but they evince a significant underlying similarity as well. What is assumed and unquestioned in both perspectives is that the therapeutic ethos does foster a strengthening and freeing of the self, however one weighs the good and the ill of that liberation. 'Freedom' in the form of greater autonomy, self-direction, and flexibility of response and choice, is problematic – it may not be sufficient for good social order (it may even serve to undermine it) or indeed for the self's fulfilment – but it is real and, for some at least, it has increased.

The second type of perspective taken towards therapy and analysis differs from the ones I have discussed above in that what is challenged here is the allegedly liberated character of the therapeutic subject.[5] Following the political theorist William Connolly, I call these 'genealogical' approaches;[6] they tend to follow, at least part of the way, the ideas of Michel Foucault. On this view, the free subject is truly an illusion, since, in the words of psychologist Nikolas Rose, all of our 'thoughts, feelings and actions ... are socially organized and managed in minute particulars'. According to genealogists, this is as true (more so, actually) of the rational autonomous subject as of the weaker or less-developed ego. And it is more true in the modern era than in pre-modern times, because, as Rose puts it:

> the later development of modern democracy is dependent upon the existence of certain types of subjects who did not require a continual external policing. The external constraint of the police was to be translated into an internal constraint upon the conduct of the self, the formation of subjects who were prepared to take responsibility for their actions and for whom the ethic of discipline was part of their very mental fabric.[7]

The ostensibly free subject is seen as the pre-eminent site of social discipline and political control. Thus, the genealogists claim, it is an
illusion that psychoanalysis strengthens anything but the hold of the
social order on the soul.

It is not really surprising that this duality can be identified in analyses
of the social meanings of therapy and psychoanalysis, because it reflects
a duality in the nature of the modern subject. As William Connolly has
written, the subject is 'an essentially ambiguous achievement of modernity'.[8] The modern subject is ambiguous because it embodies, simultaneously, not only freedom (or at least the prospect of freedom), but also
constraint so profound as to undercut and contradict such liberty.
Connolly explains that liberal democratic society aims to foster as its
ideal citizen an autonomous and rational self who expects, and accords to
others, respect and dignity; such respect includes (in principle at least) a
toleration of differences and thus some degree of pluralism. Such a self,
moreover, is inclined to be sceptical of authority and does not submit
unreflectively to received regulations and traditional rationales of legitimacy. The modern subject is 'less willing than members of other societies to be a mere stone in an edifice'.[9]

What is ambiguous – contradictory, actually – about the subject-selves
of democratic society is that 'an opposing element in the democratic ideal
nevertheless functions to grind them into material for use'.[10] Drawing
here on the work of Foucault, Connolly explains that modern liberal
regimes have aimed to ensure their legitimacy not through the external
forms of constraint that characterized pre-modern societies, but rather,
most often, by ensuring that the will of the people comes to be more
closely harmonized with the social order. State governance is enacted
and takes effect within the innermost reaches of the 'soul', shaping and
'disciplining' the self. Viewed in this light, then, the modern subject is
'subjected' to institutional and intra-personal surveillance in a manner
that belies its self-understanding as an autonomous and self-directed
entity.

The intrusion of modern social discipline into the self's very core is
seen by the genealogists (and Connolly in this respect is one) to be
effected through a process called 'normalization', as well as through
related practices that Foucault calls 'individualization', 'discipline' and
'confession'. Connolly points to 'normalizing pressures inherent in a
democracy' which 'draw a larger portion of life into the fold of thema-
tized norms'.[11] In order to ensure that subjects will not only act in
accord with, but also will experience themselves as endorsing, the social

order, 'others' must be identified both within and outside the self, others that serve to more sharply delineate the character and boundaries of the positive 'normal' self. These others are then marginalized and excluded, or contained, rehabilitated or 'cured', so that the self comes to experience itself and to be perceived as more closely harmonized with the 'normal' order.

These normalizing pressures are enacted in great measure through the human sciences and helping professions and, increasingly, are diffused ever more widely throughout popular culture and everyday discourse. During the past hundred years, there has been an exponential increase in the proliferation of what psychologist Kenneth Gergen calls 'vocabularies of deficit'.[12] While some argue that our society has become increasingly lax, with fewer sanctions against deviance, from another perspective one can see that there has been a veritable explosion of more and more categories of deviance, with every sort of behaviour and experience being caught and classified in formal and informal psychologizing and medicalizing nets. Thus there has been both an underlining, and in some cases a creating, of differences and 'others' in a manner that excludes and marginalizes such others as well as correspondingly 'other' portions of the self.

Psychoanalysis is considered by genealogists to participate in this general normalizing process. Through analysis by an expert we are taught to recognize and control those 'others' (the child, the invert, the pervert) and dangerous forces that are within us. Sexuality and other such dangerous forces are 'produced' within the self in order to strengthen it as a subject – as a self-observing and self-controlling entity that we think of as enhancing our freedom but which, according to Foucault, further ensnares us in social discipline. According to Foucault, what pass under the guise of the lifting of repression and the inducement to live more flexibly are in fact parts of a system of 'insidious leniencies' which promotes ever more effective management and policing of the self.

It has been argued that Foucault's depictions of the medicalization of madness and neurosis are inadequate because in these depictions one loses sight of the patient. The claim here is that Foucault's focus on the disciplinary functions of psychiatry gives inadequate attention to the patient's distress and difficulties in living. I would suggest that there is a similar inadequacy and incompleteness in his depiction (or lack thereof) of the analyst. That is, there may well be more genuine ambiguity and irony regarding normalization to be found in psychoanalytic discourse and practice than the Foucaultian account would indicate.[13]

Before briefly considering the nature of that ambiguity, I wish to raise the question of what – if anything – is so problematic about normalization in the first place. Clearly any social order requires limitations and boundaries. And concomitant with the endorsement of certain standards there will be a demarcation and devaluation of apparently antithetical forms of behaviour, experience and selfhood. Thus, as Connolly suggests, 'some forms of otherness' are 'the unavoidable effect of socially engendered harmonies'. What is problematic, argues Connolly, is that the proliferation of normalizing strategies in modern life, the naming of more and more segments of the populace and aspects of the self as 'others', has resulted in the marginalization and exclusion of these groups and aspects of self in a manner which runs counter to those democratic ideals which (at least in principle) affirm tolerance and inclusion of difference. This contradiction is difficult to acknowledge; as things now stand there is inadequate attention paid among the normalizing disciplines to the ambiguous, tragic and in some respects arbitrary and unjust effects of othering and normalization. Thus there is little opportunity to face, address or attempt to mitigate these effects. Hence Connolly argues that although othering is inevitable in any social order, and normalization is inevitable in modern democratic society, we would do well to reflect upon and attempt to attenuate these dynamics because when unchecked they can work to de-democratize social life. He suggests that the solution is not to throw social and conceptual order and ordering overboard, but rather to be more self-conscious about them and their effects. He advocates an ideal of reflexivity and self-consciousness 'which allows us to glimpse the limits of our own categories of classification and treatment and to confront, if obliquely, the defensive impulses that help to sustain them':[14]

> Such an orientation ... encourage[s] us to adopt a more ironic stance toward standards we endorse, striving to detect arbitrary elements within necessary limits and to discern the shadow of injustice haunting existing norms of rationality. It also encourages us to project an ideal of order that can sustain itself without drawing so massively on the forces of punishment, incentive systems, therapy, self-containment, and civic virtue.[15]

For Connolly the political theorist, this enhanced reflexivity – if it were really to make a difference in how society functions – would have to be part of a restructuring of the present political-economic order. My concern in this chapter is much more limited and modest; it is simply to ask whether there are elements of this more ironic and reflexive stance that are already detectable in some of our allegedly normalizing discourses. Specifically, are there not elements within the psychoanalytic system that potentially mitigate or at least complicate the difference-excluding tendencies of normalization?

Of course, psychoanalysis does have normalizing dimensions. In a very basic and undeniable sense, psychoanalytic therapies express and enact the pervasive societal imperative of self-surveillance and self-management. This imperative both brings people to therapy and analysis and is promoted and enhanced by the analytic process. Moreover, psychoanalytic frameworks do evince a normalizing orientation in the sense that the individual who goes for treatment comes to be understood by the analyst in terms of a defective, deficient or underdeveloped self or ego structure and object relations. Types of defects in the self are usually ranked hierarchically, although the degree to which they are ranked and the particular typology vary from system to system and indeed from analyst to analyst. The truths of the self and its modes of relating (in actuality and in fantasy) are what must be probed, uncovered and mastered, through interpretation or remedial relationship. All this is done in the service of elevating the self to a more 'normal' (at once more autonomous and more connected) position.

Yet there are other strains in psychoanalysis that tend to give a somewhat more ironic cast to such norms; and if these strains are not always evident in the practices and theories of analysts, they have nevertheless been present from the beginning. Put most generally, Freud as well as many of the post-Freudians have tended at times to blur the boundaries between normal and abnormal, natural and civilized, and even rational and irrational. All forms of psychic organization are to be understood as different solutions to the same inescapable and tragic situation (the vicissitudes of Oedipus, or of separation–individuation and disillusionment). Analytic perspectives stress the inescapability of that situation, and the imperfect and compromised nature of all possible solutions. Certainly few who call themselves analytic would assert that there is any absolute or ideal normality. Granted, analytic theories do tend to rank the compromises in terms of 'sicker' and 'less sick'. But alongside such bifurcation and hierarchicalization, there is also evident a kind of perceived continuity between 'normal' self and 'different' other, and among the varieties of others. This perception of continuity makes of difference – even that which is designated eccentric, odd, or maladaptive – something that is neither so sharply 'other', nor so unequivocally in need of a particular set of prescribed interventions (in need of being remade in a particular way), as the normalizing scenario would suggest.

Possibly this is an ingenuous depiction of the analytic orientation – perhaps the only thing that matters, for modern social life, about this apparent blurring and ironization of difference is that ultimately it is used in the service of furthering just the sort of 'subjected' self-management of which Foucault wrote. But to thus reduce away the tensions and contradictions that exist within psychoanalysis would entail an avoidance of ambiguity, the sort of avoidance that is decried by analysts and postmodernists alike. If, on the other hand, such ambiguity is not boiled down to some normalizing essence, but is taken instead as an invitation to probe its varieties and effects, then questions can be raised regarding analysts' understanding of the meanings and functions of their work. Are the tensions and contradictions between normalizing and non-normalizing dimensions recognized as such by analysts? When attention is called to such tensions, how do analytically oriented therapists attempt to reconcile or rationalize them? I conclude this chapter, then, with a call to systematic exploration of psychoanalytically oriented clinicians' patterns of reflection on 'mental health', 'normalcy', 'adaptation', and related concepts. Such exploration could serve not only to illuminate the ways in which these tensions are (or are not) acknowledged and dealt with, but also to further explain and sharpen the reflexive and ironic dimensions of psychodynamic discourse.

In an era dominated by biological psychiatry and the bureaucratization of medical care, it may seem impractical or irrelevant to make so much of talk and practices that go against normalizing and bureaucratizing forces. But one could also argue that it makes it all the more important to highlight such ambiguities, and to explore the alternative or supplementary visions of difference that still live alongside the more visible and powerful disciplines of contemporary society.

NOTES

1. Of course, this is a relative and limited sort of freedom, since absolute freedom was seen by Freud to be antithetical to individual and societal survival. Moreover, throughout its history, psychoanalytic thought has embodied a tension between

Freud's essentially deterministic view of human action and his depiction of success-ful psychoanalytic treatment as engendering strengthened capacities for rational reflection, self-mastery and choice. This tension persists; however, a majority of American psychoanalytic therapists would concur with ego psychologist Robert Holt's assertion that Freud's dictum, '"where id was there shall ego be" makes no sense if we do not include under it the recognition that mature, non-neurotic people usually have the capacity to make free choices' (Holt 1989, p. 247). See Kirschner (in press).

2. Philip Rieff, *Triumph of the Therapeutic: Uses of Faith after Freud*. Chicago: University of Chicago Press, 1987.

3. Robert Bellah, Richard Madsen, William M. Sullivan, Ann Swidler and Stephen Tipton, *Habits of the Heart: Individualism and Commitment in American Life*. New York: Harper and Row, 1986.

4. See, e.g., Louis A. Sass, 'The self and its vicissitudes: an archaeological study of the psychoanalytic avant-garde', in *Social Research* 55 (Winter 1988), pp. 551-607; Mark Freeman, *Rewriting the Self*. New York: Routledge, 1993.

5. A generation or so ago one might have included under this class the anti-psychiatry writers who argued that there was little genuine freedom in adjustment to a 'sick' or impoverished society; one also would have included members of the 'Freudian left' (Marcuse, Brown, Reich *et al.*) who accepted most of the premises of Freud's metapsychology but stunningly reversed his resigned pessimism, proposing instead that we could achieve a radically less repressive civilization. And of course the Frankfurt School, with their dismantling of the bourgeois subject, could also be included within this group. The genealogists whom I focus on embody a rather different set of attempts to 'unmask' the liberatory self-image of the therapeutic; according to them, the utopias envisioned by left-wing Freudians were yet another instance of what Foucault called the 'deployment of sexuality' for the purpose of disciplining the modern self.

6. See, e.g., Nikolas Rose, *Governing the Soul: The Shaping of the Private Self*. New York: Routledge, 1990 and Ian Parker, 'Disciplining psychology', in John Shotter and Kenneth J. Gergen (eds), *Texts of Identity*. New York: Routledge, 1990. The work of Nietzsche is considered to be an important source of genealogical approaches.

7. Rose 1990, p. 223.

8. *Politics and Ambiguity*. Madison, WI: University of Wisconsin Press, 1987, p. vii.

9. Ibid., p. 4.

10. Ibid.

11. Ibid. p. 5.

12. 'Therapeutic professions and the diffusion of deficit', *Journal of Mind and Behavior*, Summer and Autumn 1990, vol. 11, nos. 3–4, pp. 353–68.

13. There is a passage in the *History of Sexuality*. Vol. 1. (New York: Vintage, 1990) that suggests a more nuanced view:

> It is very well to look back from our vantage point and remark upon the normalizing impulse in Freud; one can go on to denounce the role played for many years by the psychoanalytic institution; but the fact remains that in the great family of technologies of sex, which goes so far back into the history of the Christian West, of all those institutions that set out in the nineteenth century to medicalize sex, it was the one that, up to the decade of the forties, rigorously opposed the political and institutional effects of the perversion-heredity-degenerescence system. (Ibid, p. 119)

14. Connolly 1987, p. 109.

15. Ibid., p. 110.

BIBLIOGRAPHY

Bellah, R.N., Madsen, R., Sullivan, W.M., Swidler, A. and Tipton, S. (1986) *Habits of the Heart: Individualism and Commitment in American Life*. New York: Harper and Row.

Connolly, W.E. (1987) *Politics and Ambiguity*. Madison, WI: University of Wisconsin Press.

Foucault, M. (1990) *History of Sexuality. Vol. I.* New York: Vintage.

Freeman, M. (1993) *Rewriting the Self*. New York: Routledge.

Gergen, K.J. (1990) 'Therapeutic professions and the diffusion of deficit', *Journal of Mind and Behavior*, 11, 3–4, 353–68.

Holt, R. (1989) *Freud Reappraised*. New York: Guilford Press.

Kirschner, S.R. (in press) *Autonomy and the Problem of Suffering: Tragedy and Transcendence in Psychoanalytic Discourse*.

Parker, I. (1990) 'Disciplining psychology', in J. Shotter and K.J. Gergen (eds), *Texts of Identity*. New York: Routledge.

Rieff, P. (1987) *Triumph of the Therapeutic: Uses of Faith after Freud*. Chicago: University of Chicago Press.

Robinson, P. (1990) *The Freudian Left: Wilhelm Reich, Geza Roheim, Herbert Marcuse*. Ithaca, NY: Cornell University Press.

Rose, Nikolas (1990) *Governing the Soul: The Shaping of the Private Self*. New York: Routledge.

Sass, L.A. (1988) 'The self and its vicissitudes: an archaeological study of the psychoanalytic avant-garde', *Social Research*, 55, 551–607.

2

Freud-baiting[1]

Paul Williams

Since the late 1970s, and the publication of a scholarly critique of psychoanalysis by Adolf Grunbaum in the 1980s, together with the release of much of Freud's personal correspondence from the Freud archive, the number of experts on Freud has proliferated. Many, like Grunbaum, are serious scholars attempting to grasp Freud's place in our modernized world. Others, like Frederick Crewes, Jeffrey Masson, Robert Wilcocks, Allen Esterson ('The Culture Essay', 29 May) and Gloria Steinem, to name a few, are noteworthy for their efforts to denigrate and, if possible, to undermine Freud's reputation. Why are these people so bitter? I shall argue that there exists a misguided campaign of vilification against Freud which derives from intellectual rivalry, an ideological worship of 'science' (a characteristic of our era) and profound ignorance of psychoanalysis, especially the workings of the unconscious mind.

To say that Freud exerted enormous influence on twentieth-century culture is so obvious as to seem banal. His ideas concerning the power of sexuality on our identity and the way we relate to ourselves and others (from infancy onwards), and his studies of the complexity of the unconscious mind, have rendered 'the internal world' an accepted currency among clinicians, philosophers, scientists, writers, artists and the public. At the same time, psychoanalysis has been subjected to criticism. This is usually on the lines that it is not proper science. The criticism comes in sporadic waves (remember Eysenck?), and we are currently enjoying a bout of it, of which Esterson's article is an example, albeit of a personal and rather nasty variety. These assaults are not, as they would have us believe, solely concerned with questions of scientific respectability. The objective bears more widely on our ideas of freedom of expression and intellectual democracy, in an age when the power of science and access to control over knowledge have never been more prized. Those who wish to smear and dismantle Freud's work seek opportunities to define and manage what the rest of us think and believe about the ways our minds and bodies function. Freud-baiting is above all a *political* activity. Groups representing certain (often reactionary and ideologizing) branches of science, literature and politics spare no effort to legitimize and monopolize 'truth'. For them Freud is a special target, not just because he overturned certain preconceptions of conventional science, but because he had the audacity to try to demonstrate how human minds work – something orthodox science, including medicine and psychiatry, has failed to achieve. In addition, he was a literary master who also had a brilliant translator in James Strachey, to the dismay of certain literary professionals. To distinguish more valid criticisms of Freud from the institutional and political bigotry, we must examine the charges against psychoanalysis.

FREUD IS NOT SCIENTIFIC. This chestnut could have been heard cracking in any Viennese drawing-room fire a century ago. How valid is the charge? Grunbaum's recent critique of the psychoanalytic scientific method is the most impressive ever undertaken. He concluded that although Freud's theories are capable of meeting the requirements for falsifiability laid down by Karl Popper (criteria justifying the title 'scientific'), these cannot be confirmed within the clinical psychoanalytic setting. This is significant criticism (physics has suffered from comparable difficulties), yet few psychoanalysts would argue with it, let alone feel abashed. This is because Grunbaum's study did not set out to address the hermeneutic complexity, in addition to the empirical rigour, with which psychoanalysis observes and interprets mental phenomena. In addition, analysts know that psychoanalysis has come a long way since the time of Freud. Existing theories have evolved, new theories have emerged and many of Freud's ideas have been proven to be true through overwhelming clinical observation, while others have not. Psychoanalysts themselves have been lax in presenting the substantial body of evidence that now exists to support the scientific validity of psychoanalysis. It is within their capacity to do so and it would help their cause.

If critics of Freud know that modern psychoanalysis is not the same as Freud's original work, why do they get worked up? Their witch-hunt is not simply about *how* Freud worked but about *what* he discovered. By attacking the founder of psychoanalysis, they hope ultimately to destroy the discovery, which has enabled human beings to alter radically the way they think about themselves and the world. Freud struggled to approach an astonishing domain of human existence – *the unconscious mind* – for

which no systematic explanation was available. Of course, the unconscious mind existed before Freud, but he was the first to try to properly
explain it in psychological terms. Think of your own fantasies. Grudges,
daydreams, sexual and aggressive imaginings. These are *conscious*
thoughts, and unpredictable enough, you might say. What of that subter-
ranean, mental cinema-complex where anarchy reigns, known as your
unconscious? One night, you dream you're the boss at work, chairing a
meeting, when your mother walks in and says, 'He really is quite
hopeless, you know.' The next night you are wandering along the streets
of your childhood, when a policeman tells you that half a pound of
butter is missing from your bank manager's briefcase. What on earth is
going on? Unconscious images depict, in primary form, our emotional
lives. Images join up to form unconscious fantasies. These can take the
form of dreams, and they can influence waking life. Some unconscious
fantasies last a lifetime. If they are pathological, they can give rise to
illness, even to the abuse of children, rape or murder. Other people may
spend their lives searching for Mr or Mrs Right, or convinced everyone
hates them, and so on. We *all* have unconscious fantasies, and they are
discerned through dreams.

Freud studied the unconscious, and consciousness, in the spirit of
nineteenth-century scientific inquiry. After failing to account for psychological functioning along neurological lines he created a new vocabulary
– psychoanalysis – forged from conventional scientific observation and
hermeneutical inquiry. The hermeneutic method involves interpretation
of phenomena not always immediately apparent to or measurable by the
observer, in order to acquire knowledge of their meaning(s). This branch
of science has a long and respectable history, and is used by philosophers
(Schopenhauer, Nietszche, Heidegger, Husserl, Habermas *et al.*) and by
social scientists to study culture and morality (Weber, Goffman,
Foucault). It is taught in most universities today. Certain scientists and
academics consider that anything other than 'pure' science is suspect.
Contemporary, 'pure' science has grown in iconic appeal over recent
years due to its seductive promises of certainty, thereby increasing the
numbers of people who have turned to its high-tech truths for intellectual security.

What led Freud to use the methods he did? He and subsequent
analysts found the unconscious to be immensely contradictory and labile.
It can say one thing, then promptly deny it. Black can become white,
white black. Life can feel wonderful (even though you're depressed),
good is bad, bad good. Your own dreams can confirm this. Empirical

observation and hermeneutic study by Freud and generations of psychoanalysts have revealed laws governing the operations of the unconscious.
Freud-baiters cannot deal with this evidence. They insist upon a solely
intellectualist appraisal of psychoanalysis and the unconscious. A strictly
rationalist critique is, however, inadequate to account for the surreal,
elusive phenomena of the unconscious. An inability or unwillingness to
join in any methodological debate concerning the unconscious forces
critics to remain mute regarding its existence and meaning. 'Pure'
science cannot define it: Freud's methods are discounted using elitist
truth criteria: meanwhile the unconscious continues to exist, patients
suffer and psychoanalysts try to help them.

FREUD WAS A LIAR. Here enters a shrill, last-ditch argument.
Literary Freud-baiters in particular leap on Freud's change of mind
regarding the seduction theory and the correspondence regarding case
histories is used as evidence. These charges are specious. Freud may
have had many of the faults of a Victorian patriarch, but he was not a
liar. He believed his female patients to have been seduced. He later
believed that fantasies of seduction occurred, and he was open about it.
Intellectual honesty and a willingness to change his mind were characteristics of his work throughout his life. Analysts know that many patients
do experience fantasies of seduction. Also, many patients have been
seduced and abused. The two groups are not coterminous and discerning
the truth of abuse in a given case is a delicate undertaking which takes
into account factors other than fantasies (a factor of importance in the
'false memory' debate). Extensive research over the past fifteen years has
confirmed this, and even despite this work, the analyst may never know
the full truth.

Freud 'the liar' is accused of claiming therapeutic successes which
were later proved not to be so (Anna O. and Serge Pankejeff, 'The Wolf
Man', are sometimes cited). Has a clinician never before believed a
patient to be improved, even cured, only for the patient to fall ill again,
often years later? Does this constitute a scandal, or a lie? To suggest, as
Esterson does, that Freud should have had the clinical knowledge we
have today to enable him to discern his patients' more complex
pathology (or more absurdly, that he had it and didn't use it), is like
castigating the inventor of the horse and cart for not having come up
with the motor car while he was at it.

The 'Freud the liar' argument derives from a limited, *cognitive*
appraisal of Freud's work by literary critics, an approach which parallels

in narrowness the objectivism of the 'pure' scientists. Both groups choose to remain oblivious to the dimensions of unconscious mental life, including, it would seem, their own. The result has been a series of shallow, one-dimensional and partisan critiques which sound more like mechanical descriptions of a Cézanne or a Vermeer than the paintings themselves. A list of colours, chemical compounds of the paint and number of brushes used are given, from which the work is judged. Absent is any embrace of the forces which impel these creations in the first place, or of the technical achievements involved. Practising psycho-analysis is akin to restoring a painting, in fact. Patient and analyst attempt together to lift the grime and wear of the years without damaging the original underneath. Where damage appears, repair is carefully undertaken in accordance with, as far as is possible, the inten-tions of the creator – the self or the patient. The process is a science, and an art.

PSYCHOANALYSIS DOESN'T WORK. This brings us to the final criticism by the Freud-baiters, and one that is not only erroneous but offensive to analysts and patients. It would be foolish to say that there are not bad analysts or failed analyses – of course there are, as there are failures in any professional group. However, in competent hands, psycho-analysis is, for many patients, a very powerful and successful treatment method. In addition, Freud and psychoanalysis effectively invented the 'talking treatments' which, in the past thirty years, have acquired a central place in psychiatry, including in the H.H.S. We now *talk* to people about their disturbed behaviour and their mental problems.

Human beings grow and flourish psychologically when their inner selves experience and assimilate the deepest emotional truths that being alive arouses. They need to be bonded to others to achieve this. To acquire psychological health is no less than a creative *œuvre*, requiring an appropriate setting. For many this is the home. Others, whose formative years fail them, never settle in their personalities until they re-find themselves. The careers of many artists, scientists and ordinary people are testimonies to this search. It can be a difficult and painful under-taking which many people avoid. In the past fifteen years reactionary politics, behaviourism, 'pure' science and high-speed, high-tech con-sumerism have striven to deter us from the complex task of maturing. Illusions of gratification and success are commodities peddled to maintain this deception, and they can now include 'truth', whether religious, scientific or political. The commercialization of everything affects knowledge as much as any other area of life. In reality, understanding the world and oneself is immensely difficult. Psychoanalysis is committed to this task using scientific skills of an observational and interpretive nature, art and, unfashionably, patience.

Why are so many attacks on Freud occurring now? I think that the period since 1989 has been horribly sobering. Take away the Cold War and what do you get? Peace? Fraternal Love? Generosity of Spirit? No, you get, as Freud observed, the return of the (literally and militarily) repressed. We are now having to face in more complex forms the destructive, envious, ungenerous and murderous side of human nature. The desiccation of compassion is apparent in the escalation of drug-related killings, mass and serial murders, the Bulger case, the annihilation of children on the streets of Brazil, Dahmer, Frederic West, the Soviet Mafia, Yardies and so on. Remove the evil empire as a scapegoat in which to locate everything negative and you must face up to the destructive impulses of your own country, your region, your city, your neighbourhood, your ethnicity, your kids' school, your self. I think this leads to a hatred of the way of thinking which has most to say about these things – psychoanalysis. So let's get Freud. He brought up all this stuff. He said that civilization was a veneer over polymorphous perversity, incest, rapaciousness, man as a wolf to other men. He said neurosis was the price of civility, goddamn him. He must be a cheat, a liar, and anyway all his followers f— their patients, don't they? The analysts and therapists are held responsible for evoking those things *that I cannot bear to know about my friends, my family and myself.*

Unless the Freud-baiters provide a coherent critique of psychoanalytic methodology, particularly in relation to the unconscious mind (and perhaps propose their own alternative at the same time) they should shut up. Otherwise their legacy will be that brand of unbridled, destructive moralizing and cynicism which too often characterizes the age in which we live.

NOTE

1.   This is a newspaper article which was produced at the request of *The Sunday Times* in reply to Allen Esterson's 'The Culture Essay' in *The Sunday Times* of 29 May 1994. In his essay, Esterson, a writer and critic, portrayed Freud as a scientific fraud, dissembler, hypocrite and liar. This reply appeared on 19 June 1994. The opinions given are mine, and I informed the publisher that I was speaking on my behalf only. I was asked to write in the style of 'elevated pub conversation'.

3

What is a Psychoanalyst?

Haya Oakley

PROLOGUE: THE SECOND WIFE

Let us start at the end. George Groddeck (1917) wrote a letter to Sigmund Freud which concludes: 'Here is the point where I begin to doubt whether or not I have the right to set myself up as a professional psychoanalyst' (Grossman and Grossman, 1965, p. 73). Groddeck is concerned that his desire to extend psychoanalytic understanding to physical ailments is outside Freud's limits on the concept. Freud replies emphatically:

> I notice that you urgently petition me to give you official confirmation of the fact that you are not a psychoanalyst, that you are not one of a group of followers ... I would apparently do you a great favour if I reject you, push you away to where Adler, Jung and others are standing, but I can't do that. I must lay claim to you and must state that you are a splendid psychoanalyst, whose thorough understanding of the essence of the matter is permanent. (ibid.)

Freud is not bestowing a privilege, but instead makes a claim that Groddeck belongs to psychoanalysis. Indeed, to the question 'what is a psychoanalyst?', Freud answers in the same letter: 'anyone who has recognised transference and resistance as the focal points of therapy belongs irretrievably to the mad horde. It does not matter if he calls the unconscious "the It" '(ibid.)

This would be the 'end of the session', were it not for the question of authorization. Who is to say who among us does or does not recognize transference and resistance, and who is authorized as the absolute owner of their definition? Who is authorized to transmit such knowledge and thus to claim membership of the 'mad horde'? Who may determine the rules of membership of such a 'horde' and, in Groddeck's words, who has the right to set themselves up as a 'professional psychoanalyst'? In short, who are the decision-makers and the true inheritors of the Freudian mantle?

In his novel *A Journey to the End of the Millennium* (1999), Abraham B. Yehoshua writes about a successful and happy Jewish merchant who takes his two wives and a local rabbi on a dangerous boat journey from Tangier to Paris to challenge a French relative's view that it was wrong of him to marry a second wife, despite the fact that the two wives are content. The merchant, a Sephardic Jew, has lived amongst the Arabs and like many Sephardic Jews adopted some of their customs. His relatives, including a much-loved cousin, are Ashkenazi Jews, living in Europe and believing in monogamy. Legally, the merchant does not need their consent, but his cousin's French wife demands that her husband break off his relationship with the merchant unless he gives up the second wife. The merchant knows that if he fails in his challenge, he risks the current estrangement becoming a formal excommunication, and yet he is compelled to follow it through.

This story is about identity, difference, acceptance, exclusion and the need for recognition. No sooner is the stage set for the first round than the merchant and his rabbi begin to wonder, 'But who will be the judges?' The relatives produce three professional copiers of religious texts. They, claim the relatives, have copied the good books so many times that they know them better than anyone:

> They would be able to judge on the basis of what was written in books. 'But what books? and what was the point of books?' Rabbi Elbaz protested vehemently. If the answer was written explicitly in a book, would it have occurred to him to leave his city and to have entrusted himself to the ocean to demand justice for his employer? Would he have allowed Ben Attar to put his wives at risk for something that was written in a book? (Yehoshua, 1999, pp. 117–18)

It could be said that members of the psychoanalytic community are currently re-staging a foregone conclusion that has been staged and re-staged for a hundred years, since Freud first handed out rings to members of his inner circle. What is that conclusion? That each of us is already a member of what the philosopher Jacques Derrida calls 'a band' and that neither the Sephardic nor the Ashkenazi bands 'will change as a result of this encounter ... in this saloon overflowing with all kinds of

bands that are more or less bankable, more or less ready for détente'
(Derrida, 1987, p. 501). And yet, like the Jewish merchant, we set out in
our personal and institutional boats again and again and, in the throes of
a relentless repetition compulsion, we risk it all, lured – perhaps by our
collective transference to the psychoanalytic project itself – to confront
our own 'judges'. Judges who, as 'experts' in 'a basically humanistic
discipline [which] has conceived and touted itself as a positive science
while organising itself institutionally as a religion' (Kirsner, 2000,
p. 233), will legislate issues of identity, difference, acceptance and exclusion, and answer the question: 'What is a psychoanalyst?' At times it
even appears as if the re-staging has an effect:

> The confrontation effect which ... has to do with the
> deconstruction of the so-called psychoanalytic institution ... is
> signaled ... by the fact that the partition of the allegiances within
> the [four French] groups is no longer ... the rule. It is no longer
> completely impermeable ... and airless, as previously. (Derrida,
> 1987, p. 508)

This may well be why certain groups refuse to debate while others have,
through debate, affected a turn in the tide.

To address the question 'What is a psychoanalyst?' one needs to
consider psychoanalysis:

a. As a cultural term of reference, a discourse, with its claimed 'body of
   knowledge'.
b. As a community which is politically organized.
c. As a clinical practice or therapy.

For the three, in my estimation, are inextricably linked in the 'making' of
a psychoanalyst.

PSYCHOANALYSIS AS A DISCOURSE : WHO WILL PAY FOR FREUD'S TRANCHE?

Psychology historian Sonu Shamdasani claims:

> In popular culture, Freud and Jung have become proper names for
> psychology ... icons and sign-systems ... founders and legitimators

of psychotherapy ... [The] function of a legitimator is to act as if a field has been founded, something discovered, some basis that offers an epistemological and professional security. (Shamdasani, 2000)

If one had to summarize what Freud is alleged to have discovered and on which is founded the psychoanalytic era and its discourse, it would be the words 'unconscious' and the 'talking cure'. As an avid reader of philosophy, Freud must have been aware that the sixteenth-century philosopher Spinoza had suggested that the cause for physical and mental disease was the existence of unclear ideas which caused bondage and suffering. Freud re-claimed the concept, and re-introduced it in a manner which totally revolutionized man's view of his own consciousness. If you accept the notion of unconscious process, nothing is ever only what it seems. If you don't accept it, you have a lifetime of fighting against its effects. While psychoanalysis set about putting the rest of the world through its mostly reductive lens, other disciplines began to scrutinize psychoanalysis – its philosophical premises, practices, therapeutic efficacy, political organizations and the way it has strayed on occasion from pursuing truth to claiming to have discovered an absolute truth.

Psychoanalysis as a discourse is open to all, yet is rarely welcomed by psychoanalytic institutions who seem to have fostered and perpetuated Freud's original privileging of the 'movement' over the discourse, keeping the latter a closely guarded in-house secret open exclusively to the loyal initiates. Like Freud for whom there existed two groups, the unquestioning friends and the doubting enemies, non-initiates are seen as 'outside' psychoanalysis and their often-learned comments as irrelevant, uninformed and 'illegitimate'.

In a public discussion entitled 'Confrontation' Derrida faces René Major on the possibility of the concept 'non-analyst':

Suppose that there was a founder ... of psychoanalysis, a first analyst. Let us take the name Freud as an index ... Suppose now that this founder, this so called institutor of the analytic movement, had need of a supplementary *tranche* [in French psychoanalytic slang, *une tranche* is the period of time one spends with a given analyst] ... Then this unanalysed remainder which in the last analysis relates it to the absolute outside of the analytic milieu will not play the role of a border, will not have the form of a limit around the psychoanalytic, that to which the psychoanalytic as

theory and as practice would not, alas, have had access. Not at all.
This unanalysed will ... have been that upon which and around
which the analytic movement will have been constructed so that
this unanalysed might be inherited, protected, transmitted intact,
suitably bequeathed, consolidated ... encrypted. It is what gives its
structure to the movement and to its architecture ... The question
then becomes: Who will pay for Freud's *tranche*? Or ... who has it
paid to whom? The bidding has been opened for some time ... on
the scene in which the attempts to occupy the place of [absolute
knowledge] are multiplying ... simultaneously all the places, those
of the seller, the buyer, and the auctioneer. (1987, pp. 520-1)

As a discourse, psychoanalysis poses fundamental questions about the
nature of the human psyche. It is the answers given to these questions
which other disciplines seek to problematize. Yet within its own
confines, it is the question of training and authorization rather than
fundamental ideologies which seems to be the cause for the institutional
discontent and creative impoverishment of psychoanalysis.

THE PSYCHOANALYTIC COMMUNITY: ANORAK OF FIRE

In a witty one-man show, the anti-hero, a compulsive train-spotter (a
nerd or, in Britain, an anorak), regales us with the trials and tribulations
of his life. At one moment, he whispers conspiratorially to the audience:
'Do you know? Rumour has it that in Huddersfield, there are people
who spot busses. Imagine!' He exclaims incredulously, 'Who would be
daft enough to spot busses?'

Being part of the psychoanalytic fabric, it is often difficult for us to see
just how irrational and destructive our politics and institutions can be. If
psychoanalysis is in danger, it is from its own institutions. When one
attempts to point this out, one is invariably seen as being disrespectful,
enviously attacking, not fully or properly analysed, or merely refusing to
take up one's rightful place in the psychoanalytic pecking order, often
given to parochial cultural variations.

One fact is clear: since its inception, the international psychoanalytic
community has been united in war. Splits have been its main form of
procreation and the source of much of its passion. The simultaneous
absence of and yet common belief in a so-called 'standard edition' by
which we could measure ourselves and which could act as a manual for

all therapists for dealing with all patients, have often driven us to a rigidity which masquerades as erudition or scholarship. This common belief has survived because it has hidden itself in exclusive little enclaves occasionally forced open by external challenge (e.g. state intervention) or internal combustion (leading to a split).

The unanalysed Freud left us with a legacy open to questioning and interpretation. One of his wishes was expressed in 1914:

I considered it necessary to form an official association because I feared the abuses to which psychoanalysis would be subjected as soon as it became popular. There should be some headquarters whose business it would be to declare: 'all this nonsense is nothing to do with psychoanalysis, this is not psychoanalysis'. (Freud, 1914, p. 7)

Australian Michael Kennedy points out that Freud's wish

serves as a salutary reminder to members of the diverse psychoanalytic traditions that 'associations' per se perform another function which is not psychoanalysis. Perhaps, the function of the association is closely linked to politics and the intrigues of nonsense. (1995, p. 12)

Derrida provides a vivid portrait of the state of affairs in France, where he sees:

the schisms, the seisms whose cracking is heard everywhere today, amplified in proportion to the extension without border of the psychoanalytic field, these movements of dividing grounds, crossing and multiplying *tranches* in every sense, in an accelerated, accumulating, abyssal fashion. (1987, p. 520)

Dany Nobus, in turn, expands on

the extraordinary amount of institutional schisms that have occurred in the Lacanian landscape since 1980. Every institution that has been created since Lacan dissolved his Ecole Freudien de Paris in 1980 is eager to conquer the world, to become as influential as possible, and to make clear that it represents the true Lacanian position. In this sense, every institution incorporates dogmas of Lacanian doctrine and has difficulty tolerating resistances. A mildly

critical lecture at a Lacanian conference is enough to be asked the
question: Have you ever been analysed? In contrast to its age, the
psychoanalytic movement in Belgium has been marked by a high
degree of turbulence both on an institutional and a theoretical level.
Within a time span of forty years, five different societies were
established. (1997, p. 16)

In the USA, the in-fighting coalesced around the issue of 'Lay Analysis'
and culminated in a court case, which was won by the lay analysts of the
American Psychological Association. Robert Wallerstein (1988) has
explored the issues which this fight highlighted including the attempts to
restrict entry to psychoanalytic trainings in the USA to medical physi-
cians, especially those with psychiatric training (adopted in 1938), which
were 'partly motivated by fear of lay competition for patients during the
lingering Depression as well as traditional desires to make psychoanalysis
as medically and thus scientifically respectable' (Hale, 1999). In different
parts of the USA the inter- and intra-institutional fights again centred
around the issue of training and authorization (see Kirsner, 2000).

In Europe in the early 1940s, the controversy about the 'training
analyst' raged between the camps of Melanie Klein and Anna Freud.
The former believed that transference should not be interpreted until
the defences had been reduced while the latter advocated analysing the
transference from the start. Despite this fundamental disagreement, the
British Psycho-Analytic Society (BP-AS) and its Institute did not split.
Instead, the Institute of Psycho-Analysis divided into two trainings (later
to develop the Middle Group).[1] A compromise was reached, namely,
that ideological differences co-exist in the same institution through
different trainings, but with rigid adoption and maintenance of the
technical rules, e.g. the length of the analytic session, the use of the
couch and the frequency of sessions. According to Elisabeth Roudinesco:

The unity that prevailed during the forties in the empire that Freud
founded was due entirely to this condition, which acted with the
force of a generally accepted law. So while different theories as to
how treatment should be conducted were tolerated, any breach of
the rules about times might result in expulsion. (1997, p. 202)

In Britain today, there are about 35 psychoanalytic organizations, most
of which belong to the national umbrella body for psychotherapy, the
United Kingdom Council for Psychotherapy (UKCP). A handful of

organizations, including the BP-AS, has created a 'breakaway' group, the British Confederation of Psychotherapists (BCP), that might be termed elitist. The groups belonging to the BCP see themselves as 'second to the Institute' which is where they draw their analysts from and to whom they remain transferentially attached clinically and politically. In 1992 the UKCP carried out site visits to all trainings to establish similarities and differences and to draw up the minimum requirements that psycho-analytic trainings would need for their graduates to gain entry to the National Register. With minor exceptions most training organizations within the Psychoanalytic Section of UKCP required the same of their trainees. Many of the same 'names' appeared in most trainings as teachers, supervisors and analysts whatever their formal associations. The absence of visible differences in the criteria of selection, training, academic or clinical requirements failed to distinguish the self-proclaimed elite from other schools of psychoanalysis.

In the eight years since its formation, the BCP has not produced a statement that substantiates the reason for the split. No coherently different minimum criteria have been published to justify the claim of superior training; a curious state of affairs which is echoed by two of its members:

> By assembling colleagues who agree with them and with whom perhaps, they can write books on a clinical topic, psychoanalysts can create the illusion that true science has taken place. But technical papers, conference appearances, and statistics about patients presumably suffering from a given syndrome are the trappings of expertise, not the substance. (Bollas and Sundelson in Kirsner, 2000, p. 237)

In Britain, the psychoanalytic field appears to be modelled on the British class system, which assumes a royal point of orientation, the 'real thing' in relation to which everyone else 'knows their place'. Likewise, it is preoccupied with titles. The BP-AS claims sole ownership of the use of the label 'psychoanalyst' and of the right to train psychoanalysts. The Institute refuses to have its criteria scrutinized by UKCP, does not allow non-members to observe the way it deals with ethical complaints and does not allow appeals to be heard elsewhere. While many trainings in Britain accept that candidates should be in analysis, they believe in the candidate's right to choose the analyst and that the conditions of the treatment be determined by the needs of the analysis. The Institute endorses a select few as 'training analysts' by whom all trainees must be analysed under strict technical restrictions. Furthermore, 'training analysts' play an active role in the progress of their analysands as trainees, which raises serious ethical questions, given the direct financial benefit to the analyst as well as the political implications within institutions about future career opportunities for candidates analysed by certain senior members.

To the outsider, we all look alike, to ourselves, we have a great difficulty articulating how the splits are formed – so what is wrong with our institutions? Some might claim that it is rivalrous resemblance that drives us crazy. We see ourselves in the other and seek to establish our independent identity by disowning and denouncing all similarities. This acts as an effective diversion from the fact that there is no consensus within the field about the nature of psychoanalysis or about the best way to transmit it. Others, like Kirsner, think that, 'A major aspect of the problem ... is that a basically humanistic discipline has conceived and touted itself as a positive science while organising itself institutionally as a religion' (2000, p. 233).

PSYCHOANALYSIS AS A CLINICAL PRACTICE: MRS BALINT'S LAUNDRY BASKET

In *Primary Love and Psycho-Analytic Technique* (1939), Alice Balint illustrates the technical dilemmas facing the psychoanalyst of her time in relation to the inevitable 'personal' element he/she brings into the transference:

> A very typical detail of this kind is 'the problem of the cushion'. There are several solutions to this problem: (a) the cushion remains the same for every patient, but a piece of tissue paper is spread over it, which is thrown away at the end of the hour; (b) the cushion remains but every patient is given a special cover, distinguishable by its shade or design, and for each hour the cushion is put into the appropriate cover; (c) each patient has his own cushion and must only use his; (d) there is only one cushion or only two or three of them for all the patients and it is left to them to use them as they like, etc. Moreover, these possibilities have to be multiplied by at least three, because the situation differs according to whether the analyst, the patient or a servant manipulates the cushion. (1939, pp. 214–15)

When addressing the question 'what is a psychoanalyst?' regarding clinical practice, we soon run aground if we answer on the level of technique alone. The outer trappings and rituals of our trade are the easiest, most visible and concrete level of our clinical work and teaching. Technique is but a consequence of our therapeutic strategy bolstered by a particular belief system. Our understanding of and the position we take up in relation to the concept of 'the unconscious' are largely what define the difference between psychoanalytic schools and between psycho-analysis and other forms of therapy. Many training organizations claiming proximity to the one seen as 'the best' are delighted to point out the great similarities in requirements. What we see too little of is a reflective pose that asks: Why does something become a requirement at all? What are the theoretical considerations which underpin the decision that a certain component is desirable or even necessary for the training of psychoanalysts? We tend to proceed as if there were an indisputable law that we all must comply with, improve on or submit to.

The psychoanalytic field is diverse. Even within its self-proclaimed exclusion zones, divisions and sub-divisions operate mercilessly. Theoretically, the icons Freud, Jung, Klein, Object Relations, ego psychology, Phenomenology, Lacan, etc., differ fundamentally on some issues and minimally on others. We all embrace some notion of 'the unconscious' yet have different notions of its nature, structure and possible dynamics. Is it structured 'like a language' or is it the pure embodiment of non-structure? Is it a place 'inside' our individual psyche, do we all share a 'universal' one, or is it a phenomenon we are all subject to outside the myth of interiority? Is it akin to an archaeolo-gical site, which must be visited every day to avoid gathering too much dust between sessions? We all claim to work with 'repression' and 'resis-tance', yet have different ways of identifying what they mean and what one 'does' with their clinical expressions. We all claim that there is no analysis without transference, yet vary a great deal in our understanding and handling of it. While we all engage in interpretations, we have very different notions about what should be interpreted – dreams, fantasies, resistance, transference, a bit of everything?

The position one takes in relation to these and other questions will produce multiple solutions to 'the problem of the cushion' and to our training requirements. Freud saw psychoanalysis as a method of investi-gation that might, under favourable conditions, alleviate symptoms. At the same time he warned that if we did not effect 'cures' no one would come to us, apart from trainees, who are obliged to do so if they wish to join the club – which brings us to the question of the 'training analysis', the small difference which is said to make all the difference. It is still the area around which our theoretical, clinical and political lack of intelligent and dispassionate discourse tends to be exposed.

After 'the unconscious', 'transference' seems to be the most central concept in psychoanalysis. It can be seen as the ground concerning which all the basic characteristics of a given treatment play themselves out: 'The establishment, modalities, interpretation and resolution of the transference are in fact what define the cure' (Laplanche and Pontalis, 1973, p. 455). As early as 1912 it was argued that to engage in psychoanalysis, it is not enough to embark on an academic course of study. Freud and Ferenczi saw the analyst's unconscious as a therapeutic instrument that needed to be finely tuned to the unconscious of the patient so that it could receive and decipher unconscious communications. Ferenczi was also concerned that unless an analyst was fully and completely analysed, he might not be able to withstand what Ferenczi saw as the assault from the patient. And so, in the mid-1920s a 'training analysis' became mandatory.

It is not fashionable at present to hold to notions of a 'complete' analysis, yet claims are still made on the authority to determine who is 'as near as can be fully analysed'. The claim for better 'standards' due to more stringent 'requirements' is easily dismissed when you compare the actual requirements of the various training bodies rather than the prevailing fantasies about them. The latter reveal an abundance of uninformed nonsense. The real sticking point remains the split between those who think that a training analysis should be conducted by the dead and those who believe it should be conducted by the living. Or, to put it more concretely, is the training of a psychoanalyst accomplished by acquiring an education or by internalizing the unconscious of one's analyst? This question has long been masked by the so-called 'times per week issue'. It is claimed that the more sessions per week one has, the deeper, more intense and better the analysis, the ultimate mark of excellence:

> We say that if others wish to join us they must meet certain requirements in their training and ethical standards ... If this means we believe in something special and excellent, the answer is yes ... the trainees must have a long personal analysis five times a week, with a training analyst – this is the most important part of the training. (Brearley, 1997, p. 8)

Thus, frequency rather than the nature of interpretation and its relation to unconscious material becomes the criteria for a 'proper analysis'.

In the 1950s, the American Psychoanalytic Association wrangled over whether four or five times per week was good enough. During the lawsuit which followed years later, a psychologist asked if anyone ever studied whether three or four hours were more effective. Other than notions of judgment and custom, no reply was apparently elicited. In the early 1990s, the then Psychoanalytic and Psychodynamic Section of UKCP was grappling with whether a two or three times per week minimum requirement justified separate titles, one Analytic, the other Psychoanalytic. Theoretical arguments aside, analytic frequency as the deciding requirement is impossible as its own supporters negate it in two major ways. First, the International Psychoanalytic Association (IPA) recognizes trainings that 'only' require three times per week training analysis. Such trainings are allowed to join the IPA and their graduates are recognized as IPA psychoanalysts. Second, many individuals in the UK have undergone a four and five times per week analysis with a training analyst recognized by the BP-AS, yet its affiliated Institute of Psycho-Analysis is opposed to these individuals calling themselves psychoanalysts (hyphenated or otherwise) because they did not train at *their* Institute. In other words, the claim for the exclusive right to train and endow the title 'psychoanalyst' appears to have little to do with any rational difference in training criteria and more to do with membership of an exclusive club that wishes to enhance its exclusivity by limiting its membership, particularly as it awards a small minority of its members with the sole rights to control the training market of anyone who wishes to join the club.

Those who wish to stop non-IPA non-hyphenated psychoanalysts using the title must have a rational reason, one that would stand up in a court of law. Transference to an institution will not suffice. There are just as many non-IPA psychoanalysts in the world as the IPA variety, which may be why the BP-AS coined the hyphenated title as a distinguishing 'trademark' knowing full well that no one organization can have exclusive rights to the word 'psychoanalyst' – which remains a cultural term of reference. Nor can the BP-AS legally prevent anyone from training psychoanalysts outside the IPA. Suppose all training organizations in this country required all trainees to have analysis five times per week. This would not suffice either, for they will have to have been analysed by someone who was analysed by an analyst who is part of the 'apostolic' succession going all the way back to Freud, transmitted by 'internalization' from one generation of a cult to another. The 'ownership' of Freud's unconscious is what is in dispute here, for whoever claims it also claims to be the gatekeeper of 'the absolute truth of Psycho-Analysis'.

In Britain, pressure from the UKCP on the government to bring psychotherapy under state regulation is forcing the BCP and UKCP to talk. But rather than talking about the obvious contradictions in the notion of a state-regulated psychoanalysis, we fight about the rights to the title psychoanalyst. Already the Institute and the BCP are telling us that it will take them a very long time to talk among themselves before they can discuss the question of the differences between 'us' and 'them' publicly. The bidding for ownership of Freud's unanalysed bits, as Derrida so aptly called it, is indeed open, but the odds of it producing anything other than acrimonious splitting and shady deals appear very slim indeed.

Fourteen years ago, I watched a television programme on which I was interviewed. To my bemusement, the title 'psychoanalyst' appeared under my name although I was never asked what my 'title' was. This persisted over the years in other media references and in conferences abroad. Several years ago, in a cross-modalities discussion, I found my argument dismissed by a humanistic psychotherapist as 'this is the kind of nonsense you psychoanalysts believe in'. In short, whenever I opened my mouth, I was recognized as one of the 'mad horde'. I remembered how a group of French painters was dismissed by the critics as 'impressionists' and adopted the name as their trademark and accepted the label. Indeed, when I use the title psychoanalyst, I do not claim to own it but rather acknowledge that it has a claim on me. I do not claim to be a member of the BP-AS or the IPA but a member of the international psychoanalytic community and a participant in its discourse and practice. By doing so, I believe that I am following the Freudian initiative of questioning all dogma and of re-inventing psychoanalysis with every patient. To do it justice, one must think of psychoanalysis differently, outside of the British class system, for to think that all is now known about the psyche and can be packaged into a sealed identity would amount to a negation of the psychoanalytic project itself.

NOTE

1.   This is exactly what did happen in the 1950s when Jaques Lacan raised funda-
     mental questions about the nature and the transmissibility of psychoanalysis,
     about whether it should follow the authoritarian model of the medical school or the

liberalism of academics. He was expelled from the IPA for breaking the technical rules and introducing the concept and practices of the 'variable length session' and indeterminate frequency.

BIBLIOGRAPHY

Balint, A. with Balint, M. (1939) 'Love for the mother and mother love'. In *Primary Love and Psycho-Analytic Technique*. London: Maresfield Library, 1952.

Brearley, M. (1997) 'Who speaks for psychoanalysis? The UKCP/BCP debate', *The Psychoanalysis Newsletter* (Therip). **23**, Autumn 1999, p. 8.

Derrida. J. (1987) *The Post Card: From Socrates to Freud and Beyond*. Trans. A. Bass. Chicago: University of Chicago Press.

Freud, S. (1914) 'On the history of the psycho-analytic movement'. In *Standard Edition* Vol. XIV. London: Hogarth Press and the Institute of Psycho-Analysis.

Grossman, C.M. and Grossman, S. (1965) *The Wild Analyst*. London: Barrie & Rockliff (Barrie Books Ltd).

Hale, N.G. (1999) 'Book review', in *Psychoanalytic Books: A Quarterly Journal of Reviews*. **10**, 3.

Kennedy, M. (1995) 'Psychoanalysis in Australia', *The Psychoanalysis Newsletter* (Therip). **16**, Spring.

Kirsner, D. (2000) *Unfree Associations*. London: Process Press.

Laplanche, J. and Pontalis, J.-B. (1973) *The Language of Psycho-Analysis*. London: The Hogarth Press and the Institute of Psycho-Analysis.

Nobus, D. (1997) 'Zeus's awakening and the handling of the eroticised transference', *The Psychoanalysis Newsletter* (Therip). **23**, Autumn 1999.

Oakley, C. and Oakley, H. (1998) 'The Site for Contemporary Psychoanalysis'. In *The Psychoanalytic Newsletter* (Therip). **21**, Spring 1998.

Roudinesco, E. (1997) *Jacques Lacan*. New York: Columbia University Press.

Shamdasani, S. (2000) 'A mere advertising bluff?', unpublished paper given at the 'Why Jung?' conference at the Site for Contemporary Psychoanalysis, October 1999.

Wallerstein, R.S. (1988) *Lay Analysis: Life Inside the Controversy*. Hillsdale, NJ: The Analytic Press.

Yehoshua, A.B. (1999) *A Journey to the End of the Millennium*. Trans. by N. de Lange. London: Peter Halban Publishers Ltd.

4

Psychoanalysis as a Surrogate for Life Experience[1]

Simona Argentieri

As one gathers from the title, this chapter is not meant to sound a triumphant or celebratory note on the occasion of the first one hundred years of psychoanalysis; nor, however, will it contribute to the already vast and trendy literature on the so-called 'crisis' of our discipline.[2] In fact, the past several years have seen a proliferation of papers and essays – ranging from the apocalyptic and sombre to the polemical or patronizing – all of which maintain that psychoanalysis is clinically outdated, metapsychologically ill-founded and even possibly iatrogenic. In all honesty, I hardly find this kind of negative criticism disturbing; not because of any absolute faith in psychoanalysis but, to the contrary, precisely because I believe that psychoanalysis is, in and of itself, a theory of permanent crisis. This belief derives not only from the fact that, since its inception, psychoanalysis has been marked by disputes, schisms and heresies; rather, and above all else, it is because psychoanalysis is based on the very notion of conflict: of the conflict inherent in the intra-psychic, unconscious dynamics of ambivalence, which forever challenge the balancing acts of our lives.

Clinically speaking, psychoanalysis is a process which insists on the transcription and retranscription of memories, on the construction and reconstruction of meaning. Theoretically, the need to rethink concepts, to defy established certainties and to remain open to the possibilities of radical transformations is part of a background philosophy which insists on a search for truth – albeit of a modest kind, and divested of all omnipotence, namely, the truth of not lying to oneself.

Nowadays, however, the social contexts in which we live and work confront us with a troubling contradiction: we witness, alongside a general disdain for psychoanalysis, the unchecked popularization of its terms and concepts. For example, the word 'unconscious,' apart from its largely colloquial use, has become fully integrated into the languages of any number of psychological schools which – like the cognitivist and behaviourist – remain fundamentally alien to the psychoanalytic project.

Moreover, even legislative efforts to regulate the practice of psychotherapy – efforts whose merits are often questionable – push for uniformity. Psychotherapists are often lumped together, without distinction: from Freud's disciples, with their many years of training, to the recent generations of psychologists, whose training consists of brief but focused post-graduate courses. These days, almost any clinical approach based on listening is hastily defined as 'psychoanalysis', both by the public at large and, with absent-minded ambiguity, by the therapists themselves, no matter what their training or theoretical orientation. The latter, in fact, include any number of practitioners who will dilute, deform and transform psychoanalytic theory to interpret and decode dreams; or, as Freud used to say, who will 'warm their soup at our fire' even as they denigrate psychoanalysis.

But aside from recriminations and distinctions of title or merit, what I would like to address here is an insidious phenomenon, typical of our confused times, which in my view affects the whole of psychotherapy. The phenomenon is a clandestine one, equally dependent on the discipline's 'diffusion' as well as 'crisis', and involves the use of psychoanalysis as a surrogate for life experience. That is to say, psychoanalysis is no longer viewed as a treatment method to help people get on with their lives, but as an emotional experience which takes the place of real events and relationships. This holds true for patients, but also – and what is even more dangerous – for therapists.

There is no doubt that one of the basic factors in this 'improper use' of psychoanalysis concerns the initial motivation of the patient; it rests, in other words, on the very choice of therapy as the privileged vehicle through which a person in distress looks for help. It used to be that only the 'classical' forms of psychopathology (i.e. neuroses and psychoses) were considered appropriate for psychological treatment. Imperceptibly, however, a significant change has come about: on the one hand, requests for treatment are increasingly spurred by life's real, everyday challenges: by the suffering caused by love, loss, separation, and the crucial decisions we are all called on to make. On the other hand, we find requests inspired by transcendent, metaphysical problems, like the fear of death, or the existence of God ...

In this way psychoanalysis (or its derivatives) comes to occupy spaces that are not its own: I refer, for example, to those 'spaces' vacated by the forces of religion and ideology. But above all else I refer to those spaces

previously occupied by the ego, on whose resources everyone must draw
to face the challenges of growing up, of relating to others and living with
another person, of managing dependency and separation issues, and of
fulfilling, ultimately, the adult function of caring for the next generation.

Moreover, since the 'causes' of one's malaise are initially located
outside the self – either in heaven or on earth – many patients today
avoid confronting the essential premise of any treatment, namely, the
acknowledgement that they are indeed ill. This goes to compound a
distinctly perverse mechanism at work in the field. Increasingly, while
young psychologists overstep their bounds in taking on patients'
everyday problems (or in sharing those existential anxieties that are the
common lot of all humans), the severe mental illnesses, including
madness itself, are no longer treated by psychologists. But this is another
matter, albeit a dramatic one.

Whenever one does treat 'real' patients, other problems arise, related
to the effects of large-scale social transformations on people's psyches,
and on the ways we express and denote pathology. Nowadays we speak
of labile character structures and fragile super-egos; of impoverished
affects and memory deficits; of weak self-identity and intolerance to
frustration; of 'as if' personalities and 'false selves' ... These are the
human beings of our time, scarred by narcissistic anxieties and pressures;
these are the people who would benefit most clearly from a classical
analysis, but who rarely are willing to make such a commitment. As
some colleagues say, it is precisely the people who have no time who
require a longer time in treatment.[3]

It is, anyhow, rare for patients to be referred for an analysis of four or
five weekly sessions. In keeping with either our modern-day life style
(dominated by the pseudovalues of haste and result-oriented hyper-
efficiency), or with patients' legitimate constraints of time and money,
once- or twice-weekly psychotherapy is more often the rule. While such
a choice may be commendable it is, unfortunately, often based on ideological or contingent criteria, with little regard for the case-specific,
preferred form of treatment – that must necessarily vary from individual
to individual. It is in this light that we can observe the disappearance of
another value, namely, of the correct definition of 'psychoanalytic
psychotherapy', with its own specific criteria and techniques. What we
find, instead, in a majority of cases, is a kind of diluted, 'low grade'
psychoanalysis being practised.

In my experience, people with severe psychological disturbances who
resort to short-term treatment do, at times, show momentary improve-

ment; but after a while they almost invariably return for help. Time and again, 'mild' forms of psychotherapy are enlisted that can only reinforce a patient's defences – which have long proven inadequate to deal with core issues – rather than meet their deeper needs. It is a paradox, then, that for the sake of brevity, therapy turns into a sort of sequential, interminable analysis which keeps the patient in treatment for life, as they move from one treatment cycle to another.

Obviously, such a misleading and distorted expectation – that a therapist should bear the burden of living and thinking on a patient's behalf, and risk dragging frankly pathological problems through endlessly disappointing treatments – cannot persist without the therapist's unequivocal and symmetrical collusion. Or, as we used to say in the 1970s, without there being an intricate nexus between 'supply' and 'demand'.

In the past the training of a psychoanalyst was a long and tortuous process. The acquisition of a professional identity would mark the endpoint of any number of diversified career itineraries: indeed, not only medical doctors and psychiatrists, but also philosophers, historians and artists ended up as psychoanalysts. For the emergence of the desire to undertake this atypical craft would often surprise the very person in question. This was the case, for example, in the pioneering days of the polyglot Karl Abraham, the actor Ernst Simmel, the princess Marie Bonaparte ... and, later, with the 'housewife' Melanie Klein, and the pediatrician D.W. Winnicott. Among Italy's founding fathers, Emilio Servadio had a degree in law, and Cesare Musatti was a mathematician. Clearly, the shortcomings and limitations of such heterogeneous, naïve and dated ways of approaching psychoanalysis are everywhere evident, but there is no arguing that such a climate also afforded a rich variety of cultural and life experiences. Ultimately, the training process was a truly enlightening one, involving a high degree of introspection alongside often painful renunciations.

Nowadays, the training track is a rather mandatory and rigid one, a unidirectional course of study (in psychology, more often than not) which recruits students prematurely and then effectively forecloses other alternatives.[4] It is also likely that this state of affairs will become increasingly consolidated in the future. What is lost, as a result, is the opportunity to truly question and be engaged by one's professional project, by the thorny and ambiguous nucleus at the root of our so-called 'vocation'. The term itself, with its mystical evocations, locates people's motivation in the sublime rather than in the unconscious. To look to heal others is, in fact, the most formidable of defences, as it involves the projection into others of one's own damaged parts, in order to then come to their aid. It is no coincidence, in the course of an analysis, that analysands will often consider becoming analysts themselves. Fortunately, in most cases this is a passing symptom, whose aim is to elude or shortcut the anxieties that meaninglessness evokes, as well as the discovery of one's own neediness and dependency.

In sum, the direction of the maturational process is thus reversed: one's professional identity is no longer the natural outcome of the construction of a personal identity, but instead proceeds backwards, in a defensive way. It is a process through which more and more people expect to answer the question 'who am I?' with the claim 'I am a psychotherapist'. Psychoanalysis thus becomes not only a surrogate way of life, but the means for a surrogate identity as well.

If, then, a psychologist, after graduation, decides to undergo psycho-analytical training, the problem is still left unresolved. Because of the long, strenuous years that intervene between applying for training and actually beginning a training analysis, the aspiring analyst will inevitably begin to see patients in that interim. In so doing a 'choice' is enacted even before one begins to lie on the couch. Thus, when the training analysis does finally begin, it is as if an implicit agreement were already in place between analyst and analysand: everything will be analysed, except for the essential core of the project, whose enactment has – for all practical purposes – made the choice unalterable. Or, what is even worse, analyst and analysand might together stage, more or less consciously, the fiction of analysing that core motivation.

We need to add that, in the past twenty years, to undergo two analyses is practically the norm in psychoanalytic circles. For example, one might begin a personal analysis prior to training, out of a sense of responsibility towards oneself and one's patients – and, in this way, come to analyse the psychoanalytic project. Later, when the need for analysis is no longer pressing, one then begins a so-called training analysis, to comply with an institute's requirements. Additionally there are times when, upon termination of the training analysis and graduation to 'associate member-ship', one realizes that some issues have remained unresolved; at this point, free from all external and formal obligations, finally – perhaps even secretly – one can become a patient.

We thus find ourselves in an uncomfortable 'impasse': for while analysis can be a remedy for all sorts of personal issues and pathology, it is sometimes their root cause. Training matters pose enormous, complex problems, with ripple effects that institutes all across the world are trying to address through efforts to adjust their statutes and by-laws.

In my view, precisely because psychoanalysis (even in its orthodox form) is such a powerful and precious instrument, it is not a harmless one. In 'overdoses' it runs the risk of funnelling vital energies in a centripetal direction; it risks blocking action, rendering chronic any number of intellectual defences, and turning life into endless waiting. The risk is even greater for the therapist – on or behind the couch – already forced by the demands of clinical practice, to spend countless hours every day isolated from reality, in a one-on-one relationship, marked by asymmetry and abstinence. To practise psychoanalysis and only analysis full time ruins the psychoanalyst's character (which is generally bad, to begin with). In and of themselves, our authentic passion for our work and dedication to our patients make us neither ideal companions nor ideal parents; in point of fact, outside of our consulting rooms, we tend to convey a sense of fatigue, or, worse, a kind of aristocratic presumption. All this can impoverish our private lives and foster, in turn, an abuse of psychoanalysis to fill our own emotional void.

Things get even worse when senior and experienced analysts end up doing only training analyses, in an air-tight, self-referential circuit which leaves the real world and its real patients even further marginalized. Thus we have analysis, a second analysis, supervision ... and then, in our 'free time', evening study groups and seminars in which we alternate as teachers or students. We spend long weekend hours in scientific or society meetings, and take holidays attending conferences and congresses. Psychoanalysis, like no other profession, saturates the mental and emotional spaces of its practitioners' lives, and acts as a secret remedy against loneliness. While it is certainly not my intention to celebrate the figure of the 'wild' psychoanalyst, I do not consider the monk-like therapist to be a model of professional life. There is no virtue, I believe, in renouncing the everyday ingredients of an ordinary life – the affective, cultural, civic, even playful aspects of living – especially when it is the therapist's task to enable patients to experience life more fully.

All this, perhaps, is nothing but a new and insidious version of the resistances which have always accompanied the history of psychoanalysis. For while the perennial epistemological uncertainties, or a single practitioner's ignorance or errors, are forever identified as signs of crisis, we fail to confront the genuine problems facing us, which I see as follows:

- We need to define, with intellectual honesty, the therapeutic limits of psychoanalysis as well as the limits of what it can aspire to know: this, without denying the extraordinary and irreplaceable value of a tool which may yet be destined to remain – for reasons both internal and external to the patient – a method of treatment for only a minority of people.
- We need systematically to distinguish psychoanalysis – on a theoretical, technical and clinical level – both from therapeutic strategies that derive from it (i.e. psychoanalytic psychotherapy, child, couple and group psychotherapy) as well as from those strategies based on other theoretical models (i.e. cognitive and behavioural therapies).
- We must, first and foremost, look to repair the senseless schism between psychoanalysis and psychiatry which, at least in Italy, has: (1) flung open the doors to the prevailing 'counter-reformation' that has led to the indiscriminate triumph of psychotropic drugs (tranquillizers, and above all anti-depressants); (2) seen this counter-reformation thrive, thanks, in part, to the enthusiastic cooperation of its victims; and (3) even revived electroshock therapy as a fashionable treatment option, practised – ironically – principally in private clinics and therefore on the wealthiest of patients.

In point of fact, the anti-psychiatry revolution that was meant to change the status of madness in society, and to transform society itself in the process, all too often has meant the further marginalization of society's most vulnerable members. In Italy, the problems resulting from the sluggish phasing out of mental hospitals in the 1970s was compounded by both the progressive shirking of responsibility on the part of the political and medical establishments, as well as by the exceedingly low profile maintained by psychoanalysts throughout the course of the controversy. Such a reprehensible situation has mostly left the patients' families with both the blame and the responsibility to provide treatment for the most severe cases of mental illness, in a climate of resentment and loneliness.[5] And yet, something is changing.

Up until the 1980s, to declare oneself a psychoanalyst was enough to arouse the admiration of one's interlocutors. These days – luckily! – ours is a profession like any other. Freed from cumbersome idealizations, the profession now appeals to fewer candidates, who in turn need to wait less time before being admitted to training. This leads to a self-selection process which rewards those who are genuinely motivated to undergo such a long and arduous training. It is through this next generation that we can hope to effect the changes necessary to preserve the matrix of psychoanalysis.

To those who would say – with an overall sense of disappointment – that one hundred years of psychoanalysis have not changed the world, we will reply that this is true. However, we are all witnesses to those minor miracles when, through the long, painstaking work of analysis, we do manage to help change a person's life. Once upon a time psycho-analysis was upheld as a banner of the individual's right to be happy; the so-called 'pleasure principle' was interpreted as an invitation to hedonistic pursuits and a promise of the joyous liberation of the instincts. Instead, now as then, our task can only be – in line with the stern Freudian admonition – 'to transform neurotic misery into ordinary unhappiness'. This, notwithstanding the apparent pessimism of Freud's dictum, is no meagre accomplishment. I say this because, aside from the pains inflicted upon us by the harshness of the 'reality principle', we all pay a very high price – and exact a similar price from others – for the suffering generated by our unconscious neurotic mechanisms.

When deployed in the service of life – and not of its bloodless substi-tutes – psychoanalysis can help us give up our pointless suffering. It can also do more: it can help us forego, together with that neurotic suffering, our resentful demands for absolute gratification, which serve only to spare us the earnest work we all need to do to muster the modicum of happiness that life, after all, does afford us.

NOTES

1. Translated by Pina Antinucci-Mark and Anthony Molino.

2. This contribution has generated diametrically opposite reactions within Italian psychoanalytic circles. Some colleagues have in fact accused me of defeatism, of a lack of solidarity, and of not supporting the future of our discipline in these bitter and confused times. Others – in a spirit of renewal – have, to the contrary, voiced their outright approval, convinced as they are of the need for an open and critical reflection on the problems facing psychoanalysis and our society today. In both cases, I was concerned that I might be misunderstood, as my intent is neither existentially pessimistic nor 'revolutionary'. Rather, it is to invoke an attitude of watchfulness: not simply over psychoanalysis, but over the ways in which it is used – or, more frequently, misused. The risk, in fact, is that we end up dissipating its distinctive theoretical, technical and clinical legacy.

3. U. Corino and I. Caponetto, 'A nuovi pazienti nuovi analisti?', *Quaderni ASP*, V, 11 (1995).

4. In some countries (e.g. Sweden), in an attempt to help students make a more mature career choice, enrolment in a university course in psychology is not allowed

before the age of 27. It is difficult to ascertain if such expedients really help avert
the risks of early choices, or if they end up artificially extending adolescence.

5.   'In fact, the reform has sanctioned abandonment as a therapeutic practice ... While
there were one hundred thousand patients in psychiatric hospitals in 1978, they now
number less than twenty thousand; this is hardly an achievement, since sixty thousand have simply died'. (S. Rossini, *L'Espresso*, November 1996).

Psychoanalysis and the Function of Consciousness

David M. Black

The word 'consciousness' has many shades of meaning. I am going to speak about it from a psychoanalytic point of view, and I shall address two questions in relation to it. First, the question: what is the relation between consciousness and the body, or more specifically the brain? And second, the question: what is consciousness for? Why has the evolutionary process come up with animals which have the characteristic of consciousness?

The first question, of the relationship between consciousness and the brain, takes us back to the origins of psychoanalytic thought. When Freud first turned his attention to psychoanalytic matters he was aged nearly 40, and already had a considerable reputation as a neuroanatomist. He had begun by doing hard research, mapping the nervous system of the crayfish, locating the gonads of eels, and had already written some 200 scientific papers to do with neuroanatomy. His textbook on cerebral paralyses in children would be the standard medical work on the subject for 40 years.

So when he first came to what he called 'the neuroses', he was still thinking in terms of the anatomy of the brain. His initial assumption was that it must be possible to map them directly onto the physical brain, that obsessions would be caused by lesions in one area of the brain, hysteria by lesions in another, and so on. This was in accordance with Helmholtzian materialism, the creed to which Freud gave his allegiance.

However, there was also a rival picture which Freud had to digest, and this was derived from his visit to Paris in 1885, when he had worked with the charismatic French psychiatrist Charcot. Charcot gave an account of hysteria in purely psychological terms; that is to say, without reference to the brain, he described emotional events giving rise to emotional consequences, including also physical manifestations such as paralyses, rashes, fainting attacks and conversion symptoms. In other words, whereas Freud's training gave him a picture of a causal sequence running from the physical to the psychological, from brain to emotion, in Charcot he had met an impressive scientist who described causal sequences which could run in the opposite direction, from psyche to soma. Freud never, I think, gave up his Helmholtzian orientation, but his encounter with Charcot, and then his own experience, made him realize that these connections were still, at that time, unresolvable; and this emboldened him to make the step into psychoanalysis as we have since known it, that is, into a science of psychological events which have their reality and their causation in a realm that can be described in purely psychological terms.

To take a familiar sort of example: if I have a neurotic symptom, say, a fear of success, a psychoanalyst is willing to think that it has a purely psychological cause, perhaps a fantasy that if I succeed it will be a mortal wound to my unsuccessful father. Even if we enquire further, and ask why should I have such a fantasy, we stay in the psychological world. For example, we say that the fantasy of a mortal wound is constructed on a template of a deeper fantasy, for example a buried memory of my father's rage when, as a small child, I protested against his possession of my mother in a way that excluded me. This whole story is told in the psychological language of wishes and desires and passionate feelings and fantasies, and it seems self-contained: it does not seem to require any stepping across from the psychological realm into the physical realm. Psychoanalysis has set out to be something very remarkable: a responsible science, but taking as its crucial data, unlike any other science, subjective experience, perceived by introspection, and not public, sharable facts, perceived by observation.

However, as a result, psychoanalysis has always suffered from a credibility gap. Those who have experienced it, and had a reasonably good experience, have been persuaded that it contains something profoundly important, and unmistakably in some sense true to reality. Those who have not experienced it, or have not had a good experience of it, have felt entirely free to dismiss the whole edifice as pretentious or dangerous delusion. And those who reject it have not always been naïve and confused thinkers, but sometimes unmistakably competent scientific thinkers like Michael Polanyi (1958) or Peter Medawar (1967).

Meanwhile, in the past one hundred years, neuroscience has also developed, and in the past fifteen years or so immensely exciting and fertile new ideas have proliferated. For example, PET scans can now give us ever more precise pictures of the complex electrical activity in the brain as it changes from micro-second to micro-second. I am not a neuroscientist, and I can only glimpse the implications of all this, but I have no doubt at all that they are enormous. One theory, for example, is that of Gerald Edelman, and although in its detail it may be superseded, in its general form it is typical of the new understanding. I shall take a moment to speak about Edelman's theory.

Edelman (1992) has suggested that the physical structure of the brain is not, in its fine detail, determined by the genes. When a baby is born, the neurones in its brain are connected up by some fifty million million of the small electro-chemical junctions known as synapses. This number of synapses, already unimaginably vast, will multiply in the first months of life by a factor of 20, to one thousand million million, and the formation of this astronomically huge number of synapses is unpredictable: it will be in large part determined by the baby's experience of the world, and particularly by the emotion-laden experience of the baby's interaction with the human beings in its world. (Children don't learn language from being exposed to the television.)

Edelman gives the example of a child learning to catch a ball. If the child succeeds in catching the ball, this experience will enhance the development of the synapses which help him to catch balls – for example, those involved in hand–eye coordination – and it will also cause other synapses to be deleted, which might tend to impede him in catching balls. The psychoanalyst, of course, wants to ask other questions. How does the child know what constitutes success, and that success is desirable? The answer must be, that the child has been rewarded for past, similar successes by the people around it, by shining eyes, smiles, exclamations of admiration, and so on. We know how confusing it is for a child, if one parent rewards a piece of behaviour, and the other punishes it. And we know too that there are other children who don't learn to catch balls – orphans in Romanian orphanages, for example, who have never received these gratifying rewards, and who have become too inert to be interested in catching balls, or in developing skills of any kind. Nowadays, we can look at the brains of such children using PET scans, and where the brains of happy, healthy, socially active children show up as full of light, in the brains of the Romanian orphans we find large areas of darkness and inactivity.

So Edelman's example, simple as it seems, is already complex. The child who learns to experience catching a ball as a success, and therefore improves his dexterity and his social desirability, is a child who has already, in our jargon, internalized someone, probably a mother, who applauds dexterous achievement, who wills development, who believes the world is worth engaging with – it is hard to describe with sufficient generality attitudes which in normal circumstances we take for granted. Often we only realize what an achievement these attitudes are, when we experience the shock of meeting another child, perhaps a Romanian orphan, in whom these attitudes have not developed; he hasn't died, but he has developed a different brain structure. And the evidence is that even the most loving parenting and the most intensive therapy at later ages may do something but can never fully repair this early damage.

These discoveries of modern neuroscience are immensely exciting to a psychoanalyst. For many years, it has felt as if psychoanalysis alone among the sciences attempted to deal with the true complexity and depth of human experience. Related sciences, such as neuroscience, behavioural psychology, psychiatric pharmacology, etc., all portrayed a curiously simplified version of emotional life. Between the vision of B.F. Skinner, and the vision of Shakespeare, there was a great gulf. Psychoanalysis, for all its limitations, tried not to lose awareness of this complexity, and often dealt with its isolation among the sciences by turning to the arts. '*These* are my teachers', said Freud once (to Ludwig Binswanger), indicating a shelf full, not of psychological works, but of Greek tragedies and the works of Shakespeare.

With the arrival of the new neuroscience, suddenly we have an unmistakably hard science, with graphs and numbers, which shows us a physical object, the brain – the most complex material structure in the universe, as Edelman is fond of saying – which is of an order of complexity comparable to our picture of the psyche; and moreover, like our picture of the psyche, it derives its structure partly from genetic factors, but to a very great extent in response to experience. As with our picture of the psyche, there are phases of development when the brain is very adaptable, and other phases when it is less adaptable but not wholly inert. We are bound to feel, and I think we are right to feel, that this new model of brain development casts a flood of light on what we have been struggling to work with for a hundred years by way of the slippery and unreliable methods of introspection.

But, of course, the question at once arises: what is the relation between the brain and the mind? Are the neuroscientists now discovering the real thing, and is psychoanalysis now ready to slide into possibly honourable but long overdue oblivion? Francis Crick puts the case for this sort of view with characteristic verve:

You, you, your joys and your sorrows, your memories and your
ambitions, your sense of personal identity and free will, are in fact
no more than the behaviour of a vast assembly of nerve cells and
their associated molecules. (cited in Solms, 1997, p. 682)

I think we should be grateful to the Francis Cricks of this world for their
enthusiastic certainties, because they spare us from having to set up
Aunt Sallies. Psychoanalysts also have at times been naïvely reductivist,
treating every human issue as if unconscious conflict were the only
reality. The challenge for all of us in the postmodern world is to
maintain our conviction that there is such a thing as truth, and yet also
to be open to the fact that there are many languages in which truth can
be spoken, and not all of them fully translate into one another. Crick is
rightly impressed by his 'vast assembly' of nerve cells, but what his
statement overlooks is precisely the thing that makes these vast assem-
blies so interesting to us, namely, that each one is owned by someone in
particular. However vast the assembly may be, and however much it
may affect our capacity to be conscious, that fact does not explain why
this assembly of nerve cells is *mine*, and *that* assembly of nerve cells is
yours.

This extraordinary fact, that consciousness is owned by *subjects*, is
beyond the reach of objective reduction, no matter how subtle our
understanding of brain function, or the electrochemical activity at the
synapses, may become. Steven Pinker, in his engaging book *How the
Mind Works*, looks at the questions to do with subjectivity, and retreats
hastily: 'beats the heck out of me!' (1997, p. 146). He writes from a neo-
Darwinian point of view, and I admire his honesty. These questions
cannot be answered by objective science alone, not because the science is
not yet good enough, but for a purely logical reason, that objective facts
alone cannot account for subjectivity.

To show this, try asking the simple question: what differentiates my
experience from yours? It may be that our experiences are very different.
Perhaps the experience I have when I hear a trumpet is like the experience you have when you hear a violin. Unlikely, but there is no way to
be sure. But there is one unmistakable difference between our experiences, that mine is mine, and yours is yours. It is not some deficiency in
our brains which causes me not to be you, or that causes, out of the five
billion human consciousnesses on planet Earth, one alone to be Meg
Ryan, or Isaiah Berlin, or President Clinton. Subjectivity is irreducible,
not because of our ignorance, but because of its nature.

Freud famously spoke of consciousness as a sense organ: 'a sense organ ... for the perception of psychic qualities'. A colleague of mine, Mark Solms, has built on Freud's metaphor to say that the physical language description, in terms of neurones and synapses, and the psychological language description, in terms of feelings and fantasies, each derive from different modes of perception, and can no more be collapsed into one another than the flash of lightning and the peal of thunder. When we use our vision, we see lightning; when we use hearing, we hear thunder; both sensations are perfectly, and equally, valid, and both tell us of an unknown event which manifests in both modalities. Similarly, when we use vision, we see PET scans, and perceive a vast assembly of neurones; when we use conscious introspection, we perceive feelings and fantasies. Both sorts of perception are equally valid, and neither tells us of some single reality to which the other can be reduced.

Following this line of thought, Solms says: 'The supposedly mysterious distinction between mind and body thus dissolves into a simple distinction between different perceptual modalities, facing in different directions.' I think this notion, that neuroscience and psychoanalysis both describe in some sense the same *thing*, though perceiving it through two different modalities of perception which cannot be reduced to one another, gives the best model we yet have for thinking about the different approaches. It leaves us with certain difficulties, however. In the case of the lightning flash, science gives us a way of speaking which allows us to understand how the same event gives rise both to a visual and to an auditory experience in the observer. In the case of neuroscience and psychoanalysis we cannot do that. Moreover, the material constituents of the brain have a comprehensible history before and after their sojourn in the brain; subjectivity, however, so far as science knows, comes into existence only with, and vanishes following, the material complexity of Crick's 'vast assembly of nerve cells'. So I think we are still at a rather provisional stage in formulating the mind–body relation.

THE FUNCTION OF CONSCIOUSNESS

So much for subjectivity, which is the most interesting and least reducible of all the topics covered by the broad heading 'consciousness'. I want to move now to 'consciousness' in another sense, one that is more peculiar to psychoanalysis, the sense in which consciousness is often contrasted with unconsciousness.

This contrast is often, I think, made in an over-simple way, and it is rather rarely in our work that a memory or feeling comes into a patient's mind which is wholly a surprise to him. Even when there is an abrupt change of feeling in a session, and a patient who is, for example, trying to be 'brave', and claiming to be unhurt by a rejection, suddenly breaks down into tears and indignation, it may be more accurate to use some expression such as 'denial' of the feeling, rather than to speak of total unconsciousness. What *is* useful, however, is to think of an unconscious developmental history behind our current capacity for emotional experience. Examples are never simple in psychoanalysis, but I will try to give one to illustrate what I mean.

The patient is a 30-year-old woman, married to a man of about 45. She works as a secretary. She comes into a session one morning, and tells me she has just had a dream. In the dream, she went into her office, and had a sudden reaction of disgust: the office was dirty with mouse-droppings. That was the whole of her dream, and she falls silent. I have no idea what this is about, and after a moment I simply say, rather ruminatively: 'Funny to have mice in the office, one usually thinks of them in the home.' I say this because the phrase *mus domesticus* has come into my mind.

She says rather briskly: 'There's something I've been meaning to tell you for several weeks.' She then tells me that, in the past few weeks, she and her boss have begun a rather inconsequential sexual affair. Alone in the office together after 5 o'clock, they have drifted into it. Having told me about it, she then says: 'I must decide what I want to do about this.' The following session she tells me that she has spoken to her boss, and told him she wants to stop the affair.

What has happened, in this episode? In a sense, nothing seems to be very unconscious. She knew she was having the affair, she was an intelligent woman, anyone could see she needed to decide what she wanted. But she had not done so, and in rather striking contrast to her usual direct and forceful nature, she had, as she put it, 'drifted' into the sexual activity.

On the surface, I think, what happened was less in the nature of 'making the unconscious conscious', than of bringing together bits of her conscious mind that she was keeping apart. The dream, with its imagery of mouse-droppings and its emotional reaction of disgust, was bringing up elements of her reaction to the affair that she had managed to separate herself from. She felt the affair was squalid, was a bit disgusted with herself for getting into it, and she needed to bring these responses clearly into consciousness and into relation with her other feelings, of excitement, of specialness, and so on, so that she could make a decision which would not be 'drifting' but would be 'responsible' – a decision she knew the reasons for. A lot of modern psychoanalysis is principally concerned with the ways in which we can 'know and not know', know something and at the same time disavow our knowledge, or, in this case, keep something known separate from our wider knowledge of our commitments and responsibilities. We have seen recently in the Clinton impeachment an example of the huge consequences that can flow from this kind of apparently trivial splitting – which is at the same time so easy and slight to the split person, and astounding, even incomprehensible, to the onlooker, who in his role of onlooker is for the moment relatively unsplit, relatively integrated.

When things are kept apart in this way, behaviour is what we call irresponsible. 'Irresponsible' is a good word here: when someone is split, it is as if there is no one person there to answer for the behaviour. When the patient becomes unsplit, she becomes one person, she becomes responsible, and she can then make a decision about her behaviour. Unconsciousness comes in in a more systematic way when we ask more far-reaching questions: why is this woman split, when another woman wouldn't be? Why did this sexual episode blow up now, rather than six months ago? What is the relation between her choosing to have this affair with her boss, and her marriage to an older husband, her thoughts about her male analyst, her relationship with her father? Hopefully, in the course of an analysis, these wider questions will also be brought up for examination, and the far-reaching changes that we aspire to in analytic therapy depend on them.

To return to the subject of this chapter. What is the *function* of consciousness in all this? After all, as Freud and many others have said, a great deal of emotion and thinking and fantasy – in a word, of mental life – can take place perfectly well unconsciously. Freud even said, and much modern neuroscience seems to bear this out, that unconsciousness is the ordinary condition of mental events: millions of things are going on in the brain, and at any given moment consciousness, we are told, can at best grasp 7 ± 2 of them. Why should consciousness have developed? What can it do that unconsciousness cannot? If we accept an evolutionary model of the origin of species, what is the distinctive advantage brought by consciousness, despite all its splittings and failures?

I suggest that the function of consciousness is to enable us to decide what we will regard as reality, and thus to adapt to the always new and unprecedented present. Adaptability is the greatness, but also the curse, of humanity. Some animals, on other branches of the evolutionary tree, for example, insects, are governed by instincts, sometimes of breath-taking complexity and precision. In a predictable environment, instinct can be very successful. The higher birds and mammals have developed a different way of coping, more flexible, more adaptable, with some capacity to learn; and then, rather suddenly, with ourselves, we break through to an animal who is adaptable to an altogether unparalleled degree. We can live alone or in groups, we can adapt to life in the equatorial forest or above the Arctic Circle, we can be motivated to spend our life composing symphonies or to climb Everest or to build the Taj Mahal; we can concentrate for years on complex trains of logical thought, and finally map the human genome or work out exactly what went on in the first four seconds after the Big Bang. And equally, we can go off the rails. We can believe we are God himself, we can come to believe, and persuade others, that the Jews ought to be exterminated, we can sit in offices and pursue financial profit, measured in figures at the foot of a balance sheet, and be careless as we do that we are destroying the ecology of the only habitable planet. More mundanely, and as with my patient, we can spoil our lives and the lives of others by living out vague and unthought mixed motives.

A rather simple experiment illustrates the crucial difference that consciousness can make. A number of volunteers are divided into two groups. Both groups are then shown a series of Chinese ideograms (none of them knows Chinese) and asked to say which ideograms are 'good' and which 'bad'. As they look at the ideograms, a simplified face, either a smiling or a scowling button face, is projected alongside each ideogram in turn. The difference is that for one group, each face is projected for just under 0.2 seconds; for the other group, each face is projected for just over 0.2 seconds. We know that 0.2 seconds is the threshold for conscious recognition of a visual stimulus, so the first group are unconscious of the projected faces, the second group are conscious of them.

What transpires is that, in the second group, who are conscious of seeing the faces, their decisions as to whether the ideograms are good or bad do not significantly correlate with the sequence of smiling or scowling faces. With the first group, however, who are *not* conscious of seeing the faces, there is a high correlation. In other words, where there is conscious-ness, a factor can be scanned for relevance, and if it is irrelevant, discounted. Where there is unconsciousness, relevance cannot be assessed, and an irrelevant factor can be strikingly influential.

What is made possible by consciousness is a marshalling of relevant factors, and therefore responsible decision. Consciousness does not of course guarantee this; it is merely the condition without which this cannot occur. Without consciousness, or with vague and split consciousness, we remain incoherent, governed not by ourselves, which requires integration and clarity, but by other influences – by the past, in the form of habit and transference, or by wishes and overbearing impulses. Our almost unlimited adaptability means that at almost every moment, I am moving in one direction, but I might be moving in another. My patient was married; but her boss was attractive, and available; what could be more natural than to have sex with him? Or: I have work to do; but wouldn't it be nicer to stay in bed? Or, a slightly different sort of example: my friend is dead; I wish he wasn't; wouldn't it be pleasant to believe that he isn't *really* dead, he's still alive but just happens to be an invisible 'spirit'? Or wouldn't it be pleasant to believe, now Spring is here, that it will never be Winter again? Or, now peace is here, there will never again be war? It is consciousness that makes it possible to confront such thoughts, reflect on them, and decide what I will do and what I believe to be the case. It is only consciousness which makes it possible to maintain intentions, to hold values, to let go of fantasies, and to live in a real, painful, ever-changing world.

Religious specialists, who choose a life style in which many of our ordinary motives are systematically frustrated – including often, for example, the huge fundamental longings for sex, children, power, self-display, etc. – are choosing above all to be more conscious. The title of the Buddha means in essence the Awakened One. Consciousness, or awareness, is for such people a goal in itself. They know that, insofar as we satisfy our desires, we put parts of ourselves temporarily to sleep. The psychoanalyst is not concerned with consciousness in this heroic sense; only in the more limited sense in which a person needs sufficient consciousness to live in the present world, and to fulfil those of his desires which he decides, on reflection, to stand by.

BIBLIOGRAPHY

Begley, S. (1998) 'How to build a baby's brain', *Newsweek*, 7 August.
Edelman, G.M. (1992) *Bright Air, Brilliant Fire*. New York: Basic Books.

Freud, S. (1900) *Interpretation of Dreams. Standard Edition, vols. 4–5.* London: Hogarth Press.

Medawar, P. (1967) *The Art of the Soluble.* London: Methuen & Co. Ltd.

Pinker, S. (1997) *How the Mind Works.* London: Allen Lane.

Polanyi, M. (1958) *Personal Knowledge.* London: Routledge & Kegan Paul.

Solms, M. (1997) 'What is consciousness?', *Journal of American Psycho-analytical Assessment*, **45**.

PART II
At the Boundaries of Theory and Practice

6

Analysis: Growth or Cure?

Luigi Zoja

To grow: ... come naturally into existence; arise, originate, develop (as from a seed); ... Of a living thing: increase gradually in size, length, or height by natural development; ... come or pass by degrees (in)to some state or condition.

To cure: ... treat surgically or medically. Restore to health, relieve of an illness, an evil. Heal (an illness, a wound); remedy, remove (an evil).

(*The New Oxford Shorter English Dictionary*, 1993 edn)

The subject of these reflections is the epistemological arrogance of *psychodynamics* which, often seduced by the veneration accorded to the natural sciences, asserts itself as a repository of scientific truths. I would like to suggest that such an assertion be interpreted analytically: that is to say, through a study of its unconscious motivations, in line with the principal application of psychodynamics. After all, as the study of envy constitutes an important application of psychodynamics, it here inspires a legitimate suspicion: namely, that given its own limited prestige, psychodynamics may well envy the universal prestige of medicine.

We insist at times, out of force of habit, on thinking of Freud as a neurologist; as a navigator who, in the wake of his explorations, established psychodynamics in a medical context. Actually, as his compatriot Stefan Zweig had already intuited in 1931:

The fact that Freud happened to topple the Chinese wall of old psychological conceptions from a medical point of departure is, yes, historically correct, but not relevant as far as results go.

In a creative personality, the point of origin is not as relevant as the direction or the point to which one pushes himself. It does not matter that Freud's starting point was medicine, just as it does not matter that Pascal's starting point was mathematics, or that Nietzsche's was ancient philology.[1]

THE GYNAECOLOGIST AND THE PEDIATRICIAN

In the early 1990s, two issues of the *American Journal of Psychiatry* (vols 147 and 148) and a response to these which appeared in *Psicoterapia e scienze umane* (vol. 3), described how the celebrated Chestnut Lodge Clinic was ordered to pay compensatory damages to a depressed patient who had undergone extensive analysis with no remission of his symptoms. Immediately afterward, in another institution, the symptoms were successfully and rapidly treated with medication. I mention this extreme case not so much for the misleading and lone result that it describes, but for what I see as its faulty premise and as a basis for general discussion.

What had been promised to the patient before treatment? And what was the premise on which treatment was based? Apparently, the patient had been promised that he would be directed in the best way possible towards recovery ('to direct' does not mean to reach the goal, but to chart a course to follow). Just as apparently, the idea of recovery adhered closely to the traditional medical model, whereby sanity was to be restored as quickly and completely as possible. Was the institution overstepping its bounds in making such a commitment? While none of us witnessed the analytic work done, on the basis of information made public one might argue that it did not consist of alleviating the patient's suffering. To the contrary, the work consisted of bringing to light serious unconscious suffering.

It is not my intention to suggest that psychoanalysis is uninterested in fighting a patient's symptoms or suffering. In a broad sense, and as any discipline concerned with human life, psychodynamics certainly aims to help people. In a specific sense, however, it has as its goal – rather, as its central value – the transformation and growth of people whose personalities, prior to analysis, may have been hindered by unidentifiable psychological factors. Whereas for psychoanalysis the elimination of symptoms is only a desirable and welcome consequence, for traditional medicine it is the end, for which transformation and psychodynamic growth are but means.

'But,' a slightly impatient outsider might object, 'indirectly you pursue the same end as medicine. The bottom line is that you're paid to alleviate symptoms.' But no. It is exactly for this reason that it is ethically and epistemologically wrong for the analyst to promise the patient a fight against symptoms or the restoration of health. The symptom is a companion, which may well accompany the very transformation that the analyst ought to facilitate. The recovery of a previous state (*cure*) is not in the analytical order of things: for after a transformation, the patient will be in a new condition which cannot be known beforehand.

Consider the following basic example. The burst of sexuality at adolescence is often accompanied by problems of uncontrollable emotionality, insomnia, difficulty concentrating, radical oppositionalism, etc. What will the objectives of the analyst be when the parents of such an adolescent seek help for their child? More than any other phase of life, adolescence is characterized by transformation; thus, to strive for recovery, or a 'cure', at such a time becomes nonsensical if by recovery one means a return to a psychic state that preceded the disturbance. As the very word suggests, psychodynamics must privilege movement (*dynamics*) rather than a return to a previous equilibrium or the defence of an already existing one. Recovery, however, commonly understood as a return to equilibrium, might thus be termed 'psychostatic'.

Certainly the analyst and medical doctor must work closely together when treating an adolescent. The former must try to foster the adolescent's growth toward an adult sexual identity, while the latter must intervene pharmacologically if any symptom becomes unbearable or weakens the body. These two specialists, however, have different aims and different interpretative models. On the one hand, the medical doctor pursues a cure, which can usually be verified objectively in the short term; only indirectly does s/he pursue growth. The analyst, on the other hand, seeks long-term growth – validated above all else by the patient's subjective feelings; only indirectly is a cure sought in any traditional sense. Herein lies the error of Chestnut Lodge: the psychological intervention, based on values which were foreign to it, was a failure in terms of the medical model, which the institution itself used to describe the case. In this sense, there was no clinical error, but an epistemological one.

Interestingly, the article in the *American Journal of Psychiatry* suggests that, in addition to the quick pharmacological cure (or remission of the more serious symptoms), the personality of the patient also experienced long-term benefits of a maturational kind. As in most analogous cases, the patient's misfortunes present as a tangled web of suffering, in which the organic component is very difficult to extricate from the psychic one. However, if we were able to distinguish between them, we might conceive of the organic condition as largely reversible. Not so for the psychodynamic condition; as everyone knows, the birth of a child, or the sudden prospect of a new job, can set off anxiety crises or depression in the same person who, ten years later, adequately mature, would react to the same event with serenity and satisfaction. Unlike bodily growth, psychological growth can take place in adults as well, and protect a person definitively from certain kinds of suffering.

To return to the case of our adolescent, his main symptoms may well disappear in a short period of time. But, if this happens, the analyst would do well to remember that his/her objective is of a different order: namely, to foster the growth of an adult sexual identity, or the transformation of boy into man. This process will inevitably last a long time and will be judged not by the disappearance of suffering, but by the appearance of a personality that is substantially new. Whereas cure re/turns to us something that was, growth brings with it something new.

Moreover, because the disturbances that accompany adolescent maturation are more the rule than the exception, the analyst must wonder to what extent it is even appropriate to combat those disturbances. The adolescent faces a necessary passage, accompanied by necessary difficulties and suffering, which recall by analogy those of giving birth. The analyst, precisely because of his expertise in the insidiousness of the unconscious – and out of respect for that grave biblical pronouncement, 'In sorrow thou shalt bring forth children' – should not himself act unconsciously and sadistically. For to give birth (symbolically, to generate new life within oneself) *does* hurt. Alleviating pain is the right thing to do, as long as it does not conflict with the birth of the new.

To stick with the birthing metaphor, gynaecologist and pediatrician can work side by side in the delivery room, constantly reinventing their roles, even sacrificing something of their own respective aims, to make room for those of the other. By no means traitors to their respective professions in such a situation, they can serve as an example. The analyst, like the pediatrician, is concerned with new, not earlier, life. He must foster birth and growth, not maintenance or restoration. But while the tasks of pediatrician and gynaecologist, or of analyst and medical doctor, can judiciously be harmonized, they must not be confused as one and the same.

The reduction of pain and the health of the mother (that is, the conservation of an earlier form of life) are not directly the pediatrician's domain, even if his intervention ends up affecting both. Such a distinction between two functions is well known to analysts who are also medical doctors and are familiar with both professions. When pharmacological intervention is warranted, it certainly cannot be rejected because of ideological prejudice or compartmentalizations. In general, however, it is advisable to entrust this intervention to a colleague, so as not to embody split and divergent functions, and so as not to create corr-esponding split expectations in the patient (i.e., a dissociated and ambivalent transference).

A MYTH OF ORIGINS

At this point, I would like to clarify the values and attitude of the analytic model, as compared with those of the medical model. Analytic discipline – at least the Jungian one to which I refer – does not belong to the natural sciences. According to its viewpoint, much as psychic disturbance is not the ultimate obstacle to confront, so the causes of the disturbance are not of central concern. In other words, a disturbance is important not because of its origin but because of the end towards which the disturbance points. According to Jung:

A neurosis is by no means merely a negative thing, it is also something positive. Only a soulless rationalism, reinforced by a narrow materialistic outlook, could possibly have overlooked this fact. In reality, the neurosis contains the patient's psyche, or at least an essential part of it; and if, as the rationalist pretends, the neurosis could be plucked from him like a bad tooth, he would have gained nothing, but would have lost something very essential to him. That is to say, he would have lost as much as the thinker deprived of his doubt, or the moralist deprived of his temptation, or the brave man deprived of his fear. To lose a neurosis is to find oneself without an object; life loses its point and hence its meaning. This would not be a cure, it would be a regular amputation; and it would be cold comfort indeed if the psychoanalyst then assured the patient that he had lost nothing but his infantile paradise, with its wishful chimeras, most of them perverse. Very much more would have been lost, for hidden in the neurosis is a bit of still undeveloped personality.[2]

The neurosis is part of the path to be followed. It is like Ariadne's thread which, unwittingly neglected, comes to us in the form of an entangled ball of yarn. To use another image, a neurotic disturbance is not so much a cumbersome weight to unload as a dark tunnel we must pass through. Without the tunnel, we would remain on this side of an impassable mountain obstructing our life.

Let me give another example. A young man shows up for analysis in a state of profound depression. His life seems to have hit a dead end. Still, his young career is going surprisingly well, and he is admired and well liked for his creativity, integrity and sensitivity. The same seems to hold for his private life, where friends of both sexes seek him out. And yet he feels lonely. He does not know what to do with all the affection and success. More generally, he does not know what he wants from life.

From the first sessions his dreams confront us with images of homosexuality. His childhood seems typical of this sort of problem: a closed and authoritarian father, an overprotective, castrating mother. The patient is already aware of this aspect of his nature, even if he has never made room for it in his day-to-day life. Yet the simple signs in this fairly common case are enough to raise a series of questions. How far should we go in trying to discover the causes of his homosexuality? Is it fair to promise the patient that we will fight, with all available means, the suffering presently afflicting him? And if he does not know what he really wants from life, will the patient be satisfied to know what he really wants from sex?

Keeping to the distinction between the medical and psychodynamic models (between *cure* and *growth*), we can attempt some answers. We often attribute great importance to psychological causes lying in a patient's past, not because we have verified their effects, but because we attribute to such processes of verification an importance derived from the dominant model of the natural sciences, that is to say, of medicine itself. Science is the kingdom of causes; and in today's disillusioned and hero-less world, on a shrunken planet bereft of surprises, we have come to mythify the scientist, in his quest for knowledge, as the last true explorer; as the last true combatant, now that wars and warriors have proven too destructive; and as the last true saint, now that religious belief has surrendered to secular thought.

The scientist is, in all likelihood, the mythologem underlying every esteemed activity of modernity. It is s/he who fights to re/cover the origins of observed phenomena, much as Odysseus fought to re/turn to his family and re/conquer the land of his childhood; or as St Francis struggled to re/discover the simplicity that was lost by the wealthy and educated of his day. An origin could be Ithaca, or harmony with nature, or the source of a physical phenomenon: realities which, while different from one another, are all united by our conviction that s/he who regains the origin will be honoured as a hero.

Let us not mis/take, then, the role of case histories in analysis. Of course a patient should recount his/her childhood, but mainly because retelling the past stirs up great emotions in the present. Strong feelings can jolt a blocked life into motion and restore the promise of a future. What matters, though, is building symbols in the present, not reconstructing a road already taken: 'Hateful to me,' writes Goethe, 'is all that merely instructs me, without immediately enhancing or enlivening my work.'[3] Hardly any of us today needs to reach Ithaca, nor would anyone get there via the senseless course charted by Homer. And yet, people the world over continue to read *The Odyssey*, because Ulysses' return home holds a message for any person in search of him/herself.

Strictly speaking, then, causality alone, applied to the psyche, is of little help. For example, parents like those of my patient's (authoritarian father, overprotective mother) also generate incurable Don Juans as often as they do obsessively loyal spouses; they can as readily produce people satisfied with their life choices as they can a son, like my patient, dissatisfied with and afflicted by his existence. Even interpretations like 'latent' homosexuality, used to explain situations like my patient's, are ultimately based on weak causal links: often enough their very wording defines the origin being sought, as well as the cure to propose to the patient for the condition thus established.[4] More than a form of knowing, this is a form of tautology.

True, *those* parents did generate *that* son. However, the analyst cannot know the parents' uniqueness, but only a patterned account brought by the patient that *may* be applicable to other situations. An analyst might not recognize the patient's parents at all if s/he were suddenly to cross paths with them in real life – even if they are the same beings described for years. And as doubts set in and threaten to chip away retroactively at years of work, the bewildered therapist may ask: 'To what degree did my patient knowingly lie to me, or did his memory delude him? And why did my work, based on such grossly distorted premises, nonetheless help him on a course of deep personal discovery, in the course of a successful analysis?'

The reactions of the human psyche are marked more by uniqueness than by causality. Even patients' accounts of their lives do not escape this rule, as the accounts themselves become symbolic worlds, independent of both narrator and the ensemble of characters described. For instance, it can be very difficult for an analyst, who happens to accept for treatment the brother of an ex-patient, to recognize the same family of origin.

At this point, it will have become clear that, if I have reduced to three the questions raised by our patient – concerning past causes, present suffering, and future possibilities – it has been to shift emphasis gradually from the first question to the third. Psychodynamics must move (*dynamic*) with life as it unfolds; it cannot insist on looking backwards. To look backwards – that is, to base one's knowledge primarily on trodden paths – maximizes the risk of not identifying a false path *en route* to the future. Where the life of the emotions is concerned, the risk is being led to a narcissistic microcosm: to a life of recounting one's own myth of origins, in an ongoing, personal celebration of the liturgy of a Paradise Lost. While an assessment of present-day options creates in people a capacity for the exercise of responsibility (and therefore for *growth*), focusing on a patient's infancy institutionally 'invents' (from the Latin *invenire*, to find) an infantile patient.

Life is frequently unpleasant, but it is not through a return to Eden that we make it better. In keeping with this biblical image, we might remember that Yahweh, after chasing his offspring from the Earthly Paradise, also promised them redemption: not in the form of a return, however, but of a going beyond. In the same way are cure and growth differentiated: on the one hand, by concerning itself with past events, and by proposing a return to what has already been experienced, cure determines its goals and parameters in advance; growth, on the other hand, is open-ended, tending towards that which is possible and individually diversified. In sum, cure can be objectively verified and pertains to the natural sciences. Growth depends on personal experience. Thus understood, analysis enhances the personality, and the patient who uses it grows.

But analysis also should be warned against pursuing extraneous ways to knowledge. Analysis's own epistemological arrogance has often fostered the very mythic ailments it proposes to cure (structured, for example, around the myths of Narcissus and Oedipus). Years of gazing inward can favour a patient's narcissism, while a prolonged dependence on the analyst may well reactivate Oedipal experiences. Similarly, the omnipotence of the past (the power of an origin myth, or of the analytic cosmogony) encourages causal links that analysts may then be tempted to apply through interpretation. In both cases, the intended object of analysis (mythic thought) risks being inadvertently transformed into an active and deforming element of the analytic process itself.

THE CATHEDRAL AND THE QUARRY

We have claimed that the most common error of psychodynamics is not its limited therapeutic efficacy – we already know that analysis has more to do with consciousness than with cure – but its efforts to incorporate the medical model as a permanent, structural element of its own. For while this model did influence the origins of the discipline over a century ago in the office of a Viennese neurologist, psychoanalysis is not a science: not, at least, in the sense ascribed to the natural sciences. Psychodynamics is concerned with specific and unique events, not with events predetermined by fixed laws; its applications have little to do with what can be known in advance. But such considerations do not deny its value as an important form of knowledge, as a heuristic tool capable of yielding general but reliable insights into the course of a human life.

Nobody, of course, would deny the importance of history. Yet despite the fact that we speak of historical sciences, history too deals only with singular, unrepeatable events. And while history can propose to study the origins of such events, it can never truly predict the events themselves; nor can an historian make any generalizations about their nature, unlike the chemist or physicist who relies on causal models to predict a succession of events. We must, in any case, be sure to clarify what we mean by *origin*: do we mean a beginning in time or a causal principle? The verb *orio*, from which the word *origin* is derived, does not distinguish between the two. A Latin word, *orio* is much older than modern-day scientific discourse and any resultant distinctions of this kind.

Even today we continue, almost superstitiously, to make use of terms that unify temporal and causal succession, infusing the former with something of the force of the latter. (And, maybe, in the case of analysts or historians, to move closer to the natural sciences.) While this was, admittedly, more evident in languages of old, residues do persist: consider, for example, the Greek *archē*, denoting principles both of temporality and of agency. The word's bivalence is, in fact, still at the root of words like *archaeology* (study of a past with limited influence, if any, on the present) and *archetype* (a past 'type' still active in deter-mining a type in the present). Allow me, on this score, to cite an historian whose words, I believe, can also be applied to psychodynamics (that is, to the deep history of an individual): 'In any study, seeking the origins of a human activity, there lurks the same danger of confusing ancestry with explanation.'[5] Earlier in the same passage, the historian resorts to an image to explain the same idea: 'Great oaks from little acorns grow. But only if they meet favorable conditions of soil and climate, conditions which are entirely beyond the scope of embryology.'[6]

If this kind of unpredictable, individual growth is true for plant life, is it not all the more true for human life? The human element introduces an inexhaustible multiformity, yielding uniquenesses that cannot be replicated. If I were asked, for example, about the origin of Milan's cathedral, I might identify the quarries from which the stone was extracted. In this way, however, through a limited understanding of the word 'origin,' I would only have specified the church's chemical-geological basis, at the expense of its architectural uniqueness – a feature which everyone, including the chemist and the geologist, admire as the cathedral's defining characteristic. To give meaning to the structure, therefore, is to see it not only in its chemical context but in its cultural context as well: where countless psychological elements – neither predictable nor replicable – are constellated and come into play. Marc Bloch states:

> Historical facts are, in essence, psychological facts ... To be sure, human destinies are placed in the physical world and suffer the consequences thereof. Even where the intrusion of these external forces seems most brutal, however, their action is weakened or intensified by man and his mind.[7]

Earlier in the same passage Bloch states:

> Historical reasoning in contemporary practice does not differ in its procedure. However necessary they may be, the most constant and general antecedents remain merely implicit. What military historian would dream of ranking among the causes of a victory that gravitation which accounts for the trajectory of the shells, or the physiological organization of the human body without which the projectiles would have not fatal consequences? ... What is the use of dwelling upon nearly universal antecedents? They are common to too many phenomena to deserve a special niche in the genealogy of any of them. I am well aware, from the onset, that there would be no fire if the air contained no oxygen: what interests me, what demands and justifies an attempt at discovery, is to determine how the fire started. The laws of trajectories are as valid for defeat as for victory: they explain both; therefore, they are useless as a proper explanation for either.[8]

So it is for human beings, to the extent that we can reverse Bloch's statement and claim: 'Psychic facts are the facts of history; that is to say, they are the individual histories of psychic life.' Like the histories of peoples, psychic facts are also bound by fixed rules, both physical and chemical. No one would deny as much. But for the analyst, such antecedents remain for the most part implied, since they do not aid in the comprehension of what is at the heart of psychodynamic investigation: namely, the individual specificity of psychic life which, while never identical to that of any other human being, is also never identical to itself over time (precisely because of its *dynamic* quality). As in the human sciences, the study of antecedents is useful in that it aids comprehension; it cannot, however, provide us with definitive formulas for understanding. The veneration of origins is a necessity of the human mind, exercised for millennia in all cultures, including today's secular, Western societies. It is exemplified throughout the study of myth, as in the story of Ulysses' return to Ithaca. In this light, we can see how even psychodynamics' obsessive exultation of the case-history method, induced by the parasitical use of causal models, is no stranger to mythic forms of unconscious survival. But a psychodyamics configured in the context of the human (and not the natural) sciences will have to come to grips with this regressive temptation. Interestingly enough, historians have already performed this epistemological self-criticism, distancing themselves in the process from a method whose cult of origins is often exposed as a cult of the dead.

This turning point, finally, was already prefigured by Nietzsche, who contributed significantly to its articulation both as a critic of history and as a protopsychologist:

Thus: it is possible to live almost without memory, and to live happily moreover, as the animal demonstrates; but it is altogether impossible to *live* at all without forgetting. Or, to express my theme even more simply: *there is a degree of sleeplessness, of rumination, of the historical sense, which is harmful and ultimately fatal to the living thing, whether this living thing be a man or a people or a culture.*[9]

Or, as he continues:

When the past speaks, it always speaks as an oracle: only if you are an architect of the future and know the present will you understand it ... If you look ahead and set yourself a great goal, you at the same time restrain that rank analytical impulse which makes the present into a desert and all tranquility, all peaceful growth and maturing almost impossible.[10]

Nietzsche aimed these reflections at both the individual and society. Underlying them is an epistemology that privileges, in either case, the dynamics of the psyche. For history, in its own right, is not simply a list of past and unmodifiable events, but a search (*istoria*); a trying and, of necessity, an incomplete *construction of the meaning(s) of those very events*. Consequently, the parameters with which to evaluate history are not based on what has already happened, but on what is yet to come. Like the parameters of growth – as opposed to those of cure – they reside in the future, not in the past. For those among us who want to grow, the past exists to the extent that it can be overcome.

NOTES

1. Stefan Zweig, *Die Heilung durch den Geist: Mesmer, Mary Baker-Eddy, Freud*. Frankfurt: Fischer, 1982 (author's translation from the German).
2. Carl. G. Jung, 'The state of psychotherapy today', in *Collected Works*, Vol. X. Princeton, NJ: Princeton University Press, 1970, p. 355.
3. Goethe, letter to Schiller, 19 December 1798 (author's translation from the German).
4. This is a strong argument in support of Karl Popper's theory of the unfalsifiability of analysis. See his *Conjectures and Refutations: The Growth of Scientific Knowledge*. New York: Basic Books, 1962.
5. Marc Bloch, *The Historian's Craft*. New York: Alfred A. Knopf, 1953, p. 32. Translated from the French by Peter Putnam.
6. Ibid., p. 32.
7. Ibid., p. 194.
8. Ibid., pp. 191–2.
9. Frederich Nietzsche, *Untimely Meditations*. New York: Cambridge University Press, 1983, p. 62. Translated by R.J. Hollingdale (italics in original).
10. Ibid., p. 94.

The Ethic of Psychoanalysis
The Fundamental Rule
to be Honest

M. Guy Thompson

Psychoanalysis is both a collection of ideas and a method based upon those ideas whose goal is to determine the right way to live. Hence, psychoanalysis is an 'ethic' in the sense that it concerns the manner by which individuals conduct themselves. Derived from the Greek *ethike tekhne* meaning 'the moral art', *ethike* is in turn derived from the Greek *ethos*, meaning 'character'. Both the character of a person who aspires to behave ethically and the customs of a people by which one's standards are measured derive from the concept. Morality, a subsidiary of ethics, pertains to distinctions between right and wrong and good and bad, whereas ethics, according to the Greeks, concerns the pursuit of happiness, the nature of which produces a state of equanimity by obtaining freedom from mental anguish.

If psychoanalysis is an ethical system whose goal is liberation from psychic conflict, then the nature of that conflict must have something to do with the way one lives, thinks and behaves. While the character of an individual is no doubt decisive in the ultimate outcome of that person's treatment, the psychoanalytic experience essentially revolves around a kind of work that is performed and accomplished, the outcome of which succeeds or fails. By analysing the customs of a given patient – the manner by which that individual lives – the patient is in a better position to change what needs to be changed and discover a better life. If psychoanalysis is an ethic – and I submit that it is – what kind of ethic does it foster? What are the rules by which it is administered and what is the basis of its method?

In *Freud: The Mind of the Moralist* (1959), Philip Rieff argued that the basis of Freud's conception of psychoanalysis rested on what he characterized as an 'ethic of honesty'. Rieff went on to say that:

> Psychoanalysis ... demands a special capacity for candor which not
> only distinguishes it as a healing movement but also connects it
> with the drive toward disenchantment characteristic of modern
> literature and of life among the intellectuals. (ibid., p. 315)

Freud's prescription for society's overzealous efforts at controlling our
irrepressible impulses was psychoanalysis. It served to give the neurotic
a second chance for a more satisfying existence by replacing secretive
repressions with a more honest effort at coping with life's inevitable
disappointments. As Rieff points out: 'We first meet the ethic of honesty
in characteristic Freudian guise – as merely a therapeutic rule: ... the
patient must promise "absolute honesty"' (ibid., p. 315). The capacity
for candour to which Rieff refers is the basis for Freud's analytic
technique, the 'fundamental rule' of psychoanalysis. But what does the
fundamental rule consists of? What, in turn, is its relationship to free
association? Are they, as most analysts assume, one and the same; or
does a relation exist between them which serves to distinguish one from
the other, comprising separate though related concepts? Contrary to
what most analysts believe, I intend to demonstrate an inherent distinction between the two terms, a distinction that Freud himself also
employed.

Put simply, the fundamental rule is a contract that every analytic
patient is asked to enter into in the early stages of their analysis. Freud
called it a pledge or a promise. In other words, when patients agree to
free associate, they *promise* to do so. On the other hand, free association
itself is not a pledge but an uncommon form of conversation that
patients are invited to employ during the course of treatment. When
patients free associate they simply confide whatever comes to mind. If
one equates the two as synonymous, the significance of the pledge and
its ethical impact on the treatment experience is virtually lost, if not
entirely destroyed altogether.

I intend to show why this distinction is vital to the way psychoanalysis
was originally conceived and its relation to the ethic of honesty that Rieff
situated at the heart of Freud's technique. By employing this tack, I
hope I can show how Freud, perhaps unintentionally, transformed
analysis into an ethic whose reliance on psychology, though important,
has been greatly exaggerated.

First, I shall begin by asking, what is 'free association', exactly? In
fact, the term does not refer to 'associations', as such. For example, the
word association test by which one is asked to respond to a word with

the first thing that comes to mind was not what Freud intended by this term. The English term, free association, was Strachey's mistranslation of the German *freier Einfall* which combines the words 'free' and 'irruption'. In the original German it simply denotes a thought that spontaneously comes to mind as it erupts into consciousness. The word 'association' conveys an entirely different connotation which lends to the mistaken impression that patients are being asked to connect an idea with the first thing it reminds them of. This connotation transforms the original sense of *freier Einfall* into a wilful use of the mind instead of one that entails the exact opposite, i.e. the suspension of conscious control.

To free associate in the manner that Freud intended is simply an admonition to be candid during the therapy session. It entails nothing more than the willingness to speak spontaneously and unreservedly, as one sometimes does when not the least self-conscious about what is being disclosed to another person. Obviously, Freud's conception of free association does not make much sense unless one appreciates the degree to which we ordinarily conceal most of what spontaneously comes to mind in the course of conversation. Seen from this angle, the fundamental rule – wherein I *consent* to reveal the thoughts that occur to me – is a precondition for grasping the nature of free association as it was originally conceived.

Free association is less a psychological 'process' than a form of verbal meditation that requires a considerable degree of discipline to perform. It entails speaking unreservedly while remaining attentive to what is being disclosed – something we do not ordinarily do. Most of us either speak impulsively without awareness of what we say or think through everything we are about to disclose before speaking. In analysis, patients discover that they are predisposed against spontaneously verbalizing their thoughts and that they instinctively hesitate to disclose objectionable ideas when they occur. It requires relentless prodding on the part of the analyst to remind patients when they have retreated into the sanctum of their secret and inaccessible worlds. Once they discover the frequency with which they customarily resist disclosing things about themselves, patients begin to appreciate why compliance with this rule is so crucial to the analytic experience. Hence, one's *capacity* to free associate hinges on one's *willingness* to do so.

Most analysts conceive of the fundamental rule as simply a means of gaining access to the patient's unconscious, reducing it to a psychological process that enables the analyst – and by extension, the patient – to determine the latent cause of the patient's psychopathology. This conception of the fundamental rule effectively ignores the rule's ethical imperative and the crisis of conscience that compliance inevitably engenders.

Freud introduced the fundamental rule – *Grundregel* in German – for the first time in the second of his six technical papers, *The Dynamics of Transference* (1912). This was after his analyses of Dora (*c*. 1905) and the Rat Man (*c*. 1909), his most famous analytic patients. This collection of six technical papers, published between 1911 and 1915, comprised his most exhaustive statement on analytic technique. While Freud only belatedly realized the efficacy of this rule, it finally dawned on him that the need for such a rule was ubiquitous to the analytic experience. Non-compliance exemplified transference resistance. At the lectures Freud delivered at Clark University in 1911 he hinted at the need for such a rule and referred to it then as the 'main rule' of analysis. Strachey claimed that the rule was alluded to earlier still in *The Interpretation of Dreams* (1900), 'in a passage where Freud urges the patient to overcome his "internal criticisms" while reporting the content of his dreams' (in Freud, 1912, p. 107). Strachey believed this was the first time Freud explicitly invoked the fundamental rule, albeit in the context of dream analysis. Yet, he overlooks the fact that Freud made no mention on this occasion of the requisite *pledge* to disclose one's associations. The reference cited by Strachey only pertains to free associations as such, in the limited context of dream analysis. In other words, Strachey also equates free association with the fundamental rule, because he failed to grasp that neither the act of speaking unreservedly (i.e., free association) nor the pledge to do so (i.e., the fundamental rule) had crystallized in Freud's mind as early as 1900. Though Freud did admonish his patients to verbalize their thoughts once he abandoned hypnosis, even as late as 1900 he had yet to insist that his patients do so, hence compelling them to unreservedly. I believe it is the actual *promise* to bare all which is essential to the fundamental rule, not the simple *act* of doing so.

The first time Freud finally brought the two concepts together was in the fourth of his technical papers, *On Beginning the Treatment* (1913). There, Freud proposed how analysts should undertake to introduce their patients to the fundamental rule and the free association method. This brief recommendation comprises the most thorough description Freud (1913) offered on *the relationship between* the technique of free association and the fundamental rule:

What the material is with which one starts the treatment is on the whole a matter of indifference – whether it is the patient's life history or the history of his illness or his recollections of childhood. But in any case, the patient must be left to do the talking and must be free to choose at what point he shall begin. We therefore say to him: 'Before I can say anything to you I must know a great deal about you; please tell me what you know about yourself.' The only exception to this is in regard to the fundamental rule of psycho-analytic technique which the patient has to observe. This must be imparted to him at the very beginning: 'One more thing before you start. What you tell me must differ in one respect from an ordinary conversation. Ordinarily you rightly try to keep a connecting thread running through your remarks and you exclude any intrusive ideas when they occur to you and any side issues so as not to wander too far from the point. But in this case you must proceed differently. You will notice that as you relate things various thoughts will occur to you which you would like to put aside on the ground of certain criticisms and objections. You will be tempted to say to yourself that this or that is irrelevant here or that it's quite unimportant or nonsensical so that there's no need to say it. You must never give in to these criticisms, but must say it in spite of them – indeed, you must say it precisely *because* you feel an aversion to doing so. Later on you will find out and learn to understand the reason for this injunction, which is really the only one you have to follow. So say whatever goes through your mind.' (ibid., pp. 134–5)

At this juncture Freud invokes the *free association* method in his famous 'railway carriage' analogy:

Act as though, for instance, you were a traveller sitting next to the window of a railway carriage and describing to someone inside the carriage the changing views which you see outside. (ibid., p. 135)

Then, in the very next sentence, Freud introduces the *fundamental rule*: 'Finally, never forget that you have *promised to be absolutely honest* and never leave anything out because for some reason or other it is un-pleasant to tell it' (ibid., p. 135) (emphasis added). This critical sentence brings the fundamental rule into play by drawing a categorical distinc-tion between the promise to comply and the act of free associating. Freud does not limit compliance with free association to a psychological 'process' alone, but emphasizes that such compliance relies on a commit-ment that entails *a pledge to be honest with another person*. In so doing,

Freud makes a case for the ubiquitous importance of honesty, a feature of the fundamental rule that is customarily omitted from contemporary characterizations of this rule.

By invoking a pledge to be truthful, Freud crystallized the specific feature of free association that distinguishes it from conventional forms of self-reflection: the promise to hold nothing back. Whatever we are tempted to conceal, by the very incidence of our temptation to, we are compelled because of this rule to direct our attention to the things we instinctively suppress. In other words, the kind of truth that psycho-analysis seeks to determine is not wedded to a correspondence with someone else's; instead, it is determined solely by what patients typically conceal. Whatever *remains* concealed constitutes the truths that analysts seek to uncover.

Though this was a novel idea when Freud introduced it, the efficacy for doing so was a logical extension of his thesis, formulated fifteen years earlier, explaining the aetiology of neurosis: that harbouring secrets elicits a breach in our perception of reality which manifests psychical conflict. In Freud's analysis of Dora, the central theme that ran through his report of the case concerned the prevalence of secrecy in the genesis of psychopathology. When life presents us with disappointments too painful to bear, we instinctively repress our experience of those disap-pointments by momentarily forgetting them. In Dora's case, Freud attributed her hysterical symptoms to somatic displacements of forbidden desires, and concluded that the only hope for relief from her symptoms lay in 'the revelation of those intimacies and the betrayal of those secrets' (1905, p. 8). Psychoanalysis aspires to undo the effect of such secrets by baring them to someone who will not condemn the patient for harbouring them. Though patients in analysis do not really 'know' what they are harbouring, the act of spontaneously uttering what comes to mind serves to uncover those secrets that, in turn, are related to what they do know.

When Freud analysed Dora in 1900 he had only recently conceived the method he had substituted for hypnosis, the so-called 'talking cure'. But he did not realize then that only someone who is already uncom-monly honest will be willing to spontaneously disclose the contents of her mind. Dora resisted her analysis bitterly and was probably convinced throughout her brief treatment that Freud was an agent of her father. She never relented in her opposition to what she construed as efforts to bend her to his will. Freud was still a decade away from acknowledging the need to augment the free association method with a second rule that would bind his patients to him personally in common cause, by taking him into their confidence. He soon realized that unless patients agree to self-disclosure in principle, they will ultimately lack the motivation to work through their inevitable resistance to the treatment.

By inviting his patients to be honest and enlisting their pledge to do so, Freud transformed the patient at the beginning of analysis from a person who simply tells stories into a moral agent who determines what is true by *saying* it. It is significant, for example, that only the patient is in a position to determine what the truth is. Unlike a court of law in which a witness's testimony is challenged so that the jury may decide what is so, Freud advised analysts against the practice of confirming what patients say by questioning their family or their friends. The *patient's word* is the sole authority for what is true because the kind of truth psychoanalysis obtains is not objectively verifiable. It is an inherently subjective truth that is derived exclusively from the patient's experience.

Indeed, psychoanalysis has more in common with jurisprudence than it does with either psychiatry or psychology. In a court of law, for example, the goal is to get to the truth. To this end, jurors must keep an *open mind* by not permitting themselves to be swayed in their opinion by personal bias or prejudice. Instead, they are counselled to base their conclusions on the evidence presented and nothing more. Indeed, the only rationale for overturning their verdict or obtaining a new trial is if it subsequently comes to light that their decision was contaminated by the omission of evidence, false testimony, and so on.

The utter neutrality – or 'objectivity' – that jurors are expected to employ in their deliberations more closely approximates the attitude of the psychoanalyst than that of the psychiatrist who relies exclusively on his accumulated knowledge of diagnostic nomenclature. Indeed, by his behaviour the analyst endeavours to instil precisely the same attitude in his patients: an open-minded, forgiving curiosity towards their mental and emotional condition, their behaviour, the problems with which they are confronted and the means they typically employ in addressing them, however inadequate they are.

In effect, patients are invited to play the role of 'juror' at their own inquisition, while assuming the role of Inquisitor. The analyst plays the part of the 'judge' who knows what the rules are and monitors them, but leaves any conclusions to the juror/patient who must follow his own predilections. Indeed, the patient's task is to determine what ethical code to live by since, whatever it is, once adopted, it will be his and his alone, whatever the consequences may be.

Hence, the type of honesty psychoanalysis entails cannot be reduced to a conventional standard of morality, such as the claim of never telling a lie or by obedience to a given society. Since it is rooted solely in the *patient's word*, once the pledge to be honest is verbalized it becomes a matter of honour, determined by no other measure than the patient's compliance. Due to its personal nature, the truth elicited can never be empirically validated; instead, it can only be *elucidated* through its transmission from one human being to another. In other words, the task of analysis is to uncover what is hidden, not for the purpose of finally 'knowing' what is concealed, but to engender that singular form of transformation that only the act of unburdening oneself can elicit.

Hence analytic truth is a solitary truth for which each of us is, alone, responsible. Whether they like it or not, analytic patients must resign themselves to serving as judge and jury to how successful their endeavour has been. This endeavour is solitary because there is no court of appeals and no higher authority that can determine the outcome for them. This is probably the most critical factor that delays the termination of treatment.

Freud recognized that no one can be expected to embrace the fundamental rule wholeheartedly due to the anxiety that compliance evokes. But his insistence that patients make their peace with the rule to whatever degree they are able assumes that none of us can ultimately escape the moral obligation to adopt a standard of truth we can live by, and one we can live *with*. In effect, Freud held a mirror to our face and forced us to decide where we stand: whether to disclose what we are about or conceal it. The consequence of this choice continues to stare us in the face for as long as we live because no one can ever escape the weight of their accountability.

Though Freud attributed ethical values to the superego, his characterization of this agency and its origins hardly accounts for the complicated dynamics that determine one's search for the truth and the desire to be honest. In *The Ego and the Id* (1923), Freud characterized the superego and the ego ideal (which he used interchangeably) as 'heirs' to the Oedipus complex. As a consequence of the prohibition against committing incest and patricide the child gradually identifies with the same-sex parent and incorporates the parent's prohibitions, edicts and values. This provides the child with a capacity for guilt and prompts the ego to repress those wishes that the superego deems unacceptable. Consequently, the superego serves as a moral agency which becomes a sort of antenna for the customs of the society in which we live. As the child grows older and replaces the parent with other influential relationships, it fosters an increasingly sophisticated set of ideals, possibilities and limitations that help to organize each individual's definition of success, failure, and the weight of public opinion.

According to Freud, the superego serves as a conscience by which we decide what is permissible and what is not, what is likely to be rewarded and what is liable to be punished. In effect, the superego helps us to navigate through the treacherous waters of our culture in order to obtain the maximum amount of reward. Hence, it serves an inherently utilitarian purpose: it protects us from being locked up or killed or simply hated by others for being the person that we are. But how does this agency account for a patient's capacity to obey the fundamental rule to be honest?

I do not see how it can. Since the superego is driven by the dynamics that derive from the *inherent frustration of not getting one's own way*, it serves as a motive force by which the individual is prompted to renounce 'prohibited' aims and to replace them with acceptable ones. If one's capacity for honesty were regulated by the superego, the pursuit of honesty would serve an exclusively utilitarian aim: to relieve frustration. However, experience tells us that honesty can just as easily increase frustration as relieve it, because some of the ethical precepts we aspire to are not rewarded by society but are rejected by it. Since one's code of conduct always takes account of reality – whether, for example, to conform or rebel – the code one chooses to live by is ultimately determined by the ego, not the superego.

Freud said as much when he attributed a given individual's capacity to benefit from psychoanalytic treatment to one's character. By 'character' Freud meant: (1) the capacity to delay gratification 'in favour of a more distant one, which is perhaps altogether uncertain' (1915, p. 170); (2) the capacity to develop a positive transference through which a patient opts for the sacrifice that analytic work entails over and above the rewards of self-love (i.e., by abiding by the reality principle through denial of the pleasure principle); and (3) the capacity to be honest in the face of more hardship and suffering.

I could give many other examples of where Freud brings moral precepts into his argument, as they are rife throughout his writings and remained a preoccupying theme during the course of his life. Freud, as Rieff has suggested, was a moral philosopher. And character, as the etymology of the word 'moral' suggests, concerns morality in its essence since it is the means by which one becomes honest. Though one's character is no doubt influenced by the superego – and, with extremely neurotic individuals, is probably determined by it – the purpose of psychoanalytic treatment is to liberate individual patients from the punitive aspects of their superego by bringing them into direct contact with their reality and their desire.

Hence, the development of one's character transcends, properly speaking, utilitarian aims. In addition to the need to be loved and obtain success, humans also aspire to live in peace with themselves and, ultimately, to like their own person. In a word, they aspire to *live with* themselves and to make themselves at home with the person they happen to be. While the weight of frustration is probably the motive force that brings most people into treatment, once the treatment has begun, they realize that honesty is the principal means by which they learn to accept themselves and the wherewithal to do better. When one re-reads Freud's technical recommendations in this light, the sense one derives from them is refreshingly simple, yet profoundly radical when measured by contemporary standards. Indeed, Freud's technical recommendations read more like meditations on the inherent hypocrisy of our culture than a panacea for the relief of mental anguish.

The moral injunction by which the fundamental rule was inserted into the treatment situation served to enlist each patient's active participation in the analysis. Once obliged to be candid, patients realize that now they must wrestle with the extraordinary power of *their* conscience, not their analyst's. Yet, the resolve to be honest does not make our lives any less complicated; it frequently makes them even more difficult. Perhaps its only virtue is that it serves as a foil against the secrecy at the bottom of our anxieties, as it engenders a crisis of conscience that can only be resolved by unburdening ourselves of our secrets. From this perspective, psychoanalysis is rather limited in the scope of pathological conditions it is able to relieve, because only people who suffer a guilty conscience can be analysed. In other words, it is only the degree to which one is haunted by guilt that psychic change is even possible.

And what is the basis of this guilt? What terrible secret accounts for it? According to Heidegger (1985), guilt is inevitable for simply *being* who we are when we defy the forces of convention (pp. 307–20). Lacan (1992), on the other hand, proposed that neurotics feel guilty when they fail to be true to their desire (pp. 319–24). Contrary as these two views about guilt may appear, each in its own way supports Freud's rationale for the fundamental rule, but in so doing they also undermine his formulation of the superego by suggesting that guilt is the consequence of repression instead of its source. Hence, we feel guilt as a consequence of endeavouring to mitigate those anxieties that are simply a consequence of living, by resisting the anguish that our desires exact from us.

Similarly, Rieff suggested that guilt is the result of the observation that neurotics are unwilling to pay the price for the happiness they wish to obtain. Instead, they would rather hold their aspirations in check than to suffer the sacrifice that the pursuit of pleasure entails. This sorry state of affairs led Rieff to conclude that 'neurosis is the penalty for ambition unprepared for sacrifice' (1959, p. 308). Rieff noted that as early as 1885, during his long engagement to Martha, Freud had discovered the key to the neurotic personality, engendered and endlessly refined by a society that restricts its citizens to gratifications that are socially 'appropriate'. Quoting from a letter Freud wrote to his fiancée:

> We [neurotics] economize with our health, our capacity for enjoyment, our forces: we save up for something, not knowing ourselves for what. And this habit of constant suppression of natural instinct gives us the character of refinement ... Why do we not get drunk? Because the discomfort and shame of the hangover give us more 'unpleasure' than the pleasure of getting drunk gives us. Why don't we fall in love over again every month? Because with every parting something of our heart is torn away ... Thus our striving is more concerned with avoiding pain than with creating enjoyment. (cited by Rieff, 1959, pp. 309–10)

Hence the pledge to be honest about all those aspirations one secretly harbours but dare not admit is the key to overcoming the guilt we have accrued while suppressing them. That is why the kind of guilt that Freud was occupied with is not the type that is caused by the failure to conform, but rather an 'existential' guilt that is a consequence of having compromised oneself in the service of conforming to a society that is opposed to gratification in principle. Paraphrasing Freud, Rieff concluded that: 'What makes neurotics talk is "the pressure of a secret which is burning to be disclosed." Neurotics carry their secret concealed in their talk – "which, despite all temptation, they never reveal"' (ibid., pp. 316–17). Hence, the analyst's task is an unpopular one. His role is to mention the unmentionable and to elicit what is obvious but remains obstinately unspoken. Though effective as a means of disclosing unconscious repressions, the need for such a rule is also an indictment of the disingenuous society to which every neurotic belongs. This disturbing

observation was finally brought home in a paper where Freud confessed
his pessimism about the prospects psychoanalysis could expect from a
society that is predisposed against it:

> Suppose a number of ladies and gentlemen in good society have
> planned to have a picnic one day at an inn in the country. The
> ladies have arranged among themselves that if one of them wants to
> relieve a natural need she will announce that she is going to pick
> flowers. Some malicious person, however, has got wind of this
> secret and has had printed on the programme which is sent round
> to the whole party: 'Ladies who wish to retire are requested to
> announce that they are going to pick flowers.' After this, of course,
> no lady will think of availing herself of this flowery pretext, and, in
> the same way, other similar formulas, which may be freshly agreed
> upon, will be seriously compromised. What will be the result? The
> ladies will admit their natural needs without shame and none of the
> men will object. (1910, p. 149)

Rieff suggests that the analyst is the 'malicious person' in Freud's
analogy, just as the ladies represent culture. The moral to the story,
Rieff concludes, is that:

> We must accept our 'natural needs,' in the face of a culture which
> has censored open declarations of [them]. In championing a
> refreshing openness, Freud disclosed the censoring of nature, thus
> to ease the strain that had told upon our cultural capacities. (1959,
> p. 316)

What, then, can the neurotic hope to obtain from analysis if it aspires to
be at all successful? According to Freud:

> A certain number of people, faced in their lives by conflicts which
> they have found too difficult to solve, have taken flight into neurosis
> and in this way won an unmistakable, although in the long run too
> costly, gain from illness. What will these people have to do if their
> flight into illness is barred by the indiscreet revelations of psycho-
> analysis? They will have to be honest, confess to the instincts that
> are at work in them, face the conflict, fight for what they want, or
> go without it. (1910, pp. 149–50)

By insisting that candour is the precondition of every analytic treatment, Freud established an undeniable interdependence between the act of free association and the fundamental rule on which it relies. Yet, there is an undeniable risk, Rieff admits:

> in the ethic of honesty of which Freud [was] aware. Some lives are so pent-up that a neurosis may be 'the least of the evils possible in the circumstances.' Some of those 'who now take flight into illness' would find the inner conflict exposed by candor insupportable, and 'would rapidly succumb or would cause a mischief greater than their own neurotic illness.' Honesty is not an ethic for weaklings; it will save no one. (1959, p. 322)

Perhaps this explains why psychoanalysts today seem uncomfortable with the characterization of psychoanalysis as a moral enterprise whose aim is to further honesty. What do we stand to gain by becoming more honest, anyway? Does it make us better people, more generous and committed to the community where we live? Not necessarily. In fact, Rieff warns that 'psychoanalysis prudently refrains from urging men to become what they really are', in part because analysts fear 'the honest criminal lurking behind the pious neurotic' (ibid., p. 322).

Despite its dangers, Freud believed that honesty, though costly, is less expensive in the long run than its alternative, a society of morons whose ultimate glory is to cow to social convention, in the hope of being rewarded for it. After all, this is the same society Freud held accountable for making us neurotic in the first place, by compelling us to conceal the views, inclinations and aspirations society opposes.

Like the existentialists, Freud believed that being true to one's convictions should always hold precedence over blindly complying with someone else's standard of behaviour. Indeed, Rieff noted the similarity between Freud's views and Sartre's existentialism, comparing the former's ethic of honesty with the latter's notion of authenticity (1959, p. 321), a notion that Sartre derived, to a considerable extent, from Heidegger. The view that individuals and society are necessarily opposed is a key to understanding Freud's conception of analysis and the form of alienation it is capable of relieving. At bottom, it is a kind of alienation that is an inescapable consequence of living. Nietzsche, Sartre and Heidegger shared with Freud a characterization of contemporary culture in which the individual is a perpetual outsider, a romantic in a post-modernist world who must bear the burden of his convictions and make what peace he is able with the relentless forces of convention. From this perspective, psychoanalysis is unremittingly subversive. Its principal goal is to uncover the latent truth about ourselves by disclosing it. Whatever we do with that truth, and whatever effect we permit it to have on our destiny, is ultimately between ourselves and our conscience.

BIBLIOGRAPHY

Freud, S. (1905) *Fragment of an Analysis of a Case of Hysteria*. Standard Edition, Vol. 7. London: Hogarth Press, 1953, 1–22.

Freud, S. (1910) *The Future Prospects of Psycho-analytic Therapy*. Standard Edition, Vol. 11. London: Hogarth Press, 1957, 139–51.

Freud, S. (1912) *The Dynamics of Transference*. Standard Edition, Vol. 12. London: Hogarth Press, 1958, 97–108.

Freud, S. (1913) *On Beginning the Treatment (Further Recommendations on the Technique of Psychoanalysis I)*. Standard Edition, Vol. 12. London: Hogarth Press, 1958, 121–44.

Freud, S. (1915) *Observations on Transference-Love (Further Recommendations on the Technique of Psychoanalysis III)*. Standard Edition, Vol. 12. London: Hogarth Press, 1958, 157–71.

Freud, S. (1923) *The Ego and the Id*. Standard Edition, Vol. 19. London: Hogarth Press, 1961, 3–66.

Heidegger, M. (1985) *History of the Concept of Time*. Trans. by Theodore Kisiel. Bloomington: Indiana University Press.

Lacan, J. (1992) *The Seminars of Jacques Lacan: Book VII, The Ethics of Psychoanalysis – 1959–1960*. Trans. by Dennis Porter. New York: W.W. Norton and Company.

Rieff, P. (1959) *Freud: The Mind of the Moralist*. New York: Viking Press.

Thompson, M.G. (1994) *The Truth About Freud's Technique: The Encounter with the Real*. New York: New York University Press.

8

Subjects of Perversion

Noreen O'Connor

Every interpretation in psychotherapeutic work is informed by a particular conception of the 'subject'. These conceptions often remain unexamined and unconscious on the part of psychotherapists. I shall focus on the concept of perversion since it raises crucial questions regarding subjectivity and it has thus been the site of much debate among modernists and post-modernists. Both modernists and post-modernists agree that individuals exist in different cultures and traditions and that they have specific histories. However, modernists believe that, although history and culture influence us, there are, nevertheless, universal, objective standards of truth and goodness. If we achieve these we will live a healthy and happy life. Post-modernists disagree that any such universally foundationally rational rules or standards can be known outside the specificity of the individual's life, culture and historicity. Both these strands are discernible within Freud's theorizing.

My aim is to highlight the importance for psychotherapists of reflecting critically on how their view of the subject informs their work. I shall discuss Freud's theory of fetishism and also Joel Whitebook's modernist interpretations of Freud as points of comparison with my own. Through discussion of some therapeutic work with a man whom I shall call Nigel, I shall reflect on the drawbacks of both these approaches. I shall argue against the notion that the task of analysis is the development of a more rationally integrated self-knowledge. On the contrary, I believe that my aim as a psychoanalytic psychotherapist is to enable the patient to live with ambiguity, complexity and uncertainty. Furthermore, the contribution of post-modernists to a conception of the subject as contingent can enable us to respond more sensitively to the historical and cultural specificity of the individual's experiences.[1]

THE TALE OF THE BLUE RIBBON

Nigel, a young man in his mid-twenties, presented for psychotherapy because he felt 'very low' and had been so for some time. He was an intelligent and successful businessman, and he said that he worked with other young people like himself in the City (London's financial centre). Nigel had confided in a male friend about feeling so dragged down; he thought it stemmed from the ending of his relationship with his girlfriend. His friend suggested that he should seek therapy and Nigel had felt a sense of relief at the prospect of finding someone to help him. From a middle-class Welsh Methodist family, he was the youngest child with two older brothers and a sister who was the eldest. Nigel was in twice-a-week psychoanalytical psychotherapy for two and a half years.

In the early months of therapy Nigel expressed intense anxiety at his recurrent and terrifying thoughts that he would die. He spoke about his family, particularly his mother whom he adored. She had very high moral standards which, Nigel said, he felt he always fell short of. His father did not rate much; he did not feel that he had a relationship with him. He admitted hesitantly that, since his anxieties had begun, he often longed to be a little boy again and he remembered feeling safe as he curled against his mother. Nigel compared himself to his brothers; they were 'normal blokes' interested in football, cars and women, who would stay out all night. Moreover, unlike himself, they were not in thrall to their mother's high moral standards. They would shout and argue vehemently with her.

After several months of therapy, the adored mother of Nigel's childhood emerged as cold, domineering and restrictive. He felt very guilty about acknowledging this but he felt she must have been justified because he felt he was 'bad'. In the transference he experienced me as highly censorious in relation to his sexuality. He saw me as an older woman, like his mother, who was potent yet castrated, able and not able to help him and out to destroy his potency. Nigel, nevertheless, was able to speak of his pain at losing his girlfriend. He was ashamed and embarrassed that, although he loved her, he was impotent with her. His fears that this was because he was gay emerged through his increasingly negative transference to me: he accused me of being homophobic. He began to give lengthy accounts of the virtues of his gay friends whom, he had decided, I would despise as 'perverts'. For him, he insisted, they were the most 'together' people he knew. Nigel was now socializing almost exclusively with these friends and reflected about 'coming out' himself. This possibility was full of fraught excitement: at last he would have a lover of his own and, most importantly, his mother would disown him. He could be rid of her and her sermons. The notion that he was gay seemed to relieve his anxieties about his sexual identity.

Eighteen months into the therapy Nigel arrived deeply distraught, saying that he wanted to kill himself. He had come to the session because he wanted to let me see the pain he was in. He described how he had 'come out' to his friends, who had all been pleased for him. They had all gone to a gay club where one of his 'so-called mates' tried to have sex with him. Since this had repulsed and terrified him there was no future for him: he wasn't straight and he wasn't gay. Furthermore, he felt that he didn't know who or what he was. He wondered if the therapist knew what he thought. He said that his mother used to know what he thought and she would tell him that he 'was her baby'. Nigel repeatedly spoke of the terror of losing his mind. The therapist wondered aloud whether 'losing his mind' felt like the disintegration of his existence, of his bodily existence. Nigel responded by speaking of his longing to be 'out of it', free of the conflict of not knowing what he was. In an abstracted moment the therapist wondered, 'Why do you think that you should know what you are?' Long silence. 'But then what do I know?' Nigel enquired. 'You know the taste of tea and coffee, the colour of the sky on a summer's morning, the smile on the face of a friend.' Silence. 'You mean it's just living, just living every day?' he said.

Shortly after this session Nigel risked exposing the pain of his real pleasure. He arrived at a session and he sobbed and shook. In a low voice he confessed that he was afraid that he was really a transvestite. As a little boy he got excited at fondling his mother's knickers. He progressed to wearing them when she was out. Nigel's big secret was that he still dressed up in women's underwear; he had never told anybody. This disclosure gave Nigel great relief and he expressed warm feelings for the therapist. He went on to explain with great embarrassment that what gave him the excitement necessary to ejaculate was the tying of a piece of blue satin ribbon around his penis. Although he was embarrassed when talking of this, he was also triumphant. It emerged that this triumph was derived from his having a secret pleasure, one that only he knew about. I wondered to myself whether he would be able to live with the revelation of this pleasure or whether it would destroy him.

One day, after months of speaking of his pleasure, Nigel announced with dismay that his piece of satin no longer 'did the trick'. He went into a period of overwhelming depression and apathy, such that, he said, it wasn't even worth killing himself. We increased his sessions to four times a week. Nigel began to realize that his despair at his embodied existence co-existed with an unconscious and productive anger and revenge at his mother. He was furious that she wanted him to remain a baby so he couldn't be masculine like his brothers. Wearing the satin ribbon expressed his revenge towards her for confining his sexuality to 'a wank with a ribbon'. At the same time, the anger and revenge expressed in his secret pleasure also connected him to his mother. On occasions, in speaking of his secret, Nigel became very angry with the therapist, demanding to know what sort of man did she think he was.

For Nigel, his secret pleasure was both a response to his mother's demands on him and his father's absence. During this stage of his therapy he began to reflect on the cultural interpretations of gender and sexuality in the tightly knit Methodist community in which he had been raised. He reflected on how rigid these had been and how much they had constrained him: he said that he knew too well what they considered to be the differences between men and women and such knowledge left him 'nowhere'.

Several months later Nigel spoke of his loneliness. Even though he had good company there was something missing. He felt he had a 'fairly mundane life', but he didn't regret the loss of his secret drama. He then began to speak about a young woman colleague who 'fancied' him. He liked her a lot but felt nervous about going out with her. As they became closer, Nigel found that he loved their physical intimacy and the ease and pleasure of this were, he said, a revelation. The world was alive and he no longer had to hide.

FREUD'S PERVERSION

From a Freudian perspective Nigel's presenting clinical material would be diagnosed as perverse. His fetish would be interpreted as arising from a conflict in relation to his masculinity. In the 'Three Essays on the Theory of Sexuality', Freud argued that there was no difference in the sources of neurotic symptoms and perversions. They are all generated by sexual wishes which are subject to repression. What distinguishes a 'perversion' is that, unlike a neurotic symptom which is disguised through symbolism, it is directly acted out. He thus defines perversions as 'sexual activities which either (a) *extend*, in an anatomical sense, beyond the regions of the body that are designed for sexual union, or (b) linger over the intermediate relations to the sexual object which should normally be traversed rapidly on the path towards the sexual aim'.[2]

Perversion, for Freud, arises specifically from the little boy's inability and refusal to accept the difference between his and his mother's gender.[3] Freud (1927) further develops his theory in 'Fetishism' where he maintains that the fetish is paradigmatic in perversion. The fetish allows the boy to retain what, at a logical level is contradictory, namely, that his mother does, and yet does not, have a penis. Freud explains that the holding of these two positions arises from 'disavowal' whereby the ego splits to allow two contradictory attitudes to persist simultaneously without affecting each other. Freud argues that, whereas repression defends the ego against the imperious demands of the id, disavowal defends against the demands of external reality. Thus, in repression, the split is between the ego and the id and, in disavowal, the split is within the ego. According to Freud, the fetish arises as a response to the traumatic anxiety experienced by the boy when he discovers that this mother does not have a penis and assumes that she is castrated. This recognition generates anxiety that he too will be castrated, and leads him to conclude that his mother both has, and does not have, a penis. The fetish plays the role of the missing penis and allows the fetishist to maintain that women are not castrated, that castration does not exist and that he is, therefore, not at risk. It is this reassurance that enables him to experience orgasmic pleasure. The fetish thus 'remains a token of triumph over the threat of castration and a protection against it'.[4] Furthermore, according to Freud, the fetish also serves to ward off the homosexuality which arises in response to the fear of castration. The boy's insistent belief that his mother has a penis prevents him from resolving his Oedipus complex and taking up a truly heterosexual position.

Freud maintains that '*in every instance*, the meaning and purpose of the fetish turned out, in analysis, to be the same' (emphasis mine).[5] Yet, as my work with Nigel highlights, such a claim forecloses on the specific meanings of certain forms of sexual behaviour for each individual, including their socio-cultural specificity. For Nigel, there is no evidence that, in his use of the blue ribbon, he wished to retain a notion of his mother as 'having a phallus', alongside his knowledge that she did not. The blue ribbon served another purpose: it allowed him to express his rage at her desire for him to remain infantile, her 'little boy'. In re-enacting what he felt had been done to him, he was in control and he was able to symbolically punish his mother for causing him to be like this. This re-enactment also connected him to her. Furthermore, the blue ribbon expressed the contradictory demands that his mother and his religious community had made on him as a boy. They all knew who or what he should be and what he should think. If only he could know who or what he really was, he would be free of their definitions and demands. Nigel was triumphant at having this secret pleasure because it was one of the few things in his life that he knew to be his very own. This 'something' that was his very own cannot be captured by the notion of the phallus: it was the site of Nigel's articulation of his rage and a creative response to the contradictory demands on his masculinity.

If I had adhered to Freud's interpretation of the fetish, I would have bypassed many of the questions that were preoccupying Nigel. I would also have been treating Nigel in the very same way that he had been treated by his mother and the Church: they both knew what he thought and told him what he should think. The crucial shift in Nigel's therapy occurred in response to my questioning why he thought that he should know what he was. It opened a space between us for ambiguity and uncertainty, possibilities of other forms of 'knowing' which allowed Nigel to speak of what had been, hitherto, unspeakable. This interpretation was informed by a notion of subjectivity as fluid and shifting and not as something which can be known. It was thus a challenge to normative notions of subjectivity in which the 'normal' subject knows himself to be heterosexual or, at the very least, 'knows' his sexual orientation as either straight or gay. Furthermore, my interpretation was informed by a commitment to hold open questions of what constitutes masculinity and femininity.

In my responses to Nigel my aim was not that he should relinquish his fetish. I do not hold the view that to give up a fetish is necessarily a sign of having achieved maturity. I do not see the task of analysis as providing a 'cure' of this type. Furthermore, this would also be a denial of the cultural specificity of the notion of the fetish and the value judgments that designate the fetish as 'unnatural' sexual behaviour. What was most important was that I offer Nigel the possibility of articulating his struggles and his despair in their unconscious aspects. The 'success' of the therapy lay in his feeling less haunted by the persecutory voices of his past and discovering that it is possible to live with ambiguity and uncertainty. That Nigel went on to have a heterosexual relationship without his blue satin ribbon is not, in my view, a measure of the success of the therapy.

PERVERSION AND UTOPIA?

The view of subjectivity that informs my work is influenced by post-modernist theorizing. This is characterized by a critique of the

Enlightenment's autonomous and self-legislating self in favour of the notion of the subject as shaped by a specific socio-historical context. Post-modernists reject universalizing theories, maintaining that knowledge and truth are perspectival. Some post-modernists argue that there are strands of post-modernism in Freud's theorizing, citing, for example, his problematization of heterosexuality. For Freud it is not a 'given', it has to be achieved through a process of precarious identifications.[6]

In contrast to post-modernist interpretations of Freud, Joel Whitebook, a philosopher and psychoanalyst, claims that what is central to Freud's agenda is the exploration of the 'irrational' in order to integrate it into an expanded notion of rationality. Whitebook is in agreement with what he reads as Freud's aim of psychoanalysis, namely the ego's integration of the instinctual forces from which it has been hitherto defined: 'Rather than abandoning the standpoint of the ego altogether, the deconstruction of naïve consciousness can instead initiate a process of creating, through the work of psychoanalysis and in alliance with the analysand's observing ego, a more adequate ... ego/consciousness.'[7] Whitebook thus insists that Freud was a modernist, a theorist of an autonomist, universally rational subject.

Whitebook characterizes post-modernism as a symptom of the groundlessness of modern living which, he argues, is expressed by identification with the irrational and the transgressive – an idealization of romanticism. By contrast, he favours 'a concept of the noncoercive integration of the self ... a necessity for countering post-modernism's manic and one-sided celebration of generalized dissolution and dispersion'.[8] Whitebook implies that post-modernist readings of Freud deny the reality of trauma and its effects. He argues that these 'utopian' psychoanalytical positions on subjectivity operate with the same denial and disavowal that Freud attributes to perversion. They are thus identified with the idealization of perverse sexuality and exclude problems of trauma, disavowal and aggression.

This raises the question as to whether my interpretations of Nigel's 'secret pleasure' denied his pain. In my view, interpretations informed by a post-modernist critique of the rational subject are not incompatible with a response to a person's suffering. Throughout the therapy with Nigel I remained attentive to his conflicts and his despair. Although I bore in mind the notion that the fetish is a culturally and historically specific term, I did not assume that what was required was for Nigel to perceive his secret pleasure as liberatory and thus idealize transgression. Post-modernist thought enabled me to challenge the universalizing features of Freud's theory of the fetish and to attend more sensitively to Nigel's suffering in its historical and cultural specificity.

Whitebook's critique raises a further question regarding the efficacy of the therapeutic work with Nigel. Nigel was terrified of what he did not know and wondered how to know it. He did not know who or what he was and whether he was gay or straight. It might appear that Nigel's dilemma would have been resolved more satisfactorily if I had taken Whitebook's view of the aim of psychoanalysis, namely the achievement of a rationally integrated self through the strengthening of his ego. It seems to me that this would be to lead Nigel further in the direction of the belief system which confined him. Nigel's problem lay in his desire for knowledge and certainty as to who and what he was. As I have described, it was crucial that I held open a space for ambiguity and uncertainty.

In his argument for the norm of subjectivity as integrated rationality Whitebook does not address the radical aspects of Freud's theorizing, such as his problematization of gender differences, heterosexuality, homosexuality and lesbianism. The integrated self that Whitebook advocates seems to be genderless and non-sexual. He also does not address the fact that some psychoanalytic writers on perversion insist that homosexuality and lesbianism are, by definition, pathological and in need of cure.[9]

CONCLUSION

Nigel's therapy ended when he discovered he could live and that living was not a matter of hiding, denying, inventing and thinking his life. I believe that this was possible for Nigel because I did not adhere to a notion of maturity in the subject as the integration of rationality, the achievement of heterosexuality, or the certainty that one is a man or a woman. I did not hold back from the challenge of questions such as: How can human embodiment be known? Why ask that question? What is the relationship between embodiment and discourse? Is there an essential femininity and masculinity?

I have argued that post-modernism analyses of identities and differences can enable psychotherapists to open out such questions and heighten their sensitivity to the specificity of their patients. The interpretation of differences need not be exclusively confined to a rigid theorizing of psychic development. Furthermore, the interpretation of differences does not preclude careful recognition of and attention to the traumas which confine people to a rigid and compulsive life of satisfactions, generating self-hatred and isolation from others. It matters very much in practice how an analyst conceives of subjectivity, masculinity, femininity, sexuality and homosexuality. As Joanna Ryan and I argued in *Wild Desires and Mistaken Identities*, 'the history of psychoanalysis does not encourage confidence in its ability to change and adapt, except by fissure and expulsion, but perhaps the pluralism that is now demanded and evident in so many other areas of thought and theory could extend to psychoanalysis'.[10]

NOTES

1. In 'Who speaks? Who listens? Different voices and different sexualities', *British Journal of Psychotherapy*, Vol. 13, No. 3 (Spring 1997), Mary Lynne Ellis emphasizes that 'to truly engage with the complexity of our patients' experience in its conscious and unconscious aspects, we must have the courage to suspend any temptation to simplify, to universalize and to colonize' (p. 383).
2. S. Freud (1905) 'Three Essays on the Theory of Sexuality', in *On Sexuality*. Harmondsworth: Penguin, 1983, p. 62.
3. For Freud, the fetish is exclusively a male phenomenon. Marie Maguire argues that, from a Kleinian perspective, the concept of perversion is applicable to both genders; whereas men direct their sexual aggression towards an objectified object, women persecute their children's or their own bodies (e.g. eating disorders). See *Men, Women, Passion and Power*. London: Routledge, 1995, p. 192.
4. S. Freud (1927), in *On Sexuality*, op. cit., p. 353.
5. Ibid., p. 262.
6. Cf. S. Freud, 'Three Essays on Sexuality', op. cit., p. 57.
7. J. Whitebook, *Perversion and Utopia*. Cambridge, MA: MIT Press, 1995, p. 131.
8. Ibid., p. 262.
9. N. O'Connor, 'Passionate differences: lesbianism, post-modernism, and psychoanalysis', in Thomas Domenici and Ronnie C. Lesser (eds) *Disorienting Sexuality*. New York: Routledge, 1995, p. 168.
10. N. O'Connor and J. Ryan, *Wild Desires and Mistaken Identities: Lesbianism and Psychoanalysis*. New York: Columbia University Press, 1994, p. 271.

9

Sexuality, Psychoanalysis and Social Changes

Juliet Mitchell

There have been considerable changes in family patterns since the 1960s, yet our work as psychoanalysts in this area uses theories either as old as our discipline (one hundred years) or as old as the work emanating from the crises of the Second World War and ending, at the latest, in the 1960s. Today, as distinct from the periods of our dominant theories, there is in the Western world, by and large, a decline in the rate of marriage, an increase in the rate of divorce, a decline in family size to less than two children, an increase in the number of children born outside marriage, an increase in single-mother families, in paternal absenteeism, in cohabitation, in serial monogamy and in a range of living arrangements including homosexual couplings with or without children. Although all these phenomena have been witnessed in other historical epochs or in other societies they were not dominant practices at the time – or times – of the creation of psychoanalytic theory.

I am interested in raising a number of what seem to me to be urgent questions about our theory and practice by exploring these in the light of social changes. For me, the problems revolve around our understanding of heterosexuality. So long as we fail to correlate our theories of psychic life with social conditions – whether these seem 'universal' or specific – these theories will, without our intending it, become reflective of these very conditions. Indeed, I think this has already happened, in relation to both the castration complex and to mother–infant relations.

As early as 1963 Alexander Mitscherlich, a psychoanalyst, wrote his book *Society Without the Father*;[1] today, descriptions such as 'fatherless America' or 'dead-beat Dads' are commonplace. I would suggest that the waning significance of the castration complex in Object Relations Theory, both for the Kleinians and British Independents (Middle Group), should be seen as an unacknowledged reflection of this social change. *Society Without the Father* translates into a theory which asserts the importance of the Oedipus complex without paying any attention to the critical role of the castration complex. Although both Kleinian and Independent practitioners subscribe to the notion of the castration complex, it is strikingly absent from both theoretical and clinical observations. To the best of my knowledge, the late Adam Limentani is one of the few psychoanalysts to reflect on the absence of the castration complex, not in our theories but in the cases that confront us.

In his paper, 'The limits of heterosexuality: the vagina-man',[2] Limentani explores something that he had learnt from his many years of clinical work, that heterosexuality – as social practice and psychic experience – was perfectly possible for individuals who showed no signs of having negotiated – or even having failed to negotiate – the castration complex (the castration complex was not even present in a symptom). Here was male heterosexuality without a castration complex, no resolution into a protective, ethical superego with coincident sublimation. Instead, Limentani's 'vagina men' had found a viable solution to their primitive 'nameless dread' (Wilfred Bion) by identifying with the woman they loved rather than electing her as their object choice.

I believe that Limentani is pointing to a possible widespread 'normal' trend: a prevalent type of heterosexuality. Limentani is convinced (and convincing) that his 'vagina man' is not, as is usually argued, defending against homosexuality, but, instead, deploying a recourse to an original fused infant–mother relationship in which the father is psychically absent. It would seem to me, although this is not part of Limentani's argument, that overt homosexuals may manifest the same psychic choice – valuing 'sameness' and intense identification rather than object choice. However, to claim that homosexuals and heterosexuals may be engaged in the same psychic practice is not at all to argue that these heterosexuals are homosexuals in disguise. The social practice of heterosexuality merely obscures the psychic identification in a way that the practice of homosexuality does not. Similarly, I would argue (again it is not part of Limentani's argument) that a woman can be a 'vagina woman' in a similar way to a man – the syndrome looks different because this 'normal-looking pathology' is so close to what she is meant to be: she has identified with a woman failed to internalize 'femininity' (see Joan Rivière, 'Womanliness as a masquerade')[3] or, perhaps more importantly, 'maternity'.

If Limentani's observation and explanation are accurate (and my own experience, both clinically and sociologically, suggests that they are), then we are left with a number of questions (and a number of problems).

If there is no castration complex in this heterosexuality, if there is no 'symbolic' father, has the father's existence been annihilated in the mind? If so, then we have an instance of a prevalent 'normal' heterosexuality whose psychic structures are psychotic. We also have a situation in which, although the heterosexuality may work well enough at the level of the couple, 'fathering' (actual and symbolic) will be very difficult or even traumatic since psychically any child of the 'vagina man' will be experienced not as the father's offspring but rather as the result of the mother's betrayal. Enormous sibling jealousy will be evoked between the father and child: the father does not psychically know his offspring is 'his', hence it must have been the result of the mother's imaginary affair. The father, a vagina man, has identified with the mother but in this fused identity he is both mother and child; so in unconscious fantasy he shares his infantile generation with his own child.

Although Limentani's portrait is benign, the combination of the absence of boundaries, necessitated by the 'vagina man's' mode of identification and his deep sense of 'being empty of his self' (Enid Balint), his primary jealousy (Joan Rivière) and the primitive untransmuted rage associated with it might well give us an identikit prototype of the child abuser. I think we need to ask if the prevalence of the 'vagina man' in the context of our changing social practices could be correlated with the apparent rise in child abuse.

At the moment our psychoanalytical theories would seem to mimic the social situation. Independent psychoanalysts (particularly Winnicottians) put all the stress on the mother–infant relation – so too does current social practice; Kleinians stress the cruel, primitive superego emanating from a maternal relationship, but the later caring, protective superego that is part of the internalization of the father of the castration complex is absent from the application of Kleinian theory as it is from aspects of social reality today. The psychic relation to social reality needs to be explained, not reflected, in psychoanalytic theory.

Limentani's 'vagina man' is a Don Juan. For the sake of coherence I am going to use the character of Don Juan to extend the argument about social practice and psychoanalytic theory.[4] A changing feature of post-1960s' sexuality has been Don Juanism among women – again this is by no means unique (one only has to think of Restoration drama) but its cultural acceptance (though not named as such) is a crucial part of our social situation in the Western world. This points to something important: if the syndrome is not gender-specific because the castration complex is missing, what is the marker of sexual difference; what symbolizes the difference between women and men if the phallus on which the castration complex turns is not subject to an inexorable law?

Thinking through the bisexuality (as subject and in object-choice) Don Juan brings another complex and perceptive clinical account to mind – Eric Brenman's 1985 article, 'Hysteria'.[5] The more I consider the portrait of a male hysteric that Brenman paints, the more I think that he is describing the same (or at least a remarkably similar) phenomenon to Limentani's 'vagina man'. Brenman's focus on the Don Juan syndrome is to illustrate how it shows 'the negation of psychic reality' (p. 423).[6] His account is of a male hysteric and is far more negative a portrait than Limentani's 'vagina man'. This negativity adds an important dimension to our picture – one that helps link it (though Brenman does not) to possible child abuse. Brenman's Mr X. is childless but is psychologically abusive of his wife.

Mr X. presented to Dr Brenman with crippling anxiety and panic states and then a miraculous recovery from these. His self-presentation continued to be contradictory – for instance, he was ruthless and caring. He tried to control both his analyst and the analysis in a highly manipulative way, constantly putting Brenman into a double-bind situation. His sexuality was not for sexuality but for triumph over the other person, 'a pseudosexuality at the service of his narcissistic conquest' (ibid., p. 423). My concern here is with Brenman's account of the object-relationship. Limentani's vagina man has regressed to a fusion with his infantile mother and as an adult Don Juan repeats this with every woman he seduces – his aim is to ward off primal dread by this safety device. Similarly of the hysteric illustrated by Mr X., Brenman writes:

> It is my belief that the hysteric is able to make an apparent relationship with live external objects. Such an external object, a person, is used to hold the hysteric together and to prevent more serious breakdown into depression or disintegration – schizophrenia.
>
> The basic theme of this paper is that the use of the external object relationship, which appears as a relationship to a whole object, is essentially narcissistic, and that an ostensibly whole object is used as a part object to prevent break-down. (ibid., pp. 422–3)

This seems to me to be the negative of the 'vagina man's' positive – both are the self-as-another, Limentani's patient thus prevents the breakthrough of 'primal dread', Brenman's disintegration, depression, breakdown. Brenman, however, is also concerned with what this means for the human 'object' thus used. In fact I believe that for this 'object' there can be a range of experiences along a continuum. Don Juan's identification with the other will make for a degree of sensitivity towards its needs; at the other end, however, the extent of projection that this entails will make for a 'takeover' that is a complete denial and abuse of the other's otherness. Where Limentani's 'vagina man' is heterosexually sensitive, Brenman's destroys the other's psychic reality. This Brenman sees as a hallmark of hysteria; these are ends of a psychic continuum ranging from fusion to extreme projective identification.

There is, however, a further aspect which I wish to emphasize – any person or any event which gets in the way of this coupling, including any action by the other that asserts its difference will bring all hell down. Mr X. demanded of his wife that she accept all his affairs as he would hers (except that she has none) but when his lover has lovers he tries to destroy her emotionally and professionally: his wife incurs his rage because, not being promiscuous, she does not see things the way he does; his mistress incurs his rage because having a further affair with another man, she indicates she is separate from him. This is at the level of childless coupling. If a child is born, then the Don Juan unconsciously (sometimes the fantasy is nearly conscious) believes it is he who has given birth and is furious if anything disturbs this notion.

Mr X. and the 'vagina man' are men projecting into or fusing with women. But women can do the same – it only seems less noticeable as this identification seems ego-syntonic with the person's gender, i.e. it is feminine. This femininity would obviously be an identification/fusion with the mother that girls like boys would seek as a defence against disintegration or a primal dread but it would also be an assertion of the girl's narcissism. We need, however, to note the factor of regression in all this. The Don Juan will be regressing to infantile bisexuality when s/he fuses or projects. The gender characteristics of woman or man are marks of the adult's contemporary psycho-social condition, not of the infantile past which is being demonstrated in the adult present.

The Don Juan syndrome is above all driven by jealousy and using sexuality for the ends of embedding this jealousy in the other's desperate response. Just as being enviable protects against the pain of envying, so being the object of jealousy protects against the madness of feeling jealous. Envy hurts, jealousy makes mad – though often concomitant states, they are not the same. The Don Juan-hysteric is enacting and trying to get rid of the madness of jealousy. Envy is about what someone has; jealousy is about where someone else stands: it is about position rather than possession.

Kleinian psychoanalytic theory has focused on the subject's primary envy – the envy in the first instance of the mother's breast for containing all the baby wants. Brenman is theoretically committed to this approach but his material, I believe, escapes these confines. To some extent the focus on envy has always obscured the jealousies of the Oedipal triangle but in its turn the Oedipal jealousies have obscured the jealousies of lateral relations. Don Juanism is sexuality without reproduction. Although the *Ur*-Don Juan murders the father figure – his fiancé's father, the Commandatore – the whole thrust of the action and passion is between 'equals'/peers not between generations.

The social factors in the Western world leading to this emphasis on lateral relations which is the background that conform to a prevalence of psychic and enacted Don Juanism are: the decline of the vertical family – grandparents, particularly with occupational mobility, are declining in status; schooling with its peer group culture is extending; step-families erode generational exactitude (a new husband or wife can be the same age as his/her step-children); male and female positions and representations are more exchangeable; sexuality in one of its central manifestations is non-reproductive (it has always been partially non-reproductive, but this aspect has been ideologically marginalized in such practices as prostitution); there are less children being born and more childfree couples.

I argued earlier that Object Relations Theory with its focus on the mother-and-baby had lost the structuring role of the father – though this is somewhat of a parody – it too had become a 'vagina man/woman' at the level of analysis and of clinical practice, interpreting from a position of maternal identification and compulsive heterosexuality. The increasing absence of the concept of a castration complex thus reflects a changing social practice which is de-centring the father in relation to the mother. We can take this further and contextualize the missing father as a feature of a move from vertical to lateral relationships which is indicated at the level of the psyche by a shift from symbolization to identification. In turn identification with the other rather than a symbolization of the other means their absence cannot be represented. The relative absence of the castration complex also implicates a different relationship to death so that now deaths haunt rather than are mourned.

Mr Z. is an amalgam of several male patients of mine, all with important hysterical features: conversion, phobia, eating disorders, compulsive

sexualization (actual or fantasized Don Juanism) and shallow identifications both feminine and masculine. The feature on which I wish to focus
is the absence of what I will call 'psychological fatherhood'. Mr Z. was
in some ways quite obsessed with his children but at another level he
simply did not know they were 'his', he could not see that they bore a
relationship to him. While puzzling how we could move beyond an
acknowledgement of this, I noted another kinship absence which seemed
pertinent: Mr Z. presented as an only child – but he was not; he had a
brother and a sister, born when he was three and five years old respect-
ively. Had he scotomized a child of his own as he had each of his
siblings, merely enacting out that common wish – if the stork brought it,
the stork can take it away?

In my pursuit of understanding hysteria, this and other factors led to
my considering that we have subjugated the significance of lateral
relationships to vertical ones to the extent almost of their exclusion – we
have not given them their place in Oedipality. The mother who screams
blue murder at her pre-verbal infant probably had a young sibling to
whom she was a 'little mother', perfect, ideal partly play-acting. For this
'little mother' of a younger sibling is deeply split, for she also wants to
murder the newcomer. She (and he) will also – like the later hysteric –
want to have given birth to her own babies parthenogenetically through
masturbation and sibling or peer play.

The first section of this chapter was addressed to the British Society of
Psychoanalysis, where Object Relations Theory is hegemonic. The focus
was thus the importance of the absence of the concept and clinical interpretation of the castration complex. The obverse can also be, if not more
socially complicit, then ideologically complicit. For instance, Lacanian
analysts argue that femininity, constructed over the absence of the
phallus, is not represented except as this absence. An absence cannot in
fact be represented thus, nor can the feminine. Only a representation can
be repressed and hence feature in the unconscious. Castration is thus
signified as a black hole into which femininity falls. To put it another way,
femininity is the black hole of castration. But it seems to me that hysterical
pregnancies and parthenogenic birth fantasies tell another story as well.

Mr Z. was fascinated with giving birth but his musical endeavours
never quite made it as a sublimation (one could say they were 'imaginary
identifacts' but not symbolic). All children want to give birth but this is
prohibited not only in relation to fantasies involving the father but also
in relation to fantasies involving only the self or replications of the self
such as we find in 'sibling'/peer play. The hysteric has not acknowledged

the prohibition on this parthenogenetic pregnancy – there is too much of him in the resultant child (or creative work), and the child (work) has not been symbolized as distinct and hence able to be related to him as a separate being – its father (or mother). If it is not distinct, how can it be one's own? – Mr Z. did not know his children were 'his'. In focusing only on the castration complex as the moment for the representation of femininity, Lacanian theory has occluded the same problem that Object Relations has missed – although from the other end. Object Relations Theory sees the enormous importance of the mother-and-baby but does not see the mother's role in prohibiting the child's 'sibling' partheno-genic desires.

Thus the dominant psychoanalytic theories echo an hysterical culture in not seeing the significance of a prohibition on giving birth to a child when a child. Unlike a realistic impossibility, a prohibition against sibling incest in which two 'likes' would reproduce must (if successful) lead to repression of the representation of the desire. In turn this repression makes possible the symbolization of a child as a separate 'object'. One has had to 'lose' the possibility of procreation in one's own child-hood and thus can regain it as a representation and a separate object in one's adulthood. (Similarly it enables sublimation.) This gives another dimension to femininity. Other than the black hole and the non-representability of castration, there is a drive and a desire to procreate which must survive as well as submit to the travails of childhood repression.

Reading in the prohibition on 'sibling' incest and murderousness to the theory also shifts the stance of transference interpretation. When the end of a lengthy treatment was in sight, Mr Z. suddenly left the wife he found so wanting for an 'ideal' woman – worryingly like his transference to my 'thin' but perfect image. With the wife absent, both children then became the focus of his dissatisfaction and there was sporadic but increasing violence towards them. Only at this stage did I really learn of earlier attacks on his first wife. Had I seen that she and I were a split of himself into the sibling who was so perfectly like him and frighteningly unlike him, we might have been able to avoid some of the subsequent enactment with the children.

Limentani considers a Don Juan character to be an exemplary instance of the 'vagina man', seeing Don Juan as heterosexual through identification with a woman rather than through object-choice. The fullest illustration of Brenman's hysteric Mr X. is a Don Juan whom he sees as promiscuous through his identifications with multiple others. Brenman

takes this back to an identification with an idealized 'breast'. The heterosexuality of the hysteric/Don Juan is a cover for an intense narcissism. If
we consider social changes, we should note that serial relationships are
now common for both genders. Brenman's patient is anxious to a point
where he fears madness; he both exploits the catastrophic situation and
denies it. He is unfaithful to his wife and outraged that she might
restrict his freedom ... he allows her to be 'free', knowing she will not be
unfaithful. When his lover is unfaithful, he wants to destroy her utterly
as she has betrayed all he gave her. For those of us who were young in
the 1960s, this is so familiar a scenario as to seem normative. But behind
it is something important: the Don Juan character, male or female, is
seeking to be adored not to love. As Brenman so aptly puts it, 'I'll make
you love me if I have to break every bone in your body' (1985, p. 425)

'Playing doctors' or Mummies and Daddies are gender flexible games;
sexual difference is not yet symbolized. This is also the moment to
which an hysterical pregnancy returns. This has been mostly mistakenly
seen as heterosexual object-relating. Freud, for example, pointed to the
moment when Anna O. believed she was pregnant. Her doctor's wife
was pregnant and Anna O. in her delusion of a similar possibility is said
to have called out with her imaginary birth-pangs, 'Dr. Breuer's baby's
coming'. Ever since this moment we have understood her to have been
fantasizing a sexual union with her doctor–father, resulting in her giving
birth to an incestuous offspring. I now believe that if the exclamation
took place, it meant nothing of the kind. Anna O. would not have been
saying that she had conceived from having been impregnated by Joseph
Breuer's sperm (the female Oedipal version), rather she was enacting
how she thought Breuer himself would have given birth and she was
imitating him. This is just like Little Hans, who reassured his father that
he too, like Hans, would be able to give birth soon. The similarity
between Hans' belief and Anna's delusion has been missed because Anna
was a young woman and heterosexuality has been assumed.

At first it seems completely nonsensical to link this vegetative or
parthenogenic 'hysterical' reproduction to Mr Z.'s inability to recognize
that his children were 'his'. In fact there is no contradiction: they are
aspects of the same situation. The child who in masturbation or sibling
play (or the hysteric who retains or regresses to this position) imagines
giving birth from himself and believes that all the children are his – the
dolls, the teddy bears, the peer playmates. However, this 'his' has no
symbolic significance. The toy-baby can be snatched away and what was
'mine' is mine no longer – the miseries of childhood squabbles. For his

children to be 'his' symbolically and irreplaceably whatever disasters of death, destruction or divorce might ensue, Mr Z. would have had to acknowledge that not all children could be his, indeed that he could not have children by himself or with someone who was the same as him, nor could he have them when a child himself. It is this renunciation or loss that enables representation and symbolization. The move would be from 'all those babies/dolls are mine' through 'they are not mine' or 'they are not babies' to 'I cannot give birth to babies yet' (girl)/'I can never give birth' (boy).

This movement from hysterical possession to renunciation/loss and symbolization may well take place Oedipally (I am not Mummy) but it also takes place laterally. There comes a moment when sibling incest is forbidden (or as with the Ptolemies, much more rarely prescribed, but subject to laws). This is the moment when boys and girls are marked as different from each other along a lateral line, this is a gender difference that is weaker than the sexual difference of the castration complex – but important nonetheless. At this point children learn lateral differentiation: I am older, younger, a boy, a girl . . Mr Z. was both loving and abusive to his children often with lightning alternation – as children are with peers, friends and siblings who are both like and unlike, but not yet symbolized as both the same *and* different.

I want to return now to Limentani's vagina man and Brenman's hysteric, Mr X. to look at one theme: the vagina man is heterosexual; indeed, he is a Don Juan – but he does not father children or if biologically he does, he does not know they are 'his'. This parentless Don Juanism which can be a psychic and behavioural state in a woman no less than a man may be actual or, as with Mr Z., only psychological. If it were always actual parentlessness as with the original Don Juan character, there would be no children to be abused. I want to link this unconscious[7] 'childfree' condition to laterality.

According to Brenman, the hysteric operates a switch between catastrophe (experienced in the symptom) and denial (expressed in the apparently healthy personality). Again one can imagine a social scenario beneath this description: the child denies that the sibling who has replaced him or was there before him is anything other than absolutely adorable or admirable, yet he stops eating, walking or talking, contracts physical illnesses, has night terrors, and so on. He 'becomes' his mother in order to have her exclusively. But is this excessive love which he displays love of the mother (and psycho-analyst as mother) or love of the sibling or both? Brenman writes: 'The pretence of being loving and friendly is not designed to achieve a loving relationship, but to be the falsely adored object of love' (1985, p. 425). Here I agree with Brenman, this I think is the mother; however, the observation continues: 'and to triumph over so-called loving objects who are then despised and annihilated' (ibid.). This, I suggest, may be the end result of the false love for the sibling rather than for the mother. Then we move back to the parent/analyst: 'the analyst is the target of conversion to agree with the patient's machinations' (ibid., p. 426). Here the mother must be seduced into believing in the sibling love and not perceive the sibling jealousy. In other words, the sibling relationship is crucially imbricated in the maternal one: it may even dominate.

Brenman elucidates the familiar observation of the labile, promiscuous, shallow identifications that hysterics make not with real but with ideal objects, commenting that these are always multiple identifications. In commenting on one of Mr X.'s dreams he notes how hard it is to tell whether the psycho-analyst (himself) is the German navy who traps the Russian navy (the patient, Mr X.) or vice versa. Again, these processes are understood by Brenman along vertical, mother–child or father–child axes. My point is not that they are not this; but that they involve lateral ones as well. It might be important to interpret confusingly interchangeable Russian and German navies as problems with fraternal relationships. It does not matter whether Brenman's Mr X. was an only child – as parents and analysts know, only children can be more plagued by 'sibling' love/hate than children with many brothers and sisters. What Mr X.'s material suggests to me is the need to read in the interpenetration of vertical and lateral relations:

> Some time later when he was improving, he re-arranged his business affairs to give more pay and a greater share to his junior partners. He realised that he was assailed by a struggle with contradictory views. On the one hand he felt that everything should be given to the business, the profits should be re-invested and he and the partners should sacrifice their salaries. He realised he was the business – both the baby who had everything and the mother who supplied the food. At the same time he hated the business that made such demands on him, and thought that he should get everything out of the business and not look after it at all and it should supply him with everything.
>
> He realised that in the conflict he was both the ideal breast who should be everything and the ideal baby who should have

everything. He was caught in the conflict of wanting to satisfy both completely, with no capacity to give and take. He linked this with what he considered to be the character of his mother ... These features show a violent greedy dependency. (ibid., p. 426)

There is room in the above account for transference interpretations (and counter-transference problems) along the lines of junior partners and siblingship. Mr X. was emotionally abusive to his wife – could she not have been a sister rather than, but as well as, a mother? His self-righteous infidelity was, among other things, a way of ensuring that it was she, not he, who was jealous – a lateral rather than vertical scenario.

I want now to make a very simple observation: when one reads case histories or clinical accounts within psychoanalysis, or indeed theoretical propositions about the construction of the mind, one cannot but be struck by their complexity. Brenman's article is an exemplary instance of this. Likewise when one reads ethnographic portraits, the social world and its relationships are intricate and nuanced, often difficult in their complexity for a lay reader to grasp *in toto*. Yet the link between these complex worlds of mind and society, from a psychoanalytic perspective, is oddly simple. The Oedipus complex and the pre-Oedipal mother–infant relationship alone is presented as the nexus that links the internal world of unconscious mentation and effects and the external social world. The triangular Oedipal pattern like the binary of Lévi-Strauss and others (in psychoanalysis, the pre-Oedipal) can go in multiple directions and reveal itself in a variety of places, but as a residual structure it is still simple. The Oedipus is presented not so much as a reductive concept as a residual one; a core complex that draws everything to it or from which everything opens out.

The Oedipus complex is key because of its wishes and the prohibitions on these. However, an ethnography reveals the multiplicities of desires and prohibitions. Even a glance at current English marriage regulations gives us a hint of this multifariousness; the rules and regulations as to whom one may or may not marry are quite extraordinarily complicated suggesting not an infinity of possibilities, but that the underlying pattern may be more than two or three.

The Oedipus complex is a metaphor for a nexus of relationships; with the acknowledgement of the castration complex both sexual and generational difference can be represented. Lateral relations – Remus and Romulus, Cain and Abel, the twins who are in various creation myths – form not a nexus but a series. Acknowledging that there is room for the next in line allows for the representation of seriality and with a recognition of the taboo on sexuality between those who socially constituted siblings, gender difference will also be represented. But the gender differences between siblings are not the same as the sexual difference which is instituted by a vertical prohibition.

In the context of the social centrality of seriality and peer group relationships, the renewed emphasis on the importance of mother-and-infant in law and ideology, or (with the obsession with health and the body) mother-and-foetus is striking. The femininization of poverty implicates single mothers as the overall poorest group and urges them to work while simultaneously demanding maternal dedication to the offspring. Such contradictions are not of course new. What is of relevance here is the psychoanalytic stance; by repeating the emphasis on the mother, it is not wrong so much as limited; by missing the lack of symbolized sexual difference, it is repeating and reflecting serial change rather than analysing it. This reflective stance leads, I believe, to psychoanalysis tending to find an outer edge for what it pathologizes and missing the pathology of the centre; in this case its endorsement of heterosexuality can hide the dangers inherent in some aspects of its practices.

NOTES

1.   A. Mitscherlich (1963), *Society Without the Father*. London: Tavistock, 1969.
2.   Reprinted in A. Limentani, *Between Freud and Klein*. New York: Free Association Books, 1989.
3.   J. Rivière, 'Womanliness as a masquerade'. In A. Hughes (ed.) *The Inner World and Joan Rivière*. London: Karnac Books, 1991.
4.   Since writing the above 'note' I have published a book about hysteria which has made me see connections between the questions I raise and the wider problematic there, see J. Mitchell, *Mad Men and Medusas: Reclaiming Hysteria and the Sibling Relationship for the Human Condition*. London: Allen Lane Penguin Press, 2000. Using the character from a different perspective – lying – the Don Juan figure is the subject of half a chapter of this book.
5.   E. Brenman, 'Hysteria', *International Journal of Psycho-Analysis*, 1985, 66, pp. 123–32.
6.   I spoke about the Don Juan as a male hysteric at an International Symposium in Cusco, Peru in 1989 (J. Mitchell, 'Whatever has happened to Don Juan? Don Juan and the Question of Male Hysteria!', *Miros Sociedad Peruana de Psicoanalysia*, 1989). I used Limentani's 'vagina man' but having been trained as an Independent Object Relations psychoanalyst, I was then, shamefully, unaware of Eric Brenman's article. This experience, however, only strengthens my sense that we were (diversely) seeing the same thing in our clinical practices.
7.   I am not referring to conscious choice childfree situations but to the unconscious determinants of psychological parentlessness which may just as easily lie beneath such phenomena as what was once called the pumpkin-eater syndrome – compulsive reproduction.

10

Cutting

Christopher Bollas

A Monday morning at an open psychiatric hospital. The therapy staff, medical director, and various nurses sit around a large conference table, its ceremonious presence dotted acne-like with plastic cups of coffee, as the psychoanalysts self-stimulate to wake from the night's slumbers. A senior nurse reads the customary lengthy report of the patients' deeds and misdeeds during the day and at night, from poignantly meaningful insights that seem newsworthy to fistfights, from complaints about the food to stolen sexual moments; each event never entirely free of the dialectic between the perceived and the hallucinated that keeps all the inhabitants of a mental hospital slightly on edge.

Today the nurse reports several incidents of cutting, the word itself stabbing into our peace of mind. 'Who?' 'How many?' 'How deep?' we wonder as another female patient is named as the latest cutter. In the last month, six of our fifty patients have begun to cut themselves on different parts of the body but mostly wrists or thighs. We always seemed to be capable of dealing with a single cutter, but now a new anxiety emerges: the women have opened a competition, daring each other on, cutting deeper, spreading the wound to the body politic, as we worry if one of *our* women – I now speak of course of our patients – will cut herself and mark our coupling with this act of ... Act of what?

'Well, clearly S cuts because she is testing limits. It is boundary testing. How far can you go before we step in to say, "Enough. Either you accept the rules against self-mutilation in our open hospital or you go elsewhere."' / 'Obviously S cuts because she poses the question "Who is to control my body, the body in question? Is it to be you? How dare you." We should ask her to speak of her feeling that this body of hers is no longer in control.' / 'We must ask the analyst, or S, or both, "What is happening in the transference to inspire the analysand to cut her analyst at this moment?"' / 'Cutting is a relief. The patient cuts to free herself of her persecutory inner contents, which she lets out concretely by bleeding, thus uniting the ego with the super-ego in an alliance of pleasure in pain.'

'S'

'My cut is secret. I create it in stolen moments. In a private place. No one is present when I do this. I slice my skin with a fine razor. I cut deftly so no one can see the finest works of this forbidden craft. I place one cut next to another, each a valley of incisions. I tell Nurse, "I want to show you something." She likes me. I speak to her about secrets. "I have cut myself," and she takes me to her room, where she bathes my inner thigh with soft light. She cannot find the cuts. Where are they? *There*, and I take her finger and put it on the place where the cuts live. She can feel them and I am relieved that she believes me. She frowns, lectures me wordlessly, gives me some soothing cream. Will she tell our secret? I hope not.

'I hear A cut across her stomach. All the way across it. A deep cut. She bled through her analytical hour, but Dr. Z knew nothing as she sheltered beneath her lovely Scottish sweater, its heavy braid soaking up the sacrament. Moments before the session's end she lifted the sweater to reveal the cut and Dr. Z's face became horror. He closed his eyes. Pathetic cuts sutured by his petty anxiety. A went to the hospital and took thirty stitches across her belly, but she refuses to talk about what it means.

'I like to cut myself. It is my private séance. Who owns this razor I use? With whose hand do I make these incisions? Is it my hand? Who cuts me? I cut deep now, to bring blood. It spurts out. Sylvia Plath cut herself in 1962:

> What a thrill –
> My thumb instead of an onion.
> The top quite gone
> Except for a sort of hinge
> of skin . . .

What do I celebrate when I cut? I love the passing of time, the interval between the incision and the arrival of the blood. I wait. Have I cut deep enough to bring up the blood? Or is this a virgin's cut, no menarche here? I must wait. I am used to such waiting. The cut in my body did not bleed until I was twelve; so I know all about waiting for a cut to bleed.

'Up it flows, up and out, spilling over my skin. Pure. No effluence of eggs. No dead babies here. No smelly stains that problematize my relation to that other cut: this blood is pure.

'How deeply have I cut? Will it run out and stop? Will it congeal, gather itself up into little balls of resistance, to arrest itself? Or do I have to stop it? Shall I mix it with pure water? Not the mixture of blood with urine but with pure spring water? Does it still flow? Shall I take my body, then, my hospital body with its new wound, to a doctor for attention? Will the mama nurse barely see it and give me her soothing female creams, or has it gone too far? Have I lost her, this pure mummy who soothed me? If the blood flows I shall lose mummy nurse to a new world, the place of Dr. Z, who frowns and puts his touchless fingers against the wound. Am I to be sutured, sewed up?

'Fuck it. It's rather nice, that. A deadening injection, no pain, and swift nimble fingers that stitch it up. Back then to mummy nurse, who removes the pieces of string, like the tiny cotton of a doll's world, and then the gentle stares and womanly kindnesses.

'Not the look of fear upon the man's face. I have not done that yet, but A did it to Dr. Z with that wonderful great cut across her belly. "Have a look at this, you coal miner of the unconscious, open your eyes to this fearsome cunt, with no pubic fleece to protect your gaze from its object: a hole that bleeds and bleeds and bleeds. Look at this, you coward!" I am not there yet. L cut herself on the upper left arm, just below her shoulder, in a very special secret place, and the blood flowed all the way down her arm, trickling off her finger into her bowl of cereal, mingling with the milk and cornflakes. She stirred and stirred. What a shock! Who could dare to look at this! It was enough to bring a horrified silence to the breakfast room. A mummy nurse led her away from her bowl of milk, but the men – ha! – they could not move. They can't take this blood, they can't deal with this, our cunt, that moves around our bodies to new secret places.

'Ah, the times I have looked and looked at my cunt. I was pure and simple, a girl, no problem, and my fine black hair, their shy locks hiding my pound of vanished flesh, grew and grew, and even my first blood was not so much a big deal. Perhaps I fool myself. I needed to see myself there but I couldn't. A man has no problem cock spotting. He can just look down, any old time, and there it is. But I can't. I tried. Many, many positions. I would just catch sight of the vulva, but I could not have a nice long, relaxed look. I was always aching in my body trying to look. I needed a long, long, relaxed look at it.

'So I borrowed a small hand mirror from my mother's closet. I lay on my bed, pillowed up from behind, and spread myself. And there it was. The famous French psychoanalyst Jacques Lacan has written an article on the mirror stage. He says the baby looks into the mirror and sees an image of pure bodily organization, a whole that unites him in the image, and divides him from his inner sense of being in pieces. What does he say of this secret mirror stage, when I gaze at my cu*t and find there a gap, a hole, a wound, a ...? Is this not the return of the *corps morcelé*? Is this the image of unity? Where do I find representations in the icons of my civilization for such a hole, an o-ffense? Greek and Roman men still walk the museums of our world with representational arrogance flaunting this penis, but where are our vaginas?

'Perhaps in the ellipses, the gaps in consciousness. The holes in minds that do not represent. In the closed eyelids of the doctors when we flash our wound. The cunt is the negative hallucination of an entire civilization. Is it?

'My cu*ts aren't the real thing, are they? Usually I just scratch the surfaces. Sometimes blood comes and I turn it into pretend surprise: Oh! Blood. But I control it. My cu*ts shock the analyst. I flash my bleeding wound and force his lids shut, but this cu*t is only a cul-de-sac, it has no interior to it, no complex foldings of skin layering its way to my insides. I present the doctors with a medical model of my cu*t, a cut version, with no inside to the body, just a surface representation for diagnostic familiarity.

'If my doctor knew me he would know when I felt like cutting. He would know before I bled myself. When I get my period, well, a day or two before it actually happens, I change. We all change differently. I feel cross, irritated by small things, and I cut myself off from my friends, as I don't want to be a pain. I get an unpleasant full-body feeling, a container stretched to its limits, about to burst its skin. My breasts, tender. Pain. It *is* pain. Every bloody month. And my close friends, one or two, they *do know*. "That time of month, eh!" or "Curse time again?" and I nod, all of this just as I start to change. But my doctor, he is an ignoramus. He knows nothing. Never once asked if I was on the rag. Occasionally he sniffs oddly, so perhaps he has smelled me, but it's far too late. He never says a thing. And they think they are so clever, these doctors. They write about psychic pain, but do they know it when it sits in front of them! Not a chance. There I am, bitchy, grouchy, tenderized by pain, and he doesn't say or know anything. I don't even think he knows when I am bleeding. Why should I tell the ignoramus? I bring my purse with me, packed with Tampax, sit it down before his very eyes, every month for a few days. Does he say anything? I kept him waiting while I linger in the women's toilet, just to make the point, but does he notice?

'He does not know me. He knows nothing of the signs of my pain, so I am delighted to shock him with my *cul-de-sacs*, my little cunts, which he takes very, very seriously. These are the true signs of pain. Indisputable marks. Inscriptions. Texts written all over my body. He reads and reads these petite cunts with all the earnestness of an anthropologist whose only fieldwork among the natives will be in the library. It gives me pleasure to laugh when he takes my little cunts so seriously. It gets him all twisted up inside. I can see his worry, his *uncertainty*. He is no longer so sure of himself. Perhaps I will create a really massive cut. Perhaps I will go to a motel, cut my wrists, get in a warm bath, take some Xanex, and go to sleep.

'So I am cutting him up. He tells me so. Well, good. That's what I desire. I want my cut to signify him. "Oh, Dr. Y," his colleagues inquire, "how is S doing?" The doctor whose patient cuts. Ha! The doctor defined by cunts, the doctor who does not know so much, who does not know when the blood comes. Let him be a cunt. A little cunt. I bleed: he bleeds. I bleed a lot: he bleeds a lot. I shallow-cut: he breathes an invisible sigh of relief. Let him be a cunt. Shall I bleed him every twenty-eight days? Shall I go all moody and silent and mysterious every twenty-eight days and see him turn into a cunt: sliced up by his anxiety? Shall I ask him if he is okay? How about "You don't look so well today, Dr. Y. You look pale. The blood has left your face." Shall I? "This seems to happen to you once a month. Dr. Y. What is it? You would call this projective identification, wouldn't you? I worry you to death every twenty-eight days or so, you thinking I shall kill myself, and yet you having this period of your month for me." Poor man. Shall I tell him this?

'No. He has no insides for me. No place for me to look inside him. Just that phallic externality, that compost heap of exposure, that medicality embodied; so why should he see inside me? Why should I open myself to him? Why show my true opening to him? He is ignorant anyway. These little cunts, these false incisions, false pains, are for him and his false cures.

'We women of the hospital should unite. We have them scared. One, two, three of us to the hospital for stitching up in one week! They say it's a record. A stream of blood from this false hospital to the true place, where they stitch up pain. We had one heck of a chance to unite: we did until R, that competitive fucked-up bitch, cut herself. In the grand manner, of course. No secrecy. No art. Just walked into the living room, cut from shoulder to wrist, and handed herself to the handsome Dr. P like the beautiful hysteric floating in Charcot's arms at the saltpeter hospital for impotent psychiatrists. She set us all against each other. A war of cunts. Who has the most hideous cunt? Whose is the biggest? Widest? Longest? Whose is attractive? Repellent? Ah. Now it is all lost, we are all hostage to our silly competition for these men, all except A, who cuts into her Carrara body with the certainty of a Tuscan: her mass was meant to be cut and she wields the razor with a sculptor's knife.'

PART III

Self and Culture

Interviews

11

Moments of the Self in Psychoanalysis and Anthropology
A Conversation with Vincent Crapanzano

Over the past two decades, Vincent Crapanzano has, perhaps more than any other scholar, refocused attention within anthropology on its problematic relationship with psychoanalysis. Employing what he calls an *agonistic* approach – that is to say, interdisciplinary, but with a critical edge that looks to fathom each respective discipline's theoretical shortcomings and methodological blind spots – Crapanzano has paid particular attention to how different cultures construct and articulate self-experience. In the conversation that follows, Crapanzano speaks of this defining research interest of his, emphasizing how the locus of selfhood and subjectivity is not everywhere oriented and determined in ways familiar to the West.

Anthony Molino: In your introduction to *Hermes' Dilemma and Hamlet's Desire*, there's a marvellous dream of yours which you cite. 'All I can remember of it,' you write, 'was a voice saying, "the I of the now is not the I of the now", and seeing the equation "I ≠ I."' This introduces for me the whole issue of what in Lacanian circles is termed the 'split' or 'decentred' subject. To what extent does your dream bespeak your own understanding of the self? And how does this, in turn, relate to contemporary understandings of the postmodern self in psychoanalysis and anthropology?

Vincent Crapanzano: I've always considered dreams a means of assessing where I am, even during fieldwork. More generally, however, I've been struck by the way in which our own particular epistemological or scientific bias has precluded the actual consideration of dreams as vehicles for ethnographic understanding. Obviously, dreams have been used, at least by some anthropologists, both in terms of monitoring personal emotional states in some sort of semi-analytic sense, as well as by analysts who happen to do fieldwork. But I am also thinking of the way dreams can serve as a kind of perceptual vehicle for alerting us to features of the society we're studying which we may not perceive consciously. Wasn't it Erich Fromm who pointed out that dreams can call attention to events that, given the dreamer's particular utilitarian concerns at the time of their occurrence, might not have been consciously registered?

But, let me get to your question. This splitting of the 'I' is extremely important, and was very much a concern of mine when writing *Hermes' Dilemma*. I was trying to put together a series of essays that did not form, in my view, a cohesive whole. You see, I was responding with anxiety to the value we place on cohesion (of self, text, outlook) that intellectually I found – and find – to be imprisoning and hardly universal. This was the immediate background of the dream, which must also be seen in terms of my long-standing personal and intellectual concern with the idea of a split self.

Already as an undergraduate I was fascinated by the split, the fragmented, the alien self. I was haunted by the idea of the double: Poe's 'William Wilson', Nerval's 'Aurélie'. I was particularly interested in Sartre, whose affinities with Lacan, by the way, are stronger than anyone was or is willing to admit. They had both studied with Alexandre Kojève and are concerned in their own ways with alienation and the processes by which we create and manipulate the Other ... Anyhow, Sartre's notion of objectification interested me; and with it, the idea of the self's split into 'I' and 'me'. At the time, alienation was all the rage. The way it was being discussed, in largely sociological terms, seemed to me to be rather pathetic attempts to avoid recognizing its inevitability. They were whining discourses of hope.

Lacan does not give us any illusions about the unity of self. He originally situated the primordial splitting of the self – his mirror phase – in a developmental process. Later, after the war, as he became more of a structuralist, his 'mirror stage' became a structural moment: a mythic event, not unlike Rousseau's social contract. It was loosened, so to speak, from a modernist perspective, from stories we like to tell about growing up. But his theory never really lost its origin-tale quality. It tells us how we become alienated from ourselves as we become human. It's less the alienation, the splitting, that interests me today than the way we tell it, the folly of trying to resolve it, of believing in unity and continuity, as somehow natural rather than as cultural artifices.

In retrospect, what I find striking about my dream is the way in which it grappled with the temporal dimension of selfhood and alienation. We are dealing not only with a kind of timeless alienation between me and *mon semblable* but also with an alienation, a split, that results from our temporal existence. There is always a moment, a difference, by and through which the 'I-of-the-now' and the 'I-of-the-then' are separated – how can I put it? – by an intervention. In one sense this intervention is simply that of an interlocutor, of someone or something other interfering. In another, it's the pause – the heartbeat, the breath – that literally inter-venes, comes between. And so the question is: when does the 'I' change? Without getting into issues of instantaneity, there has to be a kind of interference that punctuates time – that produces a gap in time: the difference between two 'I's'.

I once wrote a paper, 'Riflessioni frammentarie sul corpo, il dolore, la memoria' – on the body, pain, and memory – in which I argue, with regard to the Lacanian notion of the mirror-phase, that there is no necessary reason why the infant should see himself in the mirror. There's no reason why the child should identify with the image in the mirror. It's just a good story – a just-so story. Curiously Lacan – to my knowledge – does not see another consequence of his story: the role of contingency in the formation of the self – in the splitting. Imagine a baby crying: in the ordinary course of events, if the mother knows the baby is crying for her breast, or for a bottle, she responds (if even by denial) to the baby's cry. But think of a mirror. For the infant, it suddenly appears and just as suddenly disappears. Can the child cry for a mirror? For his *semblable*? For his self? Will the mother, will anyone, understand? What happens to the *semblable* at this point? It is not only other but contingent – wilful perhaps. And what happens to the primordial self? Is it also contingent? Wilful? Compensatorily, always there? (My language is unsatisfactory.) I am reluctant to introduce a Kleinian notion of hallucination not only because there is scant evidence for the hallucination but also because it simplifies the situation. It may appease the analyst, who doesn't have to wrestle with contingency. There is, in any case, something harrowing in this addition to Lacan's tale.

AM: Is there a way in which you see these concerns being brought to bear on contemporary anthropology, and especially ethnography?

VC: There have been enormous changes in anthropology over the last 35–40 years. We've moved away from the assumption of homogeneous societies, in which there are a series of role players – stock characters – who reflect a pervasive personality type or national character. There used to be a very strong push to homogenize 'primitive' or 'tribal' socie-ties. Clearly, though, this view, however ideologically compelling it may have been, could not be sustained. We have become disenchanted with this notion of the homogeneous society in which everyone behaves true to part and personality. It may have generated a neat vision of those other, simpler societies – one that not only appealed to our social aesthetics but also – how to put it? – to our longing, our romantic longing, for that sort of society, that *Gemeinschaft*, we never knew and could never know. It served implicitly as a basis for the criticism of the messy, heterogeneous society in which we live. We have still to work through the implications of this fantasmatic basis for social criticism. It will not be a pretty picture, I suspect.

What is interesting about this picture of society – of stock characters, of basic or model personality, of national character – was the sense of continuity it proclaimed, the ease of habituation to a particular structure it took for granted, the determinism it assumed. The self wasn't much in question. Nor human freedom. Nor freedom's relationship to the self. Look at George Herbert Mead, who exemplifies this tradition: what I see as his behaviourist dialectic of self-formation moves inexorably toward a frozen, determinate, conforming and conformist self through generalizing the other. What other? Mead doesn't even appreciate the pathetic – the tragic – dimension of the fatal process he lays out.

Anthropology at the time was engaged by questions of continuity and processes of socialization that were assumed to create *prêt-à-porter* selves. Those selves could of course be alienated from their surroundings, but such alienations were aberrant or historically contingent: the result of colonialism or other capitalist exploitations. Easy Marxism. But what about the sense of interior alienation? This dimension of human experi-ence was either denied the primitive or understood in terms of pathology. It was easier that way. Think of Roheim or Devereux. Spirit possession and shamanism were troubling because they suggested some sort of inner alienation or splitting. Of course, they were taken to be exceptional.

Today, there is certainly more interest in differing articulations of the self, but some of these articulations – socio-centric selves, dividuated selves – are really not that different from the generalizations made by the culture and personality people. I believe most Americans, despite their new-age play with them, find these possibilities terrifying.

Sometimes I think the notion of self (like that of culture) should be abandoned – or at least accepted for what it is: a native category. I would prefer if we took the self as a moment in an ongoing dialogue, exchange, or conversation – a moment in which it is rhetorically, politically, constituted and reified. We might then recognize the way in which our theories of the self – our psychologies – support certain of these constituting moments and manoeuvres. They are, as such, implicated in the plays of power that constitute the self.

As I've said, there are a number of anthropologists who have been questioning modes of selfhood. Think of the work done by Levy in Tahiti, Kirkpatrick in the Marquesas, Marilyn Strathern in New Guinea, to name a few with very different theoretical points of view.[1] They mark a change in anthropology. But I don't think they have gone far enough. I have to admit that it's difficult, for me at least, in even my most radical moods, to engage empathetically rather than intellectually with other articulations of the self. For example, I can think of a transient notion – or quality – of self, which is determined at certain junctures, within certain complicated exchanges, and treated as though it has a perduring character and then suddenly, dramatically, under new circumstances perhaps, it changes into another 'self' of a very different quality and assumption. I can imagine that neither the subject nor those about him or her would be troubled by these changes (as we are, the observers at least, in cases of multiple personality). However, when it comes to an empathetic appreciation of such a condition, I am at a loss. I simply cannot experience it, its possibility, even in meditation. Perhaps it's my weakness, my incapacity. I don't know.

I do know it's nearly impossible, if not downright impossible, to represent such moments, such processes, in our language. They are outside its 'psychology'. And what of the pragmatics and the politics of – the power plays in – 'self'-constituting exchanges? What we've done is to take too seriously those static moments of selfhood. We've fallen, if you will, for the label, for the name. We have conceptually (if not empathetically) to recognize the self as a moment, as an assumption, that serves a very complicated kind of political and moral function. I'm not saying that there isn't a self, or that a self can't exist otherwise, in a non-reified fashion. What I am saying, and what seems to me much more interesting, are the ways in which selfhood is constituted and deconstituted over periods of time.

AM: Do you then see psychoanalysis as a privileged hermeneutic or epistemological tool that can help decipher or map out those constitutive moments?

VC: Yes, when it doesn't con itself. If we had a way, as outsiders not involved in the process, to observe the entire course of an analysis, I'm sure we'd discover a whole series of dynamics and events to which both the analyst and the patient were blinded. We'd come to appreciate the role of theory in both structuring the process and in creating in different ways, for the analyst and the patient, a means to disengage from the immediacy of their relationship. Theory provides a perceptual frame. I'm hesitant to talk about Freudian, Lacanian, or any metapsychological theory about the nature of analysis, because they are too embedded in the process itself.

   So, yes, of course, psychoanalysis can and does explore these constitutive moments. We do have to ask, however, what the underlying assumptions about the nature of the self that are being enacted in the clinical hour are. They may well be different than those postulated by theory. Psychoanalysts in this country in, say, the 1950s assumed, as did their patients, a sense of self that was singular and continuous. Disturbances to that sense of self were seen as pathological, and warranted some kind of rectification or remediation so that the patient could become whole, that is, have a whole, healthy, integrated self. To this end, then, interventions and interpretations were made in light of and according to these governing assumptions. I'm not sure they are the same today, though, no doubt, there is a longing for them. Personally, I think there are other, more interesting possible directions for psychoanalysis, which do not privilege the singular self and which recognize it as a kind of artifice. They might radically problematize the nature of being human, recognizing its tragic and comic dimensions, which were ignored in much earlier theorizing. Maybe I'm being a bit of an aesthete, but I prefer the recognition of these tragic and comic dimensions to their denial.

AM: Along these lines, then, what do you see as the intrapsychic and interpersonal dynamics by which we come to recognize that otherness, or even our own otherness?

VC: That's a difficult question because the very notion of the split between the intrapsychic and the interpersonal involves an odd set of assumptions. Imagine the question being posed in a society where much of what we articulate as 'intrapsychic' would be articulated in terms of demons or spirits. Let's refuse, for sake of argument, to assume that these 'spirits' are projections, and accept them as real, as real as the table or chair in front of us. In these circumstances your question would not make sense. What we call 'intrapsychic' would be somewhere else: on another 'stage', so to speak – a demonic or spirit stage. But, for us at least, it would be external, involving a kind of 'interpersonal relationship' between self and demon. When you look at some of the descriptions of the relations among id, ego and superego in the Freudian typography, they sound very interpersonal: e.g., the 'domestication' of the superego, the 'struggle' between id and ego. What you have is a whole 'sociology' of the intrapsychic. So it's very difficult to talk about the distinction between intrapsychic and interpersonal. You have to recognize that the 'location' of agencies and functions is culturally and historically specific. The agencies and functions may be universal, but their location need not be.

Of course, we tend to universalize our particular understanding of self, other, or experience. 'You are human, therefore, you are, in a way, like me ...' I'm hesitant then to answer your question in the terms in which you pose it.

But if we were to accept the distinction between intra-psychic and interpersonal – one assumed by our sciences, by our political, pedagogical and therapeutic projects – we should look at the figurative – the metaphorical – processes within and between these two different domains. Their respective dynamics are mutually reflective: interpersonal relations are metaphorized onto the intrapsychic, just as intrapsychic relations are metaphorized, if not onto the interpersonal (though I believe they are), then onto the group. We speak of group behaviour in intrapsychic terms: of group projections, for instance.

Your question makes sense within a shared frame. The risk, however, is that the frame and its presuppositions about the nature of reality go unquestioned.

AM: To return, then, to your own statement: 'the notion of the self requires not simply the awareness of a contrasting world, but a recognition to speak awkwardly of one's own otherness in that world.' To the extent that an ethnographer can attempt, albeit awkwardly, to assume the place of the other, how can one fathom that 'Other' coming to grips

with her own otherness – if not from within a framework that posits a
self, or a distinction between the intrapsychic and interpersonal?

VC: It's a dilemma. Even Lacan stumbles here. He demystifies the self,
yes, but peeling away layer after layer of illusions of selfhood, he ends up
with the *sujet* as a kind of empty, primordial beginning. I don't think we
can avoid some such notion. It's so embedded in our language. Ironically
Lacan's demystification of the self/subject/*sujet* is like a mystic's exercise.
I simply think we can go back and back and back and postulate any
number of 'entities' until finally we arrive at an empty one that paradoxically refers – indexes perhaps – an emptiness from which an individuum
issues. Whether another language is capable of articulating these
processes differently, without a primordial sense of an individuum, I
don't know. That's really the question, isn't it?

We seem compelled to articulate the self around a notion of origin, of
origination ... It's amazing that the individuum can become so posses-
sive, so literally central, that the world itself ends up being centred on it.
Of course, you really don't begin at the beginning; you begin in the
middle. And at that point, *in medias res*, there is already a kind of
psyche, some sort of individual or subject that is acknowledged.

We write origin tales that get us up to this point, as Lacan and Freud
do. But they are origin tales. Like all stories, they offer no final explanation. No doubt they ground certain understandings. But, despite
themselves, they leave open the question: 'Where do we begin?' Any
beginning is going to be arbitrary – and privilege a moment. This does
not mean that the privileged moment is the foundational moment. It's
simply the moment to begin. That's the best way I can answer your
question. It's not satisfactory. It's contradictory.

When I use the word 'possession', for instance, I use it in a way in
which it can be and has been metaphorized: for example, incorporation,
introjection, etc. They point to the amoebic quality of possession: what's
'outside' somehow gets inside, including one's own otherness. How this
relates to spirit possession depends on a linguistic pun which, though
possible in English, French and Italian, is impossible in German,
Arabic, and a lot of other languages.

Still, with regard to the drama being enacted by the possessing spirit,
and to the specific process of its incorporation, let's accept it for a
moment as being external, as coming from the 'outside'. Let's agree to
invent a psychology in which the spirit is not a projection of the psyche
that is then internalized, but something external that wants to intrude.

This is truly a drama. The tension between being incorporated, or possessed, and resisting incorporation, resisting possession, is extremely powerful – from the perspectives of both the subject and the possessing spirit. The move is not unidirectional. I mean, the possessing spirits, insofar as they're conceived as existent, have a kind of autonomy and resistance of their own.

AM: So that in a way the subject surrenders or concedes her own capacity for possession to the possessing spirit . . .

VC: One could describe it that way. Think, for example, of Schreber's memoirs: not Freud's case, but the judge's actual memoirs.[2] There you see Schreber's struggle with the rays as they struggle to take possession of him. Sometimes he wants to expel them. Sometimes he's attracted to them. Sometimes they want to enter him. Sometimes they don't. They don't want to lose their autonomy. The struggle is continual, in both directions.

We find a similar struggle in other domains: in communicating, for example. At one level I'm confronted with the resistance of the other's, my interlocutor's, words; and at the same time I want to absorb those words, even as I want to resist them and convert them. All this at the same time! . . .

Here, with respect to possession, you see the lure of various psycho-analytic metaphors, like incorporation, which refer particularly to oral or cannibalistic qualities. They suggest a kind of primordiality. Still, referring back to our earlier reflections on origins, I would not be willing to give what they metaphorized any necessary priority – not without taking into consideration everything they, as metaphors, connote. Surely, there does seem to be a developmental process that humans go through. Clearly, the infant is not the same as the adult. Clearly, there are phenomena we observe, phenomena that we are constantly trying to interpret with resonant metaphors and narratives. But you have to be careful not to naturalize these metaphors and tales. And yet I'm afraid a lot of psychoanalysts attempt such naturalizations, supporting them by some sort of research project. And it's not just psychoanalysis that does this; it's also developmental psychology, and many other disciplines.

AM: I sense that what you're suggesting, on one level, is that while anthropology has on several occasions dipped into the treasure chest of psychoanalysis, rarely has psychoanalysis borrowed from anthropology . . .

VC: Exactly.

AM: And if there is one thing lacking within psychoanalysis, it's the capacity for self-reflexivity on which so much of anthropology is grounded . . .

VC: Exactly. For me, what's exciting about anthropology is not the elaboration of some sort of scientific understanding of culture or society but the exploration of the limits of understanding. It's a sort of post-Kantian project: a critique of knowledge that's grounded, paradoxically perhaps, in empirical reality. It's an exercise that goes back to Descartes and Montesquieu, among others, who used the ideas of the voyager, of an 'elsewhere', as vehicles for critical reflection, for postulating the possibility of otherness. In anthropology, however, it's not a fantasmatic other who engages us, but people who, in clear and dramatic ways, do seem to be different. Of course they too are given a fantasmatic dimension.

On this score, as anthropologists, we all have stories of how we became interested in the field – of our first encounter, perhaps, with the exotic. As for mine – I think it illustrates my point: When I graduated from Harvard, my grandmother gave me money with which to travel to Mexico. I went to the Yucatan, where I met a young Mayan, a guide who'd trained in Mexico City. Though I neither wanted nor could have afforded a guide, the man and I became acquainted one night, as we sat and talked on the hotel verandah. It was very dark, so dark we could hardly see each other's faces. I'd asked him some questions about the Mayans, and about himself, questions which he then asked me. The conversation went on until, at one point, with the greatest of ease, he asked, 'Where are you going to die?' Startled, I said I didn't know, a reply which startled him. How could I not know? Finally, I managed to ask him where he was going to die, and he calmly told me. It was a kind of foreknowledge he had, which went unquestioned, but astounded me.

What does it mean, really, to know the place of one's death?

I was moved and intrigued by our exchange. It was, for me, an encounter with the exotic. But what I didn't realize at the time was that I may well have been making an assumption about death in my attempt at understanding, which my friend didn't share with me. He may not have meant what I meant by 'death'. It didn't occur to me until later that night that maybe, just maybe, he might not have been referring to his physical death, but to a spiritual one. This thought, then, set up a whole train of speculations, which I never got a chance to confirm, as I was leaving the next morning and didn't see him again. Looking back, I'm not sure I could have questioned him anyway. But it was that exchange that got me started on this intellectual project of mine. It was then that I was really confronted with the limits and the artifice of my own understanding.

NOTES

1. Robert Levy, *Tahitians*, Chicago: University of Chicago Press, 1973; John Kirkpatrick, *The Marquesan Notion of Person*, Ann Arbor, MI: University of Michigan Research Press; Marilyn Strathern, *The Gender of the Gift*, Berkeley, CA: University of California Press, 1988.
2. Crapanzano refers here to Freud's 'Psycho-analytic notes on an autobiographical account of a case of paranoia', a case study of his contemporary Dr Daniel Paul Schreber, derived from the latter's 1903 autobiography *Memoirs of My Nervous Illness*. See Vol. XII of *The Standard Edition of the Complete Psychological Works of Sigmund Freud*, J. Strachey (ed.). London: Hogarth Press.

12

Protean Impulses
A Conversation with Robert Jay Lifton

Robert Jay Lifton is generally regarded as the eminent psychohistorian of our time. In his book *The Protean Self: Human Resilience in an Age of Fragmentation* (New York: Basic Books, 1993), Lifton adopts the Greek myth of the chameleon-god Proteus to illustrate what he calls the postmodern experience of 'contingency, multiplicity and polyvocality' which characterizes today's crisis/plasticity of the self. Seeing the protean impulse as an historical – indeed, as an evolutionary – development, in the following conversation with anthropologist Wesley Shumar Lifton discusses some of the major societal forces and psychological tensions shaping the advent and experience of proteanism. And, with his sombre reflections on contemporary terrorism, Lifton also alerts us, in quasi-prophetic tones, to the Armaggedon that the City of New York, and indeed the whole world, witnessed with the Sept. 11, 2001 attack on the World Trade Center.

Wesley Shumar: Can you address your attention to postmodernism, insofar as it reflects both your long-standing concern with totalitarian movements and influences, as well as the state of psychoanalysis today?

Robert Jay Lifton: One of the things that has appealed to me in much postmodern writing is the stand against totalization. My very first study on Chinese thought reform was deeply influenced by Camus. He's as influential on my work as the psychoanalysts, and *The Rebel* may be the greatest popular philosophical statement about the danger of what Erik Erikson called totalism. Most strands of postmodernism that I know of take a strong and useful stand against totalization, although they may be totalizing their own stand at times ...

When I began to think about extending the Eriksonian concept of what I called ideological totalism, and about the kind of environments in which totalism exists (American politics like McCarthyism or some graduate school training), I began to see how certain expressions of psychoanalytic training come uncomfortably close to such environments.

There can be, however, experiences or processes that absorb you into what seems to be an environment of ideological totalism, but where a little room for air persists. One might identify something like Jesuit training in that way – an environment that can be quite valuable, because it has combined the intensity of a belief system, passionately held, with some imaginative opportunity to get beyond it. Mostly, totalism closes down the imagination. It closes down symbolization and, in a sense, creates an as-if situation, as if we weren't symbolizers but simply seekers of absolute truth, which, once found, ends our search. Ultimately, I think totalism marks one of the grave dangers of our time. It's inseparable from fundamentalism, at least as I define it, and it becomes doubly dangerous when coupled with our technologies.

I recently did a study of Aum Shinrikyo, the Japanese fanatical cult that released the gas in the Tokyo subways. It's a cult of absolute totalism, where a quest for ultimate weapons combines with a training process to turn young university graduates into Nazi-like killing professionals. All the horrors that I've studied are, in small compass, condensed in Aum Shinrikyo. But in Aum totalism takes the most extreme form of guruism, which is necessary to the group's violence – and to its version of End Time/activist Armageddon, in which the group looks to create Armageddon, and doesn't just wait for it. Japan was horrified just two days ago at the discovery of more poison gas in a place that was pointed out to police by a suspect involved in the original release of the gas in a subway. So although most of its former leaders are in prison, the cult is still perceived as a threat to Japanese society. But there are similar expressions of totalism operating throughout the postmodern world, in groups quite capable of doing what Aum did and sought to do.

WS: In your discussion about the relationship between self-awareness and the awareness of one's death, you alert us to the fact that we now live in a world confronted by the reality of mass extinction. How do you imagine the response of the unconscious to such a threat?

RL: It's very hard to know how we unconsciously respond – though I'm sure that we do – to what I call imagery of extinction. The same was true in anticipating the millennial turn. No single psychological trait or symptom can be attributed to the threat of extinction in any of our lives, but there's probably nothing in our lives that's entirely free of it either. It's likely to come into play, for example, in planning long-term projects, like getting married. The threat isn't such that we cease to get

married. People get married as much as they ever did. But my sense is
that they do wonder – unconsciously, or outside of awareness in any case
– about how long everything or anything will last ... I was talking to a
psychoanalyst friend who said, 'My patients don't really talk about the
threat and its scenarios. I'm not so sure that it really has any effect on
people.' When I suggested that the effects might be indirect, he
remarked: 'You know, I have a new grandchild. I do wonder whether
she'll be able to grow up ...'

So finally nothing is free from the threat of extinction. Of course, I
also think that the imagery contributes to what I call the protean process
– by which I mean the fluidity and many-sidedness of the contemporary
self. But imagery of extinction can stifle that too, as we perceive the end
of everything, including the human mind. But the combination of our
age's extreme dislocations (and the proteanism that follows upon them)
with the threat of extinction can result in forms of End Time fundamentalism, which are very widespread and quite dangerous. End Time
fundamentalism tends to demand not just the end of history but the end
of human imagination: the end of the kind of imagination that might
help us to transcend these threats or to move toward other possibilities.
That's why totalism is so dangerous. It ties in with weapons that can do
us in, while ending imaginative thought that might help us out.

WS: You've mentioned Erik Erikson, an early mentor of yours. There
seems to be renewed interest in his work, which leads me to wonder if an
element of the postmodern was somehow prefigured in his writings ...

RL: Erikson had extraordinary influence during the 1960s and into the
1970s. Since then there's been a certain decline in his influence, at least
in America where he'd had his strongest intellectual impact. But he was,
in my view, a very special mind and I am certain that lulls of interest in
his work and thought will be followed by intense rediscoveries of him.

As for his relationship to the postmodern, I think all interesting
thinkers have a nuanced relationship to the postmodern. And, you know,
there are paradoxes. I write in *The Protean Self* that Erikson's identity
theory, as I could tell from wonderful conversations with him over
decades, was very much an effort to expand his time's dominant theory
of mind, and was very much related to self-theory in that sense. But
Erikson is still nourished by early Freudian tradition, by the European
nineteenth-century tradition ...

My own work is in tension with both Erikson and the so-called postmodern. I'm in tension with Erikson because I see the need for greater multiplicity and greater flux in relationship to a sense of self. I'm in tension with the postmodern because there's one stream of it that wants to eliminate the self. I reject that element of the postmodern that doesn't believe in the self. But I strongly believe that thoughtful scholars or writers who see themselves as working in the postmodern realm can find a lot in common with Erikson.

WS: How does your notion of proteanism both evolve out of and depart from Erikson's identity theory?

RL: My work really owes a lot to Erikson's identity theory. Erikson got me thinking about nuances and elements of identity. In early work I spoke of what I called identity elements or fragments. I began to see different subdivisions of identity, or different parts of identity, and have had, for some time, an impulse to break them down. In a very important way, then, what I wrote about the protean self stems very much from identity theory. To a degree, my ideas also break away from identity theory because of the latter's greater emphasis on sameness and continuity. There is still a strong element of continuity in the protean self, but it's very uneven and constantly subject to radical experimentation . . .

Erikson himself was ambivalent about the protean self. At first, he was made quite uncomfortable by the work. I had published a single preliminary essay long before the book, which led to a certain exchange between us. After some years he told me that he thought it was among the most important work that I'd done. I think he sensed its value and its connection to what he was doing, and yet the work was different . . . Let me put it this way: when you read his work on identity and you read it carefully, you feel the tension in it, because it was Erikson's sensibility and talent to recognize nuance and flux; and yet, his theory is always aiming to construct a whole. This marked a kind of internal tension that was very creative for Erikson. *The Protean Self* takes the tension further, out into the confusions and multiplicities of our contemporary society and history. Personally, I still feel the need to postulate and seek as desirable a kind of inner core that's moral, that functions together with the radical flux of protean experimentations. This position, or search, of mine is different however from the way other thinkers might see the struggles of the contemporary, postmodern self.

WS: You state in *The Protean Self* that we are becoming fluid, and talk about the historical emergence of this novel aspect of self-experience. At other points you talk about the protean self as being part of the modern project, and make linkages to other cultures and times. How do you see the relationship of the modern to the postmodern in terms of the development of proteanism?

RL: In the West there seems to have been a strong vision of a unitary self, though it was never as unitary as envisioned, I suspect. Modernity, beginning in the eighteenth century, has a lot to do with the strain on the unitary. The vision of the unitary self could itself survive because the world on the whole was more ordered, often by force and by authoritarian arrangements. In most places one lived out one's life in the same geographical place, within a relatively consistent set of family and cultural or subcultural arrangements. Having said this, things were never all that stable. There were upheavals, but the ideal of the ordered unitary self could be sustained and was extensively advocated in most moral, religious and philosophical writing. With modernity, this situation was radically challenged. Scientific breakthroughs and claims, geographic flux and the influence of technology, caused the vision of the unitary self to be radically questioned.

I think it would be fairly accurate to say that psychoanalysis owes its origins to the modern conflict and tension over the unitary self, and the need to question and break out from it. From the standpoint of the unitary self, Freud did something very subversive. He postulated various drives which, in the idiom of his time, he thought of as instinctual: but while consistent, the drives were themselves a source of fragments and breakdowns and conflicts. In this sense, Freud's ideas already begin to question an orderly, coherent, unitary self. Freud is often labelled as one of the great subverters of the unitary self, but the more important truth, I believe, is that he is a product of its beginning breakdown, of its important breakdown ...

My sense of the modern era, in terms of the psychology of the self, is that it was multiple from the start. Modernism is multiple. With modernism we already get the fragmentation of the self, or its breakdown into parts. It's in Freud and, suggestively, it's in Darwin. But because modernism retains a lot of eighteenth-century science, it seeks clarity and precision in cause and effect, numbers and statistics. The fragmentation of the self doesn't find much of a place in modernist science. So perhaps the degree of breakdown or fragmentation of the self that is part and parcel of modernity is less accounted for, or less recognized, because it doesn't seem to find a ready place within official modernist thought. Freud was certainly a modernist and worshipped the enlightenment – or at least thought highly of it – but he was also subversive in regard to modernism . . .

Erikson was even more subversive. One thing that he did, very importantly, was to honour subjectivity. Subjectivity breaks out all over the place in the modern period, but is not honoured by a lot of official modernist thinkers. In looking at both the life cycle and identity, Erikson breaks out of the laboratory-science aspects of modernism, but insists upon remaining a Freudian. Characteristically, he would write his extraordinary books and they would be very free and associative, but then at the end he would feel the need to re-declare himself a Freudian. One might say this reflected his allegiance to the modernist project, but it was more a reflection of Erikson's own sense of identity and his intellectual origins.

I am at least a generation removed from that era. I'm further along into what's called the postmodernist realm, that is, into a social milieu that is more clearly fragmented and many-sided, multiple. I've grown up in it in many ways, and can often feel the joy in it. And this marks a real difference from Freudianism and identity theory. Erikson sees more of the threat in fragmentation. I, too, see the threat in this aspect of the protean development, the dangers of fragmentation. That's why I talk about the quest for an integrative proteanism, that avoids the more extreme forms of fragmentation through the interaction of disparate elements with a core element of the self. But such a process is at a radical remove when compared to identity theory. That is probably why one reviewer spoke of my ideas as representing 'affirmative' postmodernism.

Part of my motivation in writing *The Protean Self* was to take stock of where we are psychologically and seize upon rather than simply condemn our predicament. In a way, the protean process has been taking place from the very beginnings of human evolution. Because in becoming human we become symbolizers, and once we're symbolizers the potential for proteanism is there. Then it's just a question of how the interactions of groups of individuals with their environments and historical forces unfold. So, dangerous things are always happening. But presently, the danger may lie less with the multiplicity of the self than with the interaction of human beings with technology. It may lie less with multiplicity than with the fear that accompanies the opening of the self, which creates fundamentalist-style reactions and closing of the mind.

WS: You talk about processes of historical dislocation that set up a quest for homeland, for a sacred place from which a spiritual sense might develop. In *Ecological Identity* Mitchell Thomashow suggests that part of the work of what he calls 'ecological identity' involves getting in touch with a sense of place.[1] Can you comment on the tensions inherent in the quest?

RL: Yes. From the very beginning I saw historical or psychohistorical dislocation as two-sided, double-edged. The element of breakdown is clear enough. Many people simply have difficulty believing inwardly, or acceding without question to religious ideas, or to ideas about authority or the life cycle or any and all of the major symbol systems. But such a predicament does open up possibilities for experimentation, and it can open up the self. In terms of place, or ecological place, what comes to mind is the threat of extermination that nuclear and other weapons present. There's the fear that we can annihilate nature, as indeed we can. I see that fear as a very important influence for many people in the return to nature, in the re-embrace of nature and the power of the ecology movement . . .

But also involved in the return to nature is a recognition, with dislocation and the threat of annihilation, of the significance of nature in its relationship to the self. There is an idea afoot of a natural setting for a sense of self. That becomes a more complicated psychological issue than it might seem. Take, for example, the teeming multitudes you saw at New York's Penn Station when you got off the train: are they experiencing a need for nature? I don't know. But, if you start humbly, it could be that many among them experience, in quiet or not-so-quiet moments, a need for something other than the crowds and noise and intensity of Penn Station. Nature, for the self, has to do with attachment to place. It is also something outside of the self and beyond the self that houses the self. What you may have been implying is that with psychohistorical dislocation, while we're banished from places and even from the very idea of place to some degree, while we move away or even flee from certain ideas and experiences of 'home', still we seek them in different ways, in different combinations. Or we symbolize home in some new way. And, yes, in that sense, among others, the protean self is born or intensified.

At our summer home, there's a view overlooking the ocean. In that place I've struggled with the most grotesque kinds of experiences and ideas in an exquisite natural setting. I've sometimes felt almost guilty over its beauty, but it's helped me to counter or cope with those struggles. It's a very vivid expression of that desire for nature or a version of nature ... and to be in a setting that has something of the infinite. I don't follow any form of religious practice, though I'm aware of and hold to my Jewishness where my identity is concerned. But in my psychological work – and in my life – I'm attentive to religion and spiritual ideas. Take my concept of symbolic immortality: it's something I see in a broadly defined scientific perspective, the need for the self to be part of something larger than the self, which begins with the emergence of humankind. Because once we're cultural animals, as we are from the beginning in becoming human, then we're symbolizers and we seek to be something, seek to be part of something larger than the self. So, yes, psychohistorical dislocation intensifies, I think, those tendencies that are inherent in us.

NOTE

1. M. Thomashow, *Ecological Identity: Becoming a Reflective Environmentalist*. Cambridge, MA: MIT Press, 1995.

13

A Challenge from Without
A Conversation with Dorinne Kondo

Dorinne Kondo is Director of Asian American Studies at the University of Southern California. The following interview, in which Kondo criticizes what she calls 'the foundationalism of the psychoanalytic project', focuses on themes from her *Crafting Selves: Power, Gender, and Discourses of Identity in a Japanese Workplace* (Chicago: University of Chicago Press, 1990). The significance of the book – where Kondo argues for the inseparability of the personal from power, culture and history – is perhaps best evidenced by the fact that it was awarded, almost ten years after publication, the 1999 J.I. Staley Prize from the School of American Research for its impact on the field of Anthropology. Her remarks are offered here as a way of providing a window onto the possible intersections between psychoanalysis and contemporary understandings of how identities are socially constructed.

Anthony Molino: You write in your book *Crafting Selves* of 'the differences, tensions and contradictions within that certain strategic assertions of self help suppress'. There's that little word, *within*, that I find intriguing and defines the space that I'd like to explore with you. How does Dorinne Kondo, as an ethnographer, experience and conceptualize the within, the inner dimension of the people and cultures she explores?

Dorinne Kondo: I guess I'm suspicious of the within. What I want is to interrogate the inner–outer boundary. All of us who've grown up within western ideology have, I think, a notion of the within: the notion that there is a self that is contained within an envelope of skin, from which then are derived certain popularized notions of the unconscious ... But while I find such notions compelling, I want to refigure them. I'd rather think in terms of nodes or points of intersection, fields where shifting, moving social forces concatenate ... sometimes pulling against each other, sometimes forming in ways that might seem coherent only for the moment ... It's that refiguration that I'm after. The 'within' I'm suspicious of ... I'm willing to adopt it, strategically, in certain moments, but it's not an idea that I can expatiate upon with any degree of conviction.

AM: Throughout *Crafting Selves*, you frequently use the terms 'self' and 'identity', along with their corresponding plural forms. At times it even seems that you use them interchangeably. How do you understand and employ these terms? And what is the relationship between selves and identities?

DK: I think there are times that I do use them interchangeably in that book. But I view 'identity' as the more general term, whereas 'self', for me, implies a notion of a corporeal 'individual' and a corresponding notion of interior space ... And, as I've suggested, my present work eschews the term. In fact, I now talk much more about identities or subjects, in the tradition of much poststructuralist work ... The idea of a 'subject' I find very compelling precisely because it articulates the contradiction of agency, on the one hand, and what is 'subjected', on the other. 'Self', on the contrary, conjures up for me the idea of an 'other' – along with an entire set of problematic binary opposites: self–other, self–society ... That's one of the reasons I no longer invoke the term, or juxtapositions like 'inner/outer'. Nowadays I'm just much more interested in what I would call a kind of performative, or narrative, production of identity ...

AM: This may explain, in part, what I found to be the conspicuous absence in your work of references to the intrapsychic dimensions of self-experience. And yet there is a very fleeting reference in your book to Object Relations Theory. What is your understanding of this turn in psychoanalysis? And, to the extent that you cite this turn at all, does it inform your work in any way?

DK: When I was a graduate student in the 1980s, people like Kernberg, Winnicott and Klein were being cited constantly, and this led to my reading all of them voraciously at that time. But I never did find the work tremendously compelling or useful in terms of my own work, and now even perceive it to be quite eccentric, in a way. I know it has also been taken up, to some degree, in feminist theory, by people like Nancy Chodorow and Evelyn Fox Keller, which certainly speaks to its

importance. But here I think of some of the critiques of the theory that
have been put forth, like Judith Butler, who questions the ways in which
the theory perpetuates a unified subject who is then in relationship to
exterior objects ... From this angle, the whole theory remains premised
upon what Judith calls an epistemological point of departure that
presumes a divide between subject and world. That's a premise I'd want
to interrogate.

AM: Central to your work are notions like 'positionings' of the subject,
which you elsewhere call 'performative contexts' ... terms which also
connote a certain physicality, a spatial and localizing quality. With
regards to the self, can you explain what you mean by these terms?

DK: This important notion of identities involves for me a sense of
intersections, which I derive from feminist and postcolonial theory. In
this context, the politics of enunciation are such that there is always a
'somewhere', a location, from which one speaks ... There's a problem,
in this sense, with 'the master subject', which propounds a view from
nowhere ... or better, a view from nowhere which really is a view
from somewhere, except that it denies its own location. Consequently,
calling attention to that position becomes an important political and
intellectual move.
   And, again, with regards to the self, that's not a term I'd use
nowadays ... I would refer to a subject position ... and I do so for a
reason, bearing in mind the contradiction of agency and subjection in
that term ... Along these lines, the performative context, or what I've
called performativity, also refers to ways in which subjects enact
themselves in a particular site, and again draws attention, I think, to the
problem of locality. To specify that location, and to talk about the
politics of location as a scrutiny of our own sites of enunciation, as
Chandra Mohanty and Lata Mani remind us, is crucial.

AM: Though you only sparingly make use of the word 'unconscious' in
your work, I wonder if you could explain its significance for you. It
seems to me crucial, not simply from a psychoanalytic perspective, but
also to understand what you situate at the core of what you call the
'theoretical/rhetorical strategy' of your work: namely, evocation. You
write in fact, again in *Crafting Selves*: 'The theoretical/rhetorical strategy
I deploy is to begin evocatively in the form of vignettes – settings and
events that lead us into a world. Evocation establishes a mood and calls

up images.' A process which, according to psychoanalysts, directly engages and stems from an agency we might call 'the unconscious' ...

DK: I would say that I think of evocation in much more literary terms. I mean, I realize that this resonates with psychoanalytic notions of the unconscious, but I'm not prepared to say anything other than that I view my strategy as being a literary strategy. In this sense, evocation would call up, literally, poetic or 'creative' forms of writing.

AM: Even if we leave psychoanalysis aside, however, we might reconsider here your challenge to the prevalent idea of an inner/outer boundary. It would seem to me, when one speaks of evocation, that there would have to be some recognition of a dimension of interiority from which one derives such creative forms of expression ...

DK: I would dispute that understanding of evocation. Why can't one think of it as being a particular kind of linguistic strategy which is absolutely, culturally and historically specific? As a strategy determined in language. I'm aware, here, of Lacanian views on the structure of the unconscious, but I simply don't see why a notion like evocation has to be understood in terms of the unconscious.

AM: What significance do you attribute to individual history in a person's lifelong definition of selfhood? Or better, to a person's (and the ethnographer's) representation of selfhood? And secondly, within the shifting fields of power and meaning, of ideology and a 'cultural unconscious', in which people craft themselves and their lives, how do you see the dialectic of desire and memory?

DK: Were I interested in selfhood, as such, I would think that individual history was fairly important, and might provide a very rich and interesting way to investigate these issues. But now that my work is much more concerned with the ways that social forces like race, gender, colonialism, and so on construct identities ... and the ways in which people can create identities on stage, in their writing, or in their everyday lives, my approach is a distinctly different one. Just recently, for example, I had the very moving experience of going to the Japanese American National Museum here in Los Angeles, where I saw the exhibit on the WWII relocation of Japanese Americans ... Both my parents, you see, were relocated ... The museum was set up as a barracks, and there were models of each of the camps. If your family was in a particular camp, you could find where they had lived. It was quite an extraordinary experience, to find the camp in which one's family was interned, to see the barracks and blocks, and have them marked ... For me, this exhibit was creating a Japanese American history, community and identity. At that level, I can be interested in history, and in the trajectories of individual histories, which are clearly important. But what I'm more interested in are questions like: how does Japanese-American identity get constructed and written? By whom? For whom, and for what ends? In this context, I'm not prepared to answer the questions you pose, in the terms in which they are posed.

AM: The issue of desire seems to be of structural significance in your writing. Without directly employing the term, you discuss your Japanese informants' difficulty in coping with your 'cultural ineptitude', and their attempts to make you over in their image. It's the same dynamic to which God subjects his human creation in the Genesis myth, and which Lacan sees as the defining moment in the construction of the 'fictional' human ego. As an anthropologist, how do you understand the 'desire of the Other'? Is it primarily an exercise in power? And what of its constitutive effects?

DK: This is a question I hesitate to answer in the terms in which it's posed ... I'm suspicious of the invocation of a kind of transcendental desire ... So I'm wondering how it could be refigured ...

AM: Small d instead of capital D? ...

DK: (*Laughing wholeheartedly.*) I guess. You see, part of my hesitation is that I'm really interested in pleasure, in the way that Roland Barthes talks about it. I'm interested in pleasure and the politics of pleasure, in how we interrogate our pleasures, take account of them and make our political interventions around them ... (*resumes laughing*) You know, Barthes has this marvellous quotation on the subject, where he talks about the psychoanalytic policemen and how they're all busy privileging desire, while the masses never seem to have desires, only pleasures ...

AM: Traditionally, when desire is invoked, crucial questions of difference are also raised. I'm thinking again of your own experience in Japan, of being 'made over', or re-made, by the people around you. To this end, you write in *Crafting Selves*: 'Over time, my increasingly "Japanese" behavior served temporarily to resolve [my friends' and co-workers'] crises of meaning and to confirm their assumptions about their own identities.' This reminds me of a comment of a professor of mine, who once said: 'It is only through cross-cultural analysis that the supremacy of the ego can be exploded.' Can you comment on this aspect of both your fieldwork and your writing activity?

DK: Other than the kind of Saussurean point about meaning arising through difference, I would say that one of the single most important things that happened in Japan was that, for the first time, I wasn't different in some ways ... at least, racially. For me, this was very important. In this sense, it called attention to the difference of being supposedly 'at home' in the United States, where instead people of colour undergo all kinds of marginalizations ... So in that way, certainly, being in another context was revealing. And I've already spoken and written at length about the process through which 'my' conventional assumptions about identity, resistance, and so on, were challenged when I went to Japan.

AM: Because of my own bias, I find it sometimes difficult to understand categories like 'meaning' or 'assumption of identity' in a context where the intrapsychic dimension is obscured or dismissed ... To talk about 'meaning' without 'mind', or outside the elaborations of consciousness, is still somewhat foreign to me as I try to bridge anthropology and psychoanalysis. Can you speak of your choice to work, for the most part, outside of the framework of an anthropology of consciousness?

DK: This is where my concerns about the foundationalism of psychoanalysis come to the fore. I find it difficult to understand how one can discuss meaning without discussing language, which is eminently historical, public, constitutive of culture, constitutive of the notion of mind ... In my view, notions of mind, notions of consciousness, and so on are quite historically and culturally specific. For me, then, meaning and language are in some ways co-extensive, as are meaning and power. Whereas 'mind' seems to be an unproblematized foundational category for you and for certain forms of psychoanalytic discourse.

AM: Can you problematize it for me?

DK: The notion of mind calls into question, and indeed calls up, opposites like 'the body' ... It fosters a Cartesian construction of sorts: mind and consciousness, mind as the locus of consciousness, agency, rationality ... 'Mind' as something bounded, separate from something else: from body, spirit, or whatever ... And that I think is a very scary proposition, to universalize something so historically and culturally specific ... My preference, then, is to think of 'meaning' in terms of linguistic articulations, and to study the various sites in which it's generated without resorting to any kind of psychological reductionism.

AM: Would it be different for you if I didn't ask of meaning without mind, but of meaning outside the elaborations of consciousness?

DK: Slightly, only slightly. But even words like 'consciousness', for me, evoke the same sort of substance metaphysics. It still connotes a bounded entity with the substance of rationality or consciousness.

AM: Alongside your work I've been reading a book by an anthropologically inspired psychoanalyst, Alan Roland ...

DK: I know him ...

AM: In a book entitled *In Search of Self in India and Japan*, Roland laments what he calls 'the overwhelming orientation of Freudian psychoanalysis to intrapsychic phenomena', as it generally ignores 'how historical, social and cultural patterns shape the inner world' – an argument which I think is part of your critique.[1] Referring to the earlier discoveries of Copernicus and Darwin, Roland goes on to suggest about Freud: 'Perhaps we should now add a further blow to the self esteem of Western man: the realization that the prevailing psychological maps and norms assumed to be universal are in fact Western-centric.' This anti-positivistic and anti-reductionist position would seem to concur to a large extent with your own. In your view, is Roland's argument a primary reason for the paucity of any innovative dialogue between psychoanalysis and anthropology?

DK: In this context, I think Vincent Crapanzano's work has been innovative and very interesting. But yes, absolutely. Roland's point is a valid one. Personally, I view certain forms of psychoanalysis as being politically very suspect, as they potentially promote forms of a colonizing discourse, or a re-inscription of a master–subject discourse. For example, in a course I was just teaching on 'Theories of the Subject', we read Carolyn Steedman's *Landscape for a Good Woman*, a marvellous book that defies genre as it engages psychoanalytic case studies, fairy tales, British working-class history, memoir, autobiography, biography ...[2] Anyway, part of Steedman's critique has to do with the way that Freudian case studies, and other forms of psychoanalytic discourse, tend to be very class-specific. They are, for the most part, applicable to the middle class, fostering notions of normativity which are also very middle-class. I see her trying to situate herself against that literature, while also wanting to deploy the literary strategies of biography, memoir, and even the invocation and critique of the psychoanalytic case study – Dora, in particular. Like myself, she too wants her work to count in a political way: in the tradition, for example, of certain British Marxisms ...

So I feel like I'm trying to steer a similar course: avoiding a kind of psychological reductionism that is always and already middle-class, white, Eurocentric, mostly male, as befits the dominant discursive regime that dismisses individual lives as not being political ... Along these lines, I view psychoanalysis as being enormously Eurocentric, enormously; but that doesn't mean that it can't be appropriated in fruitful ways. However, the ways that it's often used in the academy are really quite insidious ... For example, apparently at a fairly recent conference on psychoanalysis and race – which I did not attend – at least one of the speakers articulated a question of this kind: 'What can race tell us about psychoanalysis?' or, 'How can race help us advance our understanding of psychoanalysis?' ... To me and, I believe, to many people of colour, the question ought to have been: 'How can psycho-analysis help us understand the dynamics of racism at all?' That way of privileging a master–subject discourse, in my opinion, occurs all too often ... Again, it's not that I think that psychoanalysis has no insight to offer ... I think it does. But Eurocentricity is a perpetual problem. For example, in feminist theory, Kristeva's figuration of the pre-Oedipal, semiotic sphere is associated with very Orientalist tropes like the whirling dervish ... There's a whole chain of signification that occurs there that I find enormously problematic.

By and large, I feel that the way psychoanalysis is used is just very suspect. There are a few exceptions; Homi Bhaba's work on mimicry, for instance, can be very useful ... But there is a part of me, in any case, that still does not understand the desire to re-inscribe the father in a

certain way, in the way that Freud or Marx still operate for many people
... This need to go back to the father is something alien to me ... I want
to engage a different kind of politics of citation, in which certainly
Foucault is very important, but no more so than the discourses of
poststructuralist feminism and subaltern peoples ... It's this mode of
analysis I find most useful.

NOTES

1.   A. Roland, *In Search of Self in India and Japan*. Princeton, NJ: Princeton Univer-
     sity Press, 1988.
2.   C. Steedman, *Landscape for a Good Woman*. London: Virago, 1986.

Essays

14

Between Meaning and Madness
The Altered States of Hispanics in the USA

Patricia Gherovici

A CLINICAL VIGNETTE: MARIA'S CASE

One Friday afternoon, a woman stormed through the clinic door shouting: '¡*Mis hijos!* ... *Oh, Dios, mis hijos!*' (my sons! oh, God, my sons!). Her dishevelled aspect and dirty old clothes betrayed a homeless existence; her empty gaze and frantic behaviour frightened the other patients. I hurried down to the waiting room and spoke in Spanish to the distraught woman, suggesting she come into a side office and talk. She managed to relax a little as I asked her why she was there and how she thought we could help her.

She smiled and asked my name. As soon as I answered, she volunteered her own. Maria (as I'll call her) started to explain tearfully that her sons had been *transformados* (transformed) into *perros* (dogs), and that it was 'horrible'. I asked her to explain what she meant by her sons being 'transformed into dogs'. She sobbed: 'I would not mind them transforming my sons into *patos* (ducks) but they turned them into *perros* (dogs).'

After our brief interaction, Maria left calmer, agreeing to return for a full evaluation on Monday. She failed to keep her scheduled appointment. Three months later, Maria showed up at the clinic and asked to talk to 'Patricia'. Her return provoked many questions. Had Maria's concern with dogs been sheer madness, I wondered, or had her earlier delusion been a creative attempt to produce an explanation that would bring order to her mental chaos? Why would she not have cared about her sons being turned into *patos* (ducks, but also Puerto Rican slang for gay) yet wept about their becoming *perros* (dogs)? Was my first name, Patricia, for which the nickname in some Spanish-speaking countries is

Pato, already part of her delirium? Had Maria been confirming in her hallucinations Freud's early theories of paranoia as a defence against homosexuality?

Should I even be raising these questions? Perhaps I should simply trust the antipsychotic medications that would silence Maria's madness. Should I – as an analyst working in a *barrio* clinic – approach the deep waters of psychosis? Is psychoanalytic theory and practice suitable to treat not simply psychotics but poor Hispanic patients of inner-city public clinics?

THE SUBJUGATION OF THE HISPANIC UNCONSCIOUS

Psychoanalysis has often been seen as a luxury for economically depressed, non-white urban populations: a therapy of choice available (financially), and thus applicable (clinically) only to the upper classes, not useful for the real problems of the poor. This assumption says something both about dominant culture and practitioners' ideas about the minorities they serve. As a result, psychoanalytic clinical work in inner-city mental health centres has been discarded as futile.

The purported 'unsuitability' of psychoanalysis for poor minority groups exposes a political rather than clinical conflict. The pervasive assumption that only well-educated, sophisticated, verbal, introspective and affluent individuals meet the criteria for 'analysability' obliterates the mental health needs of underserved ethnic minorities. The implicitly racist assumption that psychoanalysis is unsuitable for poor minorities prevails among clinicians, academics and those in government regardless of racial background, a situation that demands careful examination because of its clinical, ideological and political consequences. The undemocratic character of current mental health practices is even more pronounced for Hispanic patients, a 'preference' which perpetuates a situation of marginalization and subjugation.

Distinguished Spanish-speaking mental health practitioners cast off psychoanalysis as an 'elite' treatment and exclusively endorse the Family Therapy model (Minuchin *et al.*, 1967; Inclan, 1985; Aponte, 1994). Inclan, for instance, criticizes psychoanalytic theory and its 'invididu-alist value orientation' (Inclan, 1985, p. 330). Rather than emphasizing individuation and freedom, he believes that family therapy should emphasize the value of the family as a matrix of identity, which for him is syntonic with the values of low-income Puerto Rican families. Inclan writes, perhaps unaware of the full political implications:

> Family therapy is more readily prescribed as treatment of choice for
> Puerto Ricans, Hispanics, and other minority groups. Although
> sometimes this choice is based on discriminatory reasons that
> implicitly propose 'second class' treatment to 'second class' citizens,
> the choice seems to be oriented by some level of understanding of
> the congruence of values between the therapy modality and the
> patient population ... The value orientation of conquering nature –
> physical, human, supernatural – is a relatively foreign one to poor
> people in general, and to poor Puerto Ricans in particular. While in
> the United States a middle-class value of conquering space, cancer,
> class boundaries, etc., seems to be accepted as the established value
> norm, poor Puerto Rican people are governed more by a value of
> subjugation to nature. (ibid., p. 330)

Inclan argues that the value-orientation framework allows one to see
cultural differences in a less prejudiced way even though some of the
value-orientation differences that are attributed to race and ethnicity are
the result of social class. Inclan posits a model adapted to 'poor Puerto
Ricans' using a value orientation model that replicates a discriminatory
society class-structure. The values resulting from the pathological effects
of a 'culture of poverty' (Lewis, 1966) are preserved rather than
challenged.

Rather than acknowledge that people are not as upwardly mobile as
the myth of the self-made individual promises, Americans tend to
consider poverty as evidence of either a personal failure or defect (Senett
and Cobb, 1972). These assumptions create the stereotypes that support
the alleged unanalisability of low-income patients and seep into other
therapeutic models that describe poverty as either a psychic problem or
natural cultural value. Psychoanalysis gives priority to the subject, a
model which can account for the interaction of cultural and class differences in the specificity of each individual case. The psychoanalytic
'subject' is conditioned by a social universe ruled by desire and difference, determined by a social order organized in advance of any individual appearance on the scene, ushered by language acquisition, which
introduces all socio-cultural forms. We find in each specific patient's
unconscious her particular history, that of her family members and
ancestors, her language, her culture, her social and political surround.

Yet, the complex issues revolving around race, class, language and culture which arise in mental health settings seem to exclude a consideration of the unconscious. This exclusion raises questions about the connection between the therapy 'of choice' and socio-economic position. Does such exclusion mean that the particularity of each subject and the possibility of class mobility are privileged considerations for the affluent alone? If so, doesn't this imply a disregard for the prevailing rules of the free market when it comes to the 'consumer' of mental health services?

As a way of examining the relationship between the psychological and the socio-political, I offer for consideration my six years of clinical work in the field of so-called Mental Health, within the Latino, primarily Puerto Rican, community of North Philadelphia. The precarious socio-political economies of this community, exacerbated by its cross-cultural struggles, provide a privileged context through which to explore the application of the American psychological model. My focus will be on Puerto Ricans as a group, one that dramatically illustrates the situation of the so-called Hispanic population at large.

Puerto Ricans occupy a paradoxical position; they are neither foreigners nor fully enfranchised US citizens (they cannot vote for President unless they are on the mainland). Puerto Ricans' ambiguous 'in-between' position is condensed and exposed by the regionalisms 'Newyo Rican' and 'Porto Yorkers'. This ambiguity is reinforced by a constant migration between the American mainland and Puerto Rico, earning it the denomination of 'commuter nation'.

But choices and opportunities are not the same for all Puerto Ricans. The middle class that 'commutes' often blends in with the other middle classes of American society. Once in the USA, the majority of those belonging to the poorer classes live within the closed frontiers of the ghetto, where language establishes an insurmountable limit. Many obstinately resist the passage into the dominant American culture, living in the USA for decades without speaking a word of English.

French analyst Jacques Lacan adamantly contests the emphasis American ego-psychology places on adaptation and opposes the functionally adapted subject required by the American free-enterprise system (Turkle, 1992). He rejects the idea of therapeutic improvement in terms of 'better, more functional' adaptations to reality (which can be pathological) and believes that 'adaptation' and 'reality' are concepts determined by cultural values. For Lacan there is no self-improvement of the individual in isolation; society needs to be called into question. Rather than reforming patients' behaviours with adaptational techniques or modifying patients' life performances with emotional re-education, he insists on listening to them. Against the Anglo-Saxon pursuit of adaptive 'success' or 'happiness' Lacan assigns to psychoanalysis not simply the cure of symptoms, but the creation of a passageway to truth and ethics.

THE STATES OF THE OTHER AMERICA

The mental health services available to the Hispanic community are aimed at correcting symptoms. The goal is to help – or force – the patient to comply with a capitalist model of productivity. In North Philadelphia poverty is extreme, with three generations of unemployment often present in a family (Ericksen *et al.*, 1986). Community mental health centres that serve this population offer treatment that is generally paid through government-funded health coverages. Thus it appears to the client as if the care is free. Freedom is not, however, encouraged or exercised during the treatment. Regulations require the signing of a 'treatment plan', in which the expectations of improvement are specified. These plans are written in English but discussed with the 'clients' in Spanish. 'Clients' are thus asked to sign a text that will remain unreadable. In Pennsylvania, regulations require that patients achieve the assigned goals in three months (or twelve sessions) or renew the contract, exploring with the therapist the reasons for failing to reach the 'mutually agreed upon' objectives. It is mandated that this plan be described in terms of 'observable behaviours', a process which relies on universals and suppresses the particulars of the patient. In contrast to this, psychoanalysts formulate effective interpretations by referring to a particular patient in the singularity of her symptoms. General rules or universal truths do not produce effective interpretations.

Do poor Hispanics have an unconscious? Apparently not, according to the psychotherapy mandated for inner-city Hispanic groups. In 2005, this 'non-analysable' community will have become the most numerous minority in the USA. But who are these people who speak a language that is not the official one? 'Hispanics' are not simply those who speak Spanish. 'Hispanic' excludes, for instance, Spaniards (considered 'White' or 'European'), South Americans and even 'Latinos' (a category that includes Italians, French, and even Rumanians). What kind of 'ethnic' definition should be applied to this group? A rich Hispanic, once away from the ghetto, loses most of the characteristics associated with being Hispanic (McKay, 1984, p. 4). 'Hispanics', it turns out, are the poor of the inner-city ghettos who speak 'Spanglish'. This 'symptomatic' definition is a construct of overlapping and contradicting categories of race, language and class.

The invention of 'Hispanics as a race' is a theoretical problem that has practical consequences: research is based on 'symptomatic' assumptions about Hispanics, assumptions that also provide the foundation for training models and clinical practices. Therapy planning for Hispanics not only excludes psychoanalysis but institutionally denies the existence of the Hispanic unconscious by mandating only treatments that fail to consider the unconscious. This difference in therapeutic criteria goes beyond 'cultural diversity sensitivity' and borders on what is clearly a discriminatory practice. In contrast, my clinical experience in this community showed me that the fundamental tenets of psychoanalytic practice (free-association, dream-analysis, interpretation of slips of the tongue, transference, neutrality and, above all, listening to the unconscious) worked well with low-income Hispanics, who were often in a position to achieve successful cures. Yet, within current mental health practices, any approach that listens to the Hispanic unconscious tends to be discounted and repressed.

Transference is a phenomenon that plays a predominant role in the therapeutic and analytic process. Patients come to see an analyst thinking that the analyst would know something about why they are suffering. However, this does not mean that the analyst in fact knows, but the patient's supposition of a knowledge of the analyst produces the transference that allows the analytic work to start. Transference is an expression of unconscious desires of the analysand within the analytic relationship; it is the foundation of the treatment and the territory through which the cure progresses. Since transference 'transfers' the reality of the unconscious to the analytic experience, it needs to be both analysed and resolved in a successful cure.

In the name of strengthening the ego, current mental health practices manipulate rather than resolve transference. For example, the therapist might position herself as a role-model ideal that the patient must mimic. This transference becomes unresolvable because the therapist is invested in steering the patient towards measurable behavioural outcomes that may not lie along the same route as transference resolution.

Mental health services have been reduced to an orthopaedics of behaviour: straightening up, re-educating, persuading and domesticating 'abnormalities'. No matter what the motivation of the therapist when she adopts the role of 'master' by giving advice as if she knew what is best for 'enslaved' patients, she renders 'impossible' the liberating potential of therapy. Rather than structuring treatment so that patients' particularity emerge and find a voice, such a therapist seems to be the agent of a paralysing, disempowering plot that keeps patients from facing their truth. For the treatment to progress, the patient must be able to question what she wants (rather than what the therapist wants, a wish that should remain enigmatic) and in this way articulate desire. The analyst should direct the treatment, not the life, of the patient. In this voyage of discovery, the subject can question what she wants, and find in her desire the reasons to accomplish a significant change across a lifetime.

Psychoanalysis asserts that within ourselves there is a linguistic, social, historical, cultural, other. The coexistence of two domains – conscious and unconscious – creates a fundamental discordance within ourselves. When we speak, we say something other than what we believe we are saying. We make sense, nonsense, we misunderstand. Likewise, our conscious life is determined by unconscious factors that we can only discover – always with surprise – by way of their effects.

The myth of a self-made person and the denial of the constitutional alienation of the subject enslave the subject to an impossible illusion of psychic unity. The irrelevance of this illusion is seen more acutely in the ghetto, a made-peripheral, mostly unemployed, crime-thwarted, segregated part of society. For this community, the emphasis on adaptation to a reality whose justice is not questioned and the refusal to acknowledge its traumatic experiences in the name of a perfect 'unified' psyche is yet one more disavowal of its realities. Are poor Puerto Ricans considered 'mad' because they are not 'achievers'? Are they 'sick' because instead of producing goods they produce symptoms?

Psychoanalysis reveals that the performance sanctioned by the majority as successful can be self-destructive or psychopathological. Success is expected from a 'normal' person, even at the expense of psychopathologic aberrations. 'Normality' is an equivocal, arbitrary, socially constructed concept which supposes an average, a lack of difference. By definition those who belong to a minority are 'abnormal', therefore almost 'mad', an insane exception to the sane norm.

Psychoanalysis breaks the belief that a symptom is nothing but a meaningless disruption having nothing whatsoever to do with signification. Symptoms are the evidence of unspoken statements waiting to be read between the lines. The possibility of such reading opens the way to an unconscious discourse that seeks utterance and that the analysand can put into words with the help of the analyst. Yet, the unmasking of symptoms at an individual level is not sufficient. The formation of symptoms results from the singular structure of the subject's individual and cultural history. By making symptoms readable, psychoanalysis deciphers rather than suppresses their message both at a subjective and societal level. By paying attention to the unconscious interaction of race, class, ethnicity and language, it brokers an integration of the social and psychological realms.

VOYAGES OF DISCOVERY

When Maria returned she was started on antipsychotic medication, which diminished her anxiety and allowed her to talk. In our weekly sessions, her delusional formation began to yield meaning. Maria's delusion (her incoherent talk about children, ducks or gays, and dogs) was revealed as having both a restitutive function and a defensive function in relation to an unconscious homosexual impulse. Her words were not just a paranoid construction but a message expressed in a strange language that could be decoded.

Maria used *pato* with her private meaning, an irreducible meaning not fully shared with others. On the one hand, this private meaning was an effort at explaining a situation that overwhelmed her and produced a paranoid projection: 'They transformed my sons into dogs.' On the other hand, there was the insinuation of a failed meaning, expressed by the repetitive, insistent and stereotyped concern for her sons. Her delusional symptom had a function: it offered some coherence and provided a possible answer to an impossible situation (sons turned into either ducks or dogs). The truth of Maria's symptoms resided not in their universal meaning but in their subjective specificity. I thought if I could listen attentively to Maria the nuances of her verbal expressions would reveal the story of her mental illness.

Maria never had any contact with her father. She was raised by her maternal grandmother whom she called 'mami' (mother), and referred to her biological mother, who had a peripheral role in her life, as 'Titi' (auntie). Symbolically, it seemed that her grandmother and her mother were sisters.

Maria's only father figure was her grandmother's homosexual brother, Jose, to whom she felt close. Maria's Catholic family both condemned and accepted Jose's homosexuality; her grandmother was intensely ambivalent. If Maria spent too much time with Jose, her grandmother got angry and punished her; however, the grandmother also got upset if Maria did not visit him regularly. Sometimes, she joked that Maria and Jose (Mary and Joseph) would one day 'have baby Jesus'.

The grandmother's dream that Maria would become a nun collapsed when Maria got pregnant at the age of fourteen, leading the enraged grandmother to expel her from her house. After giving birth to a son, Maria claimed that she heard voices telling her that her son was Jesus. In this delusion, Maria was fulfilling an incestuous desire for her uncle Jose, realizing a fantasy of immaculate conception, and perhaps, repeating literally her grandmother's joke (interpreted as the grandmother's desire). Her second crisis took place weeks after her second son was born.

Through listening I learned that the two signifiers *perro–pato* condensed everything that Maria rejected (pregnancy out of wedlock, homosexuality, and immaculate conception of the Virgin), yet at the same time represented her and her acceptance of homosexuality ('I would not mind if they turned my sons into *patos* [gays]'). Maria revealed the meaning of *perros* in a session where she described her grandmother's fear that Maria would turn into a *pata* (Puerto Rican slang for lesbian). Her grandmother insisted that she should look 'more feminine' and forced Maria to separate from a close adolescent girlfriend. In the grandmother's opinion, Maria was spending too much time looking *enamorada* (in love) with her girlfriend instead of learning how to become a good wife. Further associations to *perro* related to questions of maternity, out of wedlock pregnancy, and fathers neglecting their parental duty: the grandmother accused Maria's pregnant mother of being a *perra prenada* (pregnant bitch) who could not identify the father of the child. *Pato–perro* both represented Maria and symbolized her psychosis. The hallucinated perception that her sons had been transformed into dogs was her own self-portrait, a visiting card written in a strange code, a sentence couched in a foreign idiom for which we have no dictionary.

As treatment progressed, there was a marked improvement in Maria's condition: she was no longer delusional, she was able to find and keep a home, she started to interact with her relatives, she attended a church, and she started making traditional Puerto Rican paper dolls that she would sell to make money. My experience with Maria illustrates how patients' symptoms, deeply rooted in their language and culture, can be addressed and deciphered by psychoanalysis. It also demonstrates the capacity of a low-income so-called Hispanic to productively use psychoanalysis.

Lacan's theory proposes no real boundary between self and society. For him, individuals come into being via social relations, a process which occurs through the acquisition of language. Language, therefore, constitutes human beings as subjects (thus the analyst's attention to each patient's particular choice of words). Lacan insists that feelings can only be expressed through and within language and in the nuances of verbal expression.

Another analysand of mine, I'll call her Dolores, complained about a depression exacerbated by severe back pains with no apparent physical cause. The pain was unbearable, yet she did not expect a cure for her suffering. She seemed to take pride in her ailments and somehow rejoice in her complaints saying, '*Sufro por mis dolores*' (I suffer because of/for my pains). Rather than understanding this expression in its conventional sense, I asked Dolores to say whatever came to mind in reference to Dolores. Interestingly enough, her mother's name was Dolores, as was that of her favourite aunt. The bonds of Dolores and her *sufro por* had determined this connection: Dolores was a fundamental signifier. Dolores's back pain set in motion verbal associations which opened up a network of meanings concerning her relationship with her mother and her aunt. Her pains because of them and for them betrayed the ambivalence in her love, her desire to satisfy what she guessed was expected of her and the impossibility of satisfying these expectations. It became apparent to her that she experienced a certain enjoyment when enduring her affliction. It was an offering, a sacrifice as well as a testimony to her sufferings. After she was able to put her *dolores* into speech, her back pains disappeared.

Symptoms are signifiers that carry meaning and must be read in their verbal associations. The unconscious speaks in the polyphony of language illustrated by the multiple meanings of a word (e.g. Dolores/ *dolores*; *pato*/duck/gay), a slip of the tongue, a parapraxis, and the rebus of a dream. In clinical practice a homophonic reading of a word can lead us to an understanding of presenting affects. When patients speak they say more than they intend, which opens up the gateway onto the truth of unconscious knowledge.

ALTERED AS THE ONLY POSSIBLE STATE

Lacan sees the symptom both as an individual event and as the emergence of a concealed truth in social relations. The analyst reads the symptom as a knot tying together race, class and language; indeed, the symptom has several causes working together to bring about a new concept of causality.

To deny the value of the symptom as a vehicle for meaning is like the repression of the unconscious: the negation of a cultural and linguistic universe. There are evident connections linking the marginalization of Hispanics to the types of mental health services available to them. Denying a group its unconscious is also to deny its cultural, 'human' qualities, segregating them as 'abnormalities' or mere 'madness'. If the unconscious is a discourse in which meaning can be found, as I hope I have illustrated, then the denial of the unconscious silences a culture and its ways of manifesting meaning.

In post-industrial areas like North Philadelphia the poor are more prone to illnesses, accidents, depression and senile dementia. Poverty is a chronic disease that attacks the body and soul, reducing the life expectancy of someone living in a low-income urban area by 10 or 15 years. The higher rate of mental health problems among the poor is closely linked to their position on the social ladder. Traditional therapeutic interventions aimed at treating this population are not working effectively; nor have alternative procedures been explored. Given this we may wonder: Are Hispanic mental illness symptoms as useless as they seem?

Hispanics seem to serve a function in the USA – that of an 'othering' device for the majority. In official publications nearly a century ago the Puerto Rican 'native' population was characterized by US observers as 'lazy [and] easygoing' and its people as 'in the main, idle' (Robinson, 1899). This social construction of 'unproductive, lazy' Hispanics is today perpetuated in the therapeutic approaches available to them. In the adaptive approaches symptoms are never 'put to work', nor allowed 'to produce' meaningful changes by letting them speak their unconscious truth. The failure to recognize Hispanics as counterparts allows for a 'crazy' misconstruction of their problems and instead encourages adaptation and assimilation. We know that the unconscious represents language, social rules, culture; we should ask ourselves: What is the social 'secondary gain' of repressing the Hispanic unconscious?

Seemingly, Hispanics in the ghetto produce symptoms instead of producing goods. Deprived of their meaning, 'Hispanic symptoms' manifest themselves as an opaque unproductive 'madness'. The qualification of 'mad' comes from the site of the Other (embodied by the dominant American culture). Likewise, the normative modalities of mental health practices within the Hispanic communities can also be read as symptoms of 'maddening' contradictions within American society projected onto its 'margins'. Here we should keep in mind the existing connections between medical discourse and capitalist ideology, in – and for – both of which Hispanics occupy a position of 'otherness' facing the 'Other' played by the dominant American culture. Therefore, we can read between the lines that the 'Hispanic madness' reveals and exposes the madness of the 'Other' that imposes a peripheral role on some groups. The specific 'madness' allocated to Hispanics can be interpreted as a symptom – evidence indicating the existence of something else, a signifying message – of American society.

Community mental health centres can – and do – operate as a location for social control. This geosocial endeavour has severe political implications, both clinical and cultural. Currently, the imposition of Managed Care privileges behavioural approaches as the only possible efficient (therefore the only available) therapeutic modality, medically treating the psyche as if it were a sick organ. Psychoanalysis offers a non-utilitarian ethical model that is neither hedonist nor stoic. Instead of forcing patients to 'normalize' their symptoms, psychoanalysis makes the symptoms 'productive' by allowing patients to find their own subjective meanings. The 'madness' of the symptom, or its 'non-productivity' can be reversed, put to work, if we listen, if we let the symptom express itself through speech.

Through hearing themselves say what they say to their analysts, patients recognize that their subjectivity is expressed and concealed in their symptoms. This emergence of unconscious knowledge modifies the subjects' structural positions. Even if the linguistic skills of lower-income patients are different from those of higher income, this does not mean that they cannot be listened to. Experience has shown that a psychoanalytic listening is both possible and fruitful with poor patients and that their alleged limitations in terms of verbal ability, extent of vocabulary and sophistication do not prevent them from having a productive unconscious.

The economic objection to the use of psychoanalysis with low-income patients is not as simple as it looks. Contrary to common assumptions, psychopharmacology is very costly. Medications eliminate manifestations rather than curing the cause of symptoms. In most cases, once patients stop taking the medications the symptoms return. The danger of the commodification of mental health practices is exemplified by the recent Managed Care policies oriented at the control, and ultimately, the elimination of psychotherapy in favour of psychopharmacology and its side effects.

LISTENING TO THE HISPANIC UNCONSCIOUS

Contradictions abound in the Puerto Rican realities. Puerto Rico is a 'Commonwealth' in English, yet in Spanish it is an 'Estado Libre Asociado' (Associated Free State, but lacking the key element of free association – sovereignty). These two designations betray a contradiction at the core of US policy, in which the political status of Puerto Rico seems one thing in Spanish and another in English. This linguistic discordance beautifully captures the sociopolitical factors that may affect the mental health of Puerto Ricans as a group. The Hispanic unconscious may remain unheard because no one is ready to hear it in its own language. If the symptom has a function, then one can begin to interpret the Hispanic 'madness' created by the factors I have mentioned (marginality, gender, race and class problems, colonialist legacies, urban poverty, violence, pressure to acculturate, language barriers). It is the outcome of an impossible situation that cannot be symbolized, yet is seeking resolution.

According to Lacan, there has to be a peculiar configuration in the imaginary of the parents for a given child to develop a psychosis. Likewise, one may wonder what special position has been allocated to Hispanics that leads them to develop their 'madness'. We have seen that madness can be interpreted as an attempt to reach a cure and to reconstruct a meaning. For Lacan, neurotics 'believe' in the symptom: they assume that the symptom has a meaning. Psychotic patients, according to Lacan, believe in the delusion but do not question its meaning, since the delusion gives meaning to their lives. Neurotics still believe in the hope of a sane language that can cure them, while psychotics are perhaps more aware of the divisive nature of language. They live fully the 'passion' of identifying with the way the Other sees them. Without defining all Hispanics as psychotic, I would suggest that, as a group, within this schema, Hispanics become the parabolic and hyperbolic projection of the psychotic elements looming behind the neurosis of American society.

Psychotics are closer to the truth of the subject's structure: subjects come into being through the agency of the signifier. They suffer this truth in a real 'passion'. Psychoanalytic treatment tries to understand the psychotic as a 'martyr of the unconscious'. Couldn't Hispanic 'madness' retrieve its full meaning if we attempt to see it as dependent upon the function of witness or martyr? The Altered States of Puerto Ricans, who have now become the 'other' America, America's underside caught up in the double-bind of postcolonial tensions, should appear as more than a 'crazy symptom', more than a testimony to American society's current blocks. It is time for the witness to take the stand. Society needs to be called into question. The suggestion that these symptoms do have a meaning can provide a true gateway, a real via regia to the American unconscious.

BIBLIOGRAPHY

Aponte, H. (1994) *Bread and Spirit: Therapy with the New Poor*. New York: W.W. Norton.

Ericksen, E. *et al.* (1986) *The State of Puerto Rican Philadelphia Research on Philadelphia and the Greater Delaware Valley Region*. Philadelphia: Institute for Public Policy Studies, Temple University.

Gherovici, P. (1996a) 'Blocking the Hispanic unconscious: subjectivity and subjection', *Clinical Studies: International Journal for Psychoanalysis*, **2**, 2.

───── (1996b) 'The Puerto Rican syndrome: the Puerto Rican ghetto sublime hystories', *Journal for the Psychoanalysis of Culture and Society*, Fall, **1**, 2.

───── (1996c) 'The ghetto's sublime hysterics', *Bien Dire*, Volumes 2 and 3 (1995–1996).

Inclan, J. (1985) 'Variation in value orientation in mental health work with Puerto Ricans', *Psychotherapy*, Spring.

Lacan, J. (1953) 'Some reflections on the ego', *International Journal of Psychoanalysis*, **XXXIV**, 11–17.

───── (1968) *Language of the Self: The Function of Language in Psychoanalysis*. Translated by A. Wilden. Baltimore: Johns Hopkins University Press.

───── (1978) *Ecrits: A Selection*. Paris: Seuil, 1966, translated by A. Sheridan. New York: W.W. Norton & Co.

Lewis, O. (1966) *La Vida: A Puerto Rican Family in a Culture of Poverty – San Juan and New York*. New York: Random House.

McKay, E. (1984) *An Anglo's Guide to Work Effectively with Hispanics*. La Raza: National Council.

Minuchin, S. *et al.* (1967) *Families of the Slum: An Exploration of their Structure and Treatment*. New York: Basic Books.

Oral History Project (1979) *Batiendo la Olla: 'Stirring the Pot'*. Philadelphia: Taller Puertorriquenio, Inc.

Sennett, R. and Cobb, J. (1972) *The Hidden Injuries of Class*. New York: Vintage Books.

Torre, C., Vecchini Rodriguez, H. and Burgos, W. (eds) (1994) *The Commuter Nation: Perspectives on Puerto Rican Migration*. Rio Piedras: Editorial de la Universidad de Puerto Rico.

Robinson, A.G. (1899) *The Porto Rico of Today*. New York: Charles Scribner's Sons.

Turkle, S. (1992) *Psychoanalytic Politics: Jacques Lacan and Freud's French Revolution*. New York: The Guilford Press.

Žižek, S. (1989) *The Sublime Object of Ideology*. New York: Verso.

15

How Did Nietzsche Get into the Nursery?

David Marriott

[I]t is part of the essence of action to be veiled in illusion.
(Nietzsche, *The Birth of Tragedy*, 1956, p. 51)

The derived is never as perfect as the original.
(Kierkegaard, *The Concept of Dread*, 1957, p. 57)

In 1955, the psychiatrist, Frederic Wertham, published the second of his two key works on the topics of childhood, culture and crime: *Seduction of the Innocent*, Wertham's well-known (for some, infamous) study of the effects of children's comic books, echoes the themes, and preoccupations, of his previous work, *Dark Legend*, first published in 1941. Taking as his starting point the psychopathology of the everyday life of the child, in both works Wertham brought the violence of the juvenile delinquent into contact with what, in *Dark Legend*, he describes as 'the derived life of fiction' – the life which fiction borrows from the deeds, and fantasies, of its readers (Wertham, 1955, p. 87). At stake, for Wertham, are the connections between reading and acting, wishing and doing, the violence of fantasy and the violence of culture. 'Why does our civilization give to the child not its best but its worst,' he wonders in *Seduction of the Innocent*, reflecting on the apparent pervasiveness – 'on paper, in language, in art, in ideas' – of the '*über*', or 'super' in the forms of representation available to the American child: 'supermen, superwomen, super-lovers, super-boys, super-girls, super-ducks, super-mice, super-magicians, super-safecrackers.' The repetition, or hyperbole, strikes the note of Wertham's anxiety, his uncomfortable sense that there is something perverse in, *introduced into*, the child. 'How,' he concludes, 'did Nietzsche get into the nursery?' (Wertham, 1955, p. 15).

It is a question which runs throughout Wertham's career as psychiatrist and writer – and one which sustains his remarkable collaboration

with the black American novelist, Richard Wright. That collaboration is
central to this essay, its exploration of how the idea of fiction and, or in,
childhood structures the intellectual exchange between Wertham and
Wright; more specifically, their shared preoccupation with the vicissitudes of fiction and therapy, race and crime – Wertham's 'derived life'.
In their different ways, both Wertham and Wright struggle with that
life; from 1941, following the publication of Wertham's *Dark Legend*,
they will struggle together to explore how literature can contribute to a
political and therapeutic understanding of the psychopathology of the
delinquent child and youth – and, in particular, the mythic–hyperbolic
image of the black in American culture. To anticipate the argument of
this chapter, what Wertham and Wright uncover – through psychiatry,
through literature – is a type of fusion between the murderousness of the
child's fantasy life and the hatefulness of American culture, a massifica-
tion of what, in *Dark Legend*, Wertham describes as a catathymic
delusion: wedded to the pleasures, and efficiency, of violence, America
demands that its children merge their murderous fantasies with the
murderousness of the real.[1] As I want to show, the idea and (at times)
the act of matricide is central to that pleasure, its pursuit of a culture
founded, and sustained, by a loving hatred of the mother. That ambivalence can become one of the privileged points of connection, or confusion, between psyche and culture, internal life and the outside world, as
well as the (potentially catathymic?) dialogue between Wertham and
Wright – a dialogue fascinated, fixated, by the murderous potential
embedded in the relation between mother and son. It is a dialogue that,
I want to suggest, takes place over the body of a woman, a mother,
murdered by her child, a scene – both fictional and real – which structures the encounters, intellectual and amicable, between Wertham and
Wright. That scene is going to support an account of post-war American
culture as one which derives from a massive invasion of self, a possession
of the children of America by a culture saturated by images of power,
racist violence and sexuality.

On 24 October 1941, Wright pays tribute to Wertham's *Dark Legend*, his
study of a seventeen-year-old youth, Gino, who, possessed by the belief
that she has dishonoured his family, murders his mother:

> I want to thank you for making it possible for me to read this
> highly fascinating psychological study of crime. My reactions to
> Gino, his plight and his crime were so many and so varied that it

would be futile to attempt to set them down in a letter. It is enough
to say that I think it is the most comprehensive psychological
statement in relation to contemporary crime that I have come
across. Indeed, it is as fascinating as any novel. (Wright, in Fabre,
1993, p. 171)

'As fascinating as any novel': *Dark Legend: A Study in Murder* has
Wright under its spell, fascinated by its heady mix of fiction and reality,
psyche and myth: what Wertham calls his 'bio-literary method'
(Wertham, 1955, p. 95). That method – 'the detailed comparison of a
literary character with a living person' as Wertham puts it – supports his
decision to tell the story of Gino as an 'intellectual detective adventure'
which puts the psychiatrist-reader on the trail of Hamlet and Orestes as
the mythic-literary prototypes of the modern matricide (ibid., pp. 95, 12)
(I will be coming back to this). Merging a psychoanalytic commentary
with the *noir* of true crime fiction – 'The cop was standing by the candy
store,' Wertham begins. 'It was just past midnight on a spring night' –
Dark Legend seduces Wright with its rewriting of the *ur*-dramas of
psychoanalysis as well as its refusal to give up on the enigmatic connection between fiction and action (ibid., p. 7). A compelling topic for a
writer, like Wright, committed to an aesthetic of political change, to
what, I want to suggest, Wertham describes as 'the derived life of
fiction'. Fictions, Wertham suggests in a key move towards the end of
his discussion of Gino's murder of his mother, have a 'derived life, in
the spectator, the reader, and the listener' (ibid., p. 87). Part of the
problem of Gino, for Wertham, is what drives him to the *act* of matricide, to act out the fantasies that, on one (psychoanalytic) reading, are
the common property of every child-man? 'There was one specific and
actual occurrence,' Wertham concedes, at the beginning of this discussion, 'which, at the last moment, apparently helped Gino to turn his
impulse into fact. On the night of the murder he went to a movie' (ibid.).
   Let us note the drama of this moment in Wertham's narrative. Gino, a
youth possessed by an ambivalent image of his mother, goes to the
cinema. He becomes a spectator of the fiction staged on screen, the
consumer of a public fantasy which allows him to identify himself with
the (avenging) hero of the story unfolding on screen (the film told 'a
story of revenge,' Wertham tells us, 'a young man, betrayed by the
woman he loves, finds his career ruined by her connivance') (ibid.). It is
an identification which speaks Gino's displacement from his own imaginings, his preoccupation by a creative act which, though belonging to

(coming from) someone else, is able to make his unconscious wishes, and conflicts, more tolerable. More tolerable and so, perhaps, more thinkable, more do-able. 'I asked myself,' Wertham continues, 'whether fiction of that sort [cinema] can influence people in this way':

> Similar instances are not rare. Immediately before the matricide Orestes heard the Chorus recite in stirring dramatic dialogue the sequence of events concerned with his father's death and his mother's re-marriage. Immediately after hearing the Play-Within-the-Play, Hamlet goes to his mother's chamber and threatens her. In a recent murder trial a father who had performed a 'mercy killing' on his feeble-minded son testified that shortly before his deed he had seen a movie called 'Murder by the Clock', in which a weak-minded boy was led astray. 'This', he said, 'had a tremendous effect on me.'
>
> It seemed to me just as inexact to say fiction has no influence at all on people's actions as to blame crime on such fiction. Apparently anti-social impulses do not originate in this way. But when they once exist, added impetus may be given them by way of identification with a fictional scene.
>
> This is easily understandable, for literature does not exist in a vacuum. Since stories are read and listened to, it is not even entirely correct to say that they have no life. They have a derived life, in the spectator, the reader, and the listener. (ibid.)

It would be too easy, I think, to dismiss Wertham's account of the influence of fiction as a reductive one: crudely, the violence of representation reflects, and repeats, the violence of culture. (That is a common response to his analysis of the effects of violent comics on children.) Clearly, Wertham wants to avoid the dialectic of accusation and defence – fiction as cause, fiction as no cause – which so often dominates discussion, turning instead to the idea of 'identification with a fictional scene': identification as a type of *impetus*, a force deriving from fiction or, more precisely, from the *relation* between fiction and its consumers (a type of transient mesmerism, uncanny in its deferred, and unpredictable, effects). That is, words become deeds, wishes become actions, in an encounter between fiction and reader-spectator; the 'derived life' of fiction derives from a structure of identification through which fantasy – on screen, in Gino – becomes real. It is as if the odd convergence between impulse and influence, Gino's wish to kill his mother and whatever vengeful scenes he watches on screen, are there to authorize his fantasy, to bring it to life via an identification with the wish fulfilment – the hero who, against the odds, gets what he wants – at the heart of mass cultural forms. Not a repetition but a doubling of fantasy and fiction, then – in Gino, on screen – is what Wertham uncovers in his attempt to identify precisely how, and why, Gino is spurred on from the vicarious pleasures of fictional fulfilment to the *act* of matricide.

That act is startling enough. Gino, Wertham tells us, suffered from an excessive attachment to his mother – an Orestes complex, in the terms of *Dark Legend* – a 'fixation on the mother-image' which casts all women as 'mother': 'In this woman he killed all women' (ibid., pp. 94, 95). Kills all women, that is, with the thirty-two knife thrusts aimed at his mother ('that agony on the floor behind the door' in the words of the police officer who discovers her) (ibid., p. 9). Possessed to death by the image of the mother, Gino finds in the cinematic scene the means to exorcism. In the doubling between spectator and screen there is, paradoxically, a loss of fantasy and fiction; or, more precisely, both are fixated in the moment of identification with a scene which traffics a structure of fulfilment: crudely, I want to be (like) the one who gets what he wants: the superman or *Übermensch*. 'In the movie,' Wertham specifies, 'the young man succeeds', while the spectator is laid open to the imperatives of fiction – Do this! Be that! – in so far as that fiction is able to appeal to what he recognizes already in himself: Gino, Wertham concludes, was 'influenced by this picture because it fitted in so well with his own preoccupations' (ibid., pp. 87, 88). In other words, it is his very preoccupation – the fixation on the mother – which lays Gino open to the coercions of (cultural) fiction, coercions which confirm, and encourage, the reduction of fantasy to a single scene: the violent death of the mother. Intrigued by that reduction, the poverty of fantasy and fiction in Gino's psyche, Wertham presents the concept of catathymia, or catathymic crisis, as the key to his pathology: a special disturbance in the relation between thinking and feeling, a type of fixation and rigidity in the processes of thinking and wishing. 'The thought processes,' Wertham explains, 'lose their plasticity and become more and more rigid along definite lines as the result of repressed ungratified wishes, unallayed fears or any unresolved feelings' (ibid., p. 96). It is as if the mobility of the primary processes – condensation, secondary revision, displacement – supporting the work of the dream, of thought, of feeling, has been lost, the mobility of unconscious life supplanted by an *idée fixe* which, Wertham points out, casts the catathymic as a subject possessed by the belief that an act of violence is the only solution to the impasse generated by the loss of the capacity to symbolize – and so to bear – the tension between wish and frustration.

When Gino goes to the cinema, then, it is as a catathymic spectator, a youth who finds his obsessions reflected in the (equally) catathymic idiocies of post-war American film in which violence is trafficked as distraction. Fiction allows fantasy to express brutal reality; Gino has no fantasy; fiction comes in because fantasy has become fixated, rigidified. In so far as Gino finds himself mirrored on the screen, in so far as the screen appears to reflect what is already there, so the cinematic scene can begin to direct the very life in which its fictions find their purchase: the life is derived from fiction just as the fiction takes on a derived life in its spectators (no straightforward account of motive or cause here). But if fiction fascinates Gino, it also allows him to enact an unspeakable act of violence against a mother-image now representational of *all* women.

A complex relation between pathology and fiction, culture and influence, runs right through Wertham's work – and will become central both to his understanding of representation in the life of the child and to his dialogue with Wright. Wright, I think, perceives affinities. *Dark Legend* is, in its imagining, (like) fiction. Wertham is telling a story, reconstructing a psyche and a scene which catch at Wright's imagination: the writer is fascinated by Gino's plight, the crime which, I want to suggest, is a symptom of Wright's own fiction from *Native Son*, first published in 1939, to *Savage Holiday*, published in 1954 (the book which, it seems, Wright valued most). To put this another way: matricide appears as symptom in the works of one of the most important black modernists at the same time as a matricidal reading of post-war American culture is emerging through the psychoanalytic psychiatry popularized by Wertham in his analyses of crime and race, fiction and film. In this sense, *Dark Legend* fascinates, seduces Wright because it responds to the problem which haunts his life and work. Starting from the son's murderousness towards his mother, that response moves towards an account of fiction as provocative force in the lives of the modern Hamlets and Orestes: Wertham's Gino, Wright's Bigger Thomas – the protagonist of *Native Son* whose plight, or plot, anticipates the analysis of mother (image) and murder put forward in *Dark Legend*. The question of the mother as *image*, the imago or fiction of the mother in the life of the son, is worked through both *Dark Legend* and *Native Son*, the one embroiled in a real or literal act of matricide, the

other bound to repeat the symbolic murder of the mother which thema-
tizes Wright's fiction. It has become a critical commonplace in readings
of Wright's fiction that the figure of the mother is used to symbolize the
'poverty, the ignorance, the helplessness' of black lives and traditions;
similarly, that the body of the mother lies concealed behind the women
brutalized through Wright's problematic fictions (Wright, 1945, p. 111).
But what I am interested in here is a coincidence between Wright's
representation of the mother – as metaphor and fiction, mask as well as
masked – and the idea of culture as perverse intrusion on the self-
identified by both Wertham and Wright. Like the mother, culture
intrudes as fiction; fixated by the image of his mother, Gino can be
provoked to murder her by the fictions of culture; compelled by a need
to understand the fictions of American racism, Wright becomes
embroiled in a complex series of substitutions and equations between
mothering, childhood and culture. Figuring himself as Hamlet, say,
Bigger Thomas as Orestes, Wright uncovers the logic of racism as a
form of sadistic mothering, writing as a way of abreacting (and enacting)
the impulse towards matricide at the heart of contemporary life.

'Matricide,' Wertham notes towards the end of *Dark Legend*, 'is the
disease of a patriarchal society'; the murder of the mother by her son has
a 'social significance in the development of mankind' which, despite the
progressive (Wertham's term) forces of repression ranged against it,
persists 'in life and literature today' (ibid., p. 116). At once mythic and
political, symptomatic and social, then, the act of matricide explored
through *Dark Legend* becomes central to Wright's understanding of
literature and crime as *scenes* which can be used to reveal the repressed
of cultural life: the literary and the criminal are the place for that which
has no place. One of the key texts here is *Native Son*, and, in particular,
'How Bigger Was Born', the 1940 Preface to the novel delivered by
Wright as a lecture to the Schomburg Collection, New York. Wright
explains, laying his cards on the table as to how, and why, he came to
write Bigger Thomas:

> The more I thought of it, the more I became convinced that if I did
> not write of Bigger as I saw and felt him, if I did not try to make
> him a living personality and at the same time a symbol of all the
> larger things I felt and saw in him, I'd be reacting as Bigger
> himself reacted: that is, I'd be acting out of *fear* if I let what I
> thought whites would say constrict and paralyze me. (Wright, 1983,
> pp. 9, 25)

Writing Bigger rather than being Bigger, then; literature rather than crime. *Native Son* takes the place of Bigger's murders, the murderousness directed at the white and black woman sacrificed to the fear generated in a black youth by American culture. This is, I think, literature as a defence against the paralysing effects of white racism, Wright's demand that literature take on the burden of living in a hostile world. It is as if Wright is deriving Bigger from a life that might have been his own, the life that Wright has managed to divert through fiction – using fiction to derive another life for himself (fiction as a cure for fiction). What you find in fiction, then, are the traces of a life that might have been, a life avoided, or averted – 'an unveiling of the unconscious ritual of death,' as Wright puts it, 'in which we, like sleep-walkers, have participated so dreamlike and so thoughtlessly' (ibid., p. 420).

Like any form of defence, Bigger may not always secure Wright against the hostile dream that is American racism. Any reader familiar with the criticism of *Native Son* will know that Wright was quickly identified with the savagery of his literary character, condemned as the author of this living, and dangerous, personality. What goes missing here is writing as a work of transformation, a rerouting of impulse through language: in other words, writing as that which makes the difference between wishing and doing (the terms which dominate Wertham's analysis of Gino). How does one derive from, or stall, the other? This is, in fact, the question which organizes not only Wertham's reading of *Native Son* but the 'experiment' that both he and Wright undertook to 'determine where certain elements in *Native Son* were *derived from*' (Wertham, 1964, p. 321). Part of Wright's 'analysis' with Wertham – their 'discussions', as Wertham puts it, 'on the relationship of psychiatry to literature' – that experiment is written up in 'An Unconscious Determinant in "Native Son"', an essay read before the American Psychopathological Association in 1944. Acknowledging an obvious identification between Wright and Bigger Thomas, Wertham is also keen to emphasize the idea of literature as transformation and disguise. 'It has always to be kept in mind,' he insists, 'that "a literary creation is not a translation but a transmutation of human experience" (*Dark Legend*)' (ibid., p. 322). Returning to his earlier reading of *Hamlet* in *Dark Legend*, Wertham brings his bio-literary-psychiatric experiment with Wright into dialogue with his analysis of Gino: black modernism and delinquency, literature and murder, converge on the topic of matricide (the traces of matricide in the work of literature). At the same time, Wertham refers his readers, or listeners, to two specific scenes in *Hamlet* and *Native Son*, reading across the two texts to describe the matricidal impulses of their authors:

> Just as I believe that in *Hamlet* the key scene is the appearance of the father's ghost in the mother's bedroom, so the key scene in *Native Son* is when Bigger Thomas unintentionally kills Mary Dalton in the presence of her blind mother. (Bigger, as you will remember, is employed as a handyman in the house of the Dalton family.) (ibid.)

On Wertham's reading, *Native Son* is replaying the unconscious dynamics of Shakespeare's *Hamlet*, while *Hamlet* is a drama of repressed matricide – 'Shakespeare has added in the *Second Quarto* the new motif of matricide' – in which the mother figures as object of both incestuous desire *and* murderous, but diverted, wish. Echoing between *Hamlet* and *Native Son*, the two scenes are supposed to speak a matricidal desire which, however, misses the mother as object. In *Hamlet*, it is a (dead) father's command which stays the son's 'bitter business': 'Taint not thy mind nor let thy soul contrive/Against thy mother aught' (though, as Wertham points out, Hamlet initiates the circumstances which lead to his mother's death) (Wertham, 1947, p. 88). In *Native Son*, the death of a young white woman comes in place of the (wish for a) dead maternal body that, in Wertham's terms, lies buried in the text of this scene. But where is that body? In what sense is Bigger Thomas – who, at the end of *Native Son* stands trial for the murder of two women, one black, one white – a matricide? 'In this woman he killed all women': Wertham's analysis of Gino in *Dark Legend* appears to be reversed in his discussions of Wright's fiction: by killing women, he kills the one woman, the mother. That is, in the transmutation that is Wright's fiction, a son's (wish to) murder his mother is displaced by, re-presented as, the death of a daughter in the presence of her mother. A blind mother, a mother who sees but cannot see: 'And the very symbol of the seeing eye that is blind fits the mother image' (Wertham, 1964, p. 324).

What is it in Wertham's discussions with Wright which puts him on the track of this disguised matricidal scene? On the one hand, clearly, Wertham is bringing *Native Son* into dialogue with one of the *Ur*-texts of Freud's thinking on the troubling relation between mothers and sons; on the other hand, Wertham has been reading, and discussing, Wright's recent 'autobiography', *Black Boy*, a text which, Wertham declares, shows up the 'special problem' of Wright's identification with his creation, Bigger Thomas (ibid., p. 322). Let's note that *Black Boy* (first published in 1945), opens with a mother's act of violence against her son: 'But for a long time,' Wright recalls, 'I was chastened whenever I remembered that my mother had come close to killing me' (Wright, 1945, p. 13). Maternal aggression is a persistent, and painful, theme, nothing less than an intrusion which threatens the son's capacity to think and dream: 'I had once tried to write,' Wright acknowledges, 'had let my crude imagination roam, but the impulse to dream had been slowly beaten out of me by experience' (ibid., p. 272). Part of the world which helps to obliterate her child's impulse to dream, the mother is an equivocal figure in Wright's fiction – source of persecution and desire. A threat to life and imagination in *Black Boy*, she is cast as origin of both in the dedication to *Native Son*: 'To My Mother who, when I was a child at her knee, taught me to revere the fanciful and the imaginative.' There may be a bitter irony here (the mother who refuses the child's fancy and imagination may well teach him to revere it), but, if so, it is an irony which becomes more apparent when we read across from *Native Son* to *Black Boy*, from 'fiction' to autobiography: Wertham is careful to point to the work of disguise – 'almost as hard to penetrate as any novel' – in the latter (Wertham, 1964, p. 322). Or, perhaps, the mother threatens what she most reveres, censors what she most wants to liberate in her child? In each case, it is the disguise of fiction which allows Wright, finally, to dream: writing is the capacity for dream, resistance to experience. And, I want to suggest, resistance to as well as a defence against, the mother, the terror and helplessness she has come to represent:

> My mother's suffering grew into a symbol in my mind, gathering to itself all the poverty, the ignorance, the helplessness; the painful, baffling, hunger-ridden days and hours; the restless moving, the futile seeking, the uncertainty, the fear, the dread; the meaningless pain and endless suffering. Her life set the emotional tone of my life, colored the men and women I was to meet in the future, conditioned my relation to events that had not yet happened, determined my attitude to situations and circumstances I had yet to face. (Wright, 1945, p. 111)

It is in the context of this powerful, and miserable, statement that Wertham diagnoses the place of the mother in Wright's psychic life – making the connection between Wright and Shakespeare, Bigger and

Hamlet. 'In Wright's life,' Wertham suggests, towards the end of his
account of *Native Son* as a complex relation to Wright's image of the
maternal, 'it may be sufficient to say that the ego ideal was largely
derived from the mother' (Wertham, 1964, p. 324, my emphasis). But,
then, what does it mean to derive your ego ideal from a symbol of
poverty, ignorance, helplessness, suffering ... ? To internalize, or intro-
ject, an inarticulate and brutal cultural legacy, one that, as Wertham
claims, is destined to intrude like a 'nameless fate' into Wright's *œuvre* as
well as his dreams (indeed, to intrude on his ability to dream). As
symbol, or metonym, for black life in America, then, the mother is a
degraded, even abject, figure in Wright's fiction; or, to put this another
way, because she carries the riven consciousness, the dereliction, that
Wright associates with black culture in America, she is herself a figure of
that dereliction: like Bigger, in fact, the mother carries a desperate
awareness she can neither understand, nor avoid. Or, as Wright describes
it in his 1953 novel, *The Outsider*, 'Mother love had cleaved him in
twain: a wayward sensibility that distrusted itself, a consciousness that
was not conscious of itself' (Wright, 1993, p. 22).

Figuring a violence at once intimate and public – the deeply familial
aggression of a mother against her son, the residues of black experience
made derelict by racist hatreds – the matricidal attack on the *images* of the
mother in Wright's fiction is always also an attack on the racist culture
whose effects she embodies. An attack, in other words, on the experience
of growing up as a black child in racist culture. That experience becomes
central to the experiment between Wertham and Wright as Wertham
begins to probe what he describes as the 'unconscious determinant' of
Native Son, the scene(s) – real or fantasmatic, historical or imaginative –
from Wright's childhood in which Bigger is able to find his purchase:
'Was he conscious of any fantasies or daydreams from which threads
would lead to the key scene and its setting in the novel. The answer to
both these questions is "No"' (Wertham, 1964, pp. 322–3). Drawing a
blank, Wertham is forced to dig deeper, to bring Wright up against the
presence of fiction in the telling of any life. 'Did I invent these people?'
Wright wonders to Wertham, faced with the uncertain difference between
fantasy and memory in relation to the scenes and figures he is uncovering
from his past (ibid., p. 323). Gradually, against all resistance, against the
difficulty of telling the past in a way that convinces Wertham with its
'reality character' (an aesthetic, or literary, judgement on the quality of
the memories being retrieved?), Wright reveals the scene that, he tells
Wertham, 'was the soil out of which *Native Son* came' (ibid.):

As an adolescent of fifteen, Wright went to public school and worked mornings and evenings for a white family. The lady of the house was young and pretty. She lived with her husband and her mother ... In his memory the figure of the mother is very unclear. She used to get the breakfast every morning. The daughter, the lady of the house, was friendly to young Richard, and he felt this was a second home to him ... Further associative material led to the recollection of a special scene. In the early morning young Richard would carry scuttles of coal and wood into the house. On one such morning when he was carrying out his usual routine, he opened the door and came suddenly upon the lady of the house before she had dressed. She reprimanded him severely and told him he should always knock before entering. These recollections had great emotional power. They were related to much earlier emotional experiences. (ibid., pp. 323–4)

It is an abyssal structure of scenes upon scenes: through the (fictional) Dalton family Wright reworks an episode that, Wertham points out, Wright had completely forgotten while that episode, in turn, draws on the power of much earlier experiences. The sexuality, and shame, of the adolescent are projected back into earlier experiences – Wright's powerful, and ambivalent, tie to his mother – and forwards into the literature through which Wright reinvents himself, refinds his life. Let us note, again, that in this 'adolescent' scening, the mother remains a shadowy figure, 'nebulous' (Wright's word) in his memory, and apparently not able to be further delineated in his discussions with Wertham. Shadowy, and therefore, in terms of the psychoanalysis to which both Wright and Wertham are indebted, a significant and overdetermined figure. What does the shadow of the (white) mother represent here? Put the mother in the shadows, I want to suggest, and you cannot quite see her: more importantly, perhaps, she cannot see *you*. She cannot say 'no' to whatever it is you are doing which she cannot see (looking or murdering). It is not the mother who issues reprimand or prohibition here but the object of the look herself.

No limit, then, to what a blind mother can look at. It would be impossible to overstate the ambivalence and complexity of the imago of the mother (black and white) in Wright's fiction. Part of the challenge of Wright's fiction is the way in which it runs that imago into the very modern problem of 'Bigger': symbol of a black delinquency athwart American national life and the matricidal relation between black mother and son. 'I wanted the reader to feel that Bigger's story was happening now, like a play upon the stage or a movie unfolding upon the screen,' Wright explains in 'How Bigger Was Born'. 'I wanted the reader to feel that there was nothing between him and Bigger; that the story was a special première given in his own private theatre' (Wright, [1939] 1983, p. 24). Not only Wright, then, but his readers are asked to occupy the place of Bigger, to be him in order to know, from the inside out, what it feels like to suffer from and to wage war against American racism. Again, this is an understanding of literature – cinema, drama – in terms of its derived life: fiction can take up its place on the inside of its readers, grappling with, even combating, the formations of fiction and fantasy which already reside there. It is a derivation which, in the case of Wright's aesthetics of commitment to political change can be used to generate a therapeutic action against the violence of American cultural life (a derivation which cuts both ways?). 'Like a scientist in a laboratory,' Wright continues, 'why should I not ... use my imagination and invent test-tube situations ... work out in fictional form an emotional statement and resolution of this problem?' (ibid., p. 36).

A fictional resolution for a racist reality? It may be that matricide – as fiction, as act – comes as a defence against the effects of that hostility (the mother identified with the racism of cultural life) as well as the unbearable pain of a conflicted inner world. 'Regarded from the point of view of the development of his personality,' Wertham concludes in *Dark Legend*, 'the act of murder appears to have prevented consequences far more serious for Gino's mental health' (Wertham, 1947, p. 99). The question of matricide always, finally, derived from something else? A happy matricide, Gino *acts* rather than *wishes*, obeys his mother in the very act of murder: 'I killed her, I took her life away, but no one can say that I ever disobeyed her' (ibid., p. 54). What price the mother? How do we start to reckon her guilt in the filial imaginaries explored by Wertham and Wright? Is it always her fault?

NOTE

1. I will be coming back to Wertham's concept of catathymic crisis. For now, in 'The catathymic crisis: a clinical entity', he defines catathymia as a 'rutlike fixation', a disturbance between 'logic and affectivity' in which 'the patient acquires the idea that he must carry out a violent act against others or against himself'. See *Archives of Neurology and Psychiatry*, 1937, p. 976.

BIBLIOGRAPHY

Fabre, M. (1993) *The Unfinished Quest of Richard Wright*. Trans. I. Barzun. Urbana and Chicago: University of Illinois Press, 1993, p. 171.

Kierkegaard, S. (1957) *The Concept of Dread*. Trans. W. Lowrie. Princeton, NJ: Princeton University Press.

Nietzsche, F. (1956) *The Birth of Tragedy and The Genealogy of Morals*. Trans. F. Golfing. New York: Doubleday & Co.

Wertham, F. (1947) *Dark Legend: A Study in Murder*. London: Victor Gollancz.

Wertham, F. (1955) *Seduction of the Innocent*. London: Museum Press.

Wertham, F. (1964) 'An unconscious determinant in "Native Son"', in Hendrik, M.R. (ed.) *Psychoanalysis and Literature*. New York: E.P. Dutton & Co.

Wright, R. (1945) *Black Boy: A Record of Childhood and Youth*. New York and Evanston: Harper & Row.

Wright, R. ([1939] 1983) *Native Son*. Harmondsworth: Penguin.

Wright, R. (1993) *The Outsider*. New York: HarperPerennial.

Wright, R. (1994) *Savage Holiday*. Jackson: University of Mississippi Press.

16

Italy's Subjection of Psychoanalysis:
A Case-Study Look at Regulatory Politics

Anthony Molino

> Our partial and skewed imitation of the American model has grotesque consequences
> (Economist Guido Rossi, on Italy's importation of American-style capitalism. *La Repubblica*, 31 July 2001)

In their book *The New Informants: The Betrayal of Confidentiality in Psychoanalysis and Psychotherapy* (Northvale: Aronson, 1995), Christopher Bollas and David Sundelson examine the far-reaching and crippling implications of third party intrusions on American psychoanalysis, including the perversions of practice resulting from clinicians' compromises with the likes of lawyers, insurance and health care companies. In addition to voicing their concerns over the systematic dismantling of psychoanalysis' defining ethos of confidentiality, the authors also suggest that many of the deleterious compromises threatening psychoanalysis stem from the historically occasioned and distinctly American relations between psychoanalysis and its so-called 'parent professions'. In the authors' words:

> [Psychiatry, psychology and social work] may not be capable of or interested in preserving the integrity of psychoanalysis. However, psychoanalysts have not declared their independence from disciplines that have to a considerable extent allied themselves with the forces of intrusion and disclosure. (1995, p. xi)

Throughout their book, Bollas and Sundelson refer to the situation in Europe and South America, where analysts are said to be alarmed over developments in the USA but still relatively free from the day-to-day anxieties of a Faustian gambit with the dehumanizing forces of a market economy. What I'd like to suggest, however, with the following reflections on the situation of psychoanalysis in Italy, is that the rest of the world may well be fast on the heels of America's unwelcome but trend-setting example.

In 1989, in a move which sought to fill a legislative black hole in its psychotherapy landscape (even as it countered the long-standing examples of leading European countries such as France and England,[1] where psychoanalysis and most psychotherapies are not regulated), the Italian government passed legislation establishing a national registry for psychologists. A principal feature of Law #56, as the decree has come to be known, was the definition of the exclusive terms under which any and all *psychotherapies* could be practised. While leaving aside, for the moment, the crucial point of whether psychoanalysis is or is not to be considered a form of psychotherapy, the law's fundamental provisions are thus stated:

1. Any and all practitioners of any form of psychotherapy must hold a university degree in either psychology or medicine.
2. All non-medical practitioners must hold a university degree in psychology and be enrolled in the newly instituted Registry of Psychologists.
3. All psychotherapy training institutes will be state-certified and restrict admission to their programmes to holders of a university degree in either psychology or medicine.
4. The professional title of 'psychotherapist' is thus redefined as a *specialized* credential or qualification, limited to registered psychologists and medical doctors, who will have completed an additional four-year course of study at a state-certified training institute and be enrolled in the Registry's Roster of Psychotherapists.

In point of fact, such regulation is contrary to the *de facto* situation prevailing throughout much of Europe, where the title of *psychotherapist* is a generic title, pursuant to formalized training options, but not in the least subjected to prior state-approved training in psychology or medicine. As if this state of affairs were not sufficiently troubling in and of itself, there is a background situation which also warrants elucidation. Until 1970, 'psychology' did not exist as a degree-granting course of study in Italian universities.[2] One might argue that it is

precisely the needs generated by an evolving and increasingly complex
society such as the Italian one that has warranted the greater importance assumed by and attributed to academic psychology and the so-
called helping professions. Needless to say, there are enormous
economic and ideological interests invested in consolidating the place of
academic psychology as the privileged vehicle through which one must
pass if intent on becoming a psychotherapist. Among these is the
widespread and ongoing affiliation of psychotherapy training
programmes with the university system, and the resultant centralizing
function that academic psychology has come to assume *vis-à-vis* the
psychoanalytic establishment.

It would be helpful, I believe, to compare these recent developments
with their American precedents. Bollas and Sundelson help shed light on
a similarly turbulent time in the United States, when a series of laws
were implemented to order that country's extensive and irregular
landscape:

> In the early 1960s there were hundreds of different types of
> 'therapy' offered by individuals from numerous schools of
> thought. For very good reasons, the state legislatures moved
> towards the licensing of psychotherapists, demanding credentials
> that required a qualified training, the passing of an examination,
> and licensure by a state board of examiners. By the early 1970s
> there was something of a stampede by counselors and therapists
> into programs where they could obtain the needed credentials.
> Further, while clinical psychology had been the poor sibling to
> academic psychology throughout the century, suddenly schools of
> psychology were inundated by people who wanted clinical
> training in order to gain certification ... We need to keep in
> mind that one important aspect of this licensing rush was a need
> to satisfy the statutory requirements set by the state. (Bollas and
> Sundelson, p. 115)

In Italy, prior to Law #56, the practice of psychotherapy – while the
near-exclusive domain of psychiatrists and the medical establishment –
was nonetheless deregulated and admittedly vulnerable to the excesses
and abuses of 'wild' practitioners such as the notorious devotee of Lacan
Armando Verdiglione. The negative publicity heaped upon psychoanalysis by questionable characters like Verdiglione weighed heavily on
the credibility of psychoanalysts nationwide. In fact, it is no secret that

Verdiglione's scandals and widely publicized unethical behaviour prompted the kind of public and political outrage that hastened, if indeed it did not spur, the passage of Law #56.[3]

It is important to note in this context that the Italian Psychoanalytic Society – at the time, the only national institution affiliated with the International Psychoanalytic Association – strongly opposed the passage of the law. What was at stake from the start was the Society's own autonomy and integrity, given the fact that its prestigious training would be forced to close its doors to any would-be analyst whose education did not conform with the law's exclusionary provisions. Indeed, with the passage of Law #56, the Italian Psychoanalytic Society, as well as the few but select psychoanalytic psychotherapy programmes existing in Italy, were no longer free to accept as candidates anyone not trained as a psychologist or psychiatrist. Rather, they could, but their candidates thus trained would not be legally entitled to practise as psychotherapists at the end of their long and arduous apprenticeship.[4]

Thus, while not formally opting – until only recently, and only after a decade-long debate over the law's implications for its membership and future – to restrict its admission policies, the Italian Psychoanalytic Society found itself in the throes of a most peculiar identity crisis. While inspired to preserve something of the distinctiveness of the psychoanalytic tradition, the Society had to contend with the fact that a significant part of its 'lay' membership – which had always practised psychoanalysis without being trained in either psychology or medicine – was now looking to be grandfathered into the National Registry of Psychologists, via a series of accommodating provisions contained in the law.[5] What this meant, in essence, was that the American model had won. For all sakes and purposes, the most exclusionary and prejudicial aspects of the history of lay analysis in the United States – where the American Psychoanalytic and American Psychological Associations, for years at odds in their respective claims to the 'territory' of psychoanalytic training, had only some years before joined forces in their efforts to close off the field to non-IPA institutes still committed to Freud's 1926 vision of lay analysis – had been assumed, in Italy, to reflect the reality of law.[6] Indeed, the mad rush towards registration on the part of the country's psychoanalysts instituted a situation whereby, in point of fact, one could not, did not, and for the most part would not practise psychoanalysis if not as a nationally licensed psychotherapist: a title now conferred only upon certification

by a state-certified training institute, and only after prior licensing as a
psychologist or psychiatrist

> We believe that one important aspect of this transformation was an
> identification with state-sanctioned respectability, perhaps further
> galvanized by prior states of rebelliousness towards that same state.
> The fact that such professionalization of psychotherapy was right
> and long overdue only fed the sense of a righteous advance. And
> while the textures of righteousness are exceedingly complex in
> contemporary America, [one] interesting strand [is] the profession-
> alization of once-radical therapists. (Bollas and Sundelson, 1995,
> p. 115)

What Bollas and Sundelson say about the American stampede towards
credentials in the 1970s could just as easily be applied to post-1968,
post-Red Brigade, post-Christian Democratic Italy, a country where the
once-rebellious Left had come to power with sweeping regulatory
policies which left people confusing its lawmakers with traditional
standard-bearers of the authoritarian Right. An anecdote may help to
illustrate my point.

I was not always sensitive, I must admit, to the political implications
of licences and registries. As often happens, it was personal experience
that sensitized me to many of the issues I now write about. When,
after years of practising as a lay psychoanalyst in the United States, I
first planned to move to Italy, I was invited by the President of one of
the country's foremost psychoanalytic psychotherapy institutes to apply
for admission to its training programme. For several reasons, I determined that I would be well served, in a new country, by a refresher
course of sorts. As becoming part of an established psychoanalytic
culture and community was indeed a welcome prospect, I accepted the
President's invitation and travelled one spring to Italy from Philadelphia, for the sole purpose of the Society's admission interviews.
Months later, after interviewing with three of the more prominent
members of the Society, I was told in confidence by the committee's
foremost representative that the new law had precluded my membership from the very start – hence the rejection of my request to be
admitted to the Society's training. While congratulating me on a 'most
impressive' presentation – which, in the words of my counterpart,
'would have easily qualified any other candidate' – she also expressed

astonishment and earnest regret over the fact that I should have been
invited to apply to the programme in the first place. For while a
practising psychoanalyst, I was clearly not yet qualified in Italy (i.e.
licensed, or registered) as a psychologist.

[for] some psychoanalysts, who do often try to find some prior
category for their discipline, considering it either as a science, a
form of psychology, a kind of philosophy of the mind, a theology,
or a poetics, its characteristics are too overdetermined to be so
classified. (Bollas and Sundelson, 1995)

To say that analysis is the voice of stones; to say that what makes a
psychoanalysis are the flowers in the analyst's office, and that they,
the flowers, are at one and the same time both patient and analyst,
is still not enough. (Cesare Viviani, *Il sogno dell'interpretazione*)

As I have already suggested, Law #56 does not explicitly regulate
psychoanalysis in Italy. The law, in fact, makes no specific reference
whatsoever to psychoanalysis. The most astounding aspect of the law's
implementation, however, has been the near-total acquiescence of
the psychoanalytic community with its policies of registration, and
the mutation of practically all of the country's psychoanalysts into
psychologists.[7]

Even as concerned psychoanalysts in America call out for the necessary rediscovery of psychoanalysis as an independent profession[8] –
distinct and separate from its (adoptive) parents – in Italy that
independence has been all but surrendered. No better, and sadder,
example, I believe, testifies to the perversion – or better, to the ill-
concealed murder and hasty burial – of Lacan's fundamental question:
'What is the analyst's desire?' But while the perversions of the Italian
situation are particularly vexing, and return us to the lessons of that
other essential play of Sophocles, *Antigone*, they are happily not
without their critics. For the sake of brevity, I will limit myself to
introducing the work of one such voice, that of Cesare Viviani, a
Jungian analyst also influenced by Lacan. What follow are some
scattered but fertile excerpts, in my translation, from the author's far-
reaching critique of the regulatory attitude, articulated in his book *Il
sogno dell'interpretazione: Una critica radicale all'ideologia psicanalitica*.[9]
(All italics are the author's own.)

Psychoanalysis is not adherence to a code, or to a technique. (The analytic event cannot be analyzed or evaluated from the outside, on the basis of knowledge of a code: one canot know if there is *analysis* in an analytic relationship; if the *inevitable*, the *irreducible*, happens or not. One must accept this impossibility of objectification. Anyone seeking to 'clarify', or 'specify', or to 'distinguish', is in the market for guarantees. Only from within an analytic experience is it possible to know when *analysis* takes place – something which necessarily varies with individual experience. It is impossible, from the outside, to say what has taken place.)

Analysis is the space between codes. It is the precision of the *inevitable* and of the *illegible*, that regrettably and all-too-often gets confused with the precision of a code. (1989, p. 67)

The *experience of the irreducible* cannot be spoken. The relationship between this experience and consciousness cannot be spoken (i.e., is illegible). In any description of this relationship ... inheres a pressure to specify and clarify those relational possibilities which, once mediated, force the irreducible into a box: this, in an attempt to define, albeit negatively, both the *irreducible* and its locus. (ibid., p. 72)

The most seductive attempt to lure the irreducible into a box and subject the practice of psychoanalysis to the sanction of a code was, of course, Italy's institution of its National Registry and Roster. In Viviani's words:

A registry ... presupposes and guarantees the certainty (even if the certainty is never definitive) of a form of knowledge 'objectified' and formalized; it thus reflects the social exigency of a specialized control over professional practice. (ibid., p. 50)

[the soul of] psychoanalysis cannot attain to a registry: the experience of the *relative-irreducible* is neither determined nor measurable. Nor can the experience of the illegible be specified: it escapes generalizations, control, exams. It cannot be 'registered' because it cannot become a matter of 'objectivity'.

As a result, this condition can be assimilated to that of artistic labor (for which any and all 'controls' are exercised within the context of 'personal' relationships, and not by any professional organ: poets have no registry!). Or, it can be assimilated to conditions pertaining to religious experience (where the latter is free of institutional constraints). (ibid., p. 51)

To say that art and religious experience do not allow for codified regulation (but only for the illegible *order* of loss and the uncodifiable order of human relations), and are thus not subject to any professional 'ordering', may not suffice to convince my detractors: since both realities are conventionally considered 'incapable of harming the health and life of one's neighbors'. Let us then ask ourselves: who regulates, or who could ever hope to regulate, love relations? And above all, what school teaches or might teach parents how to treat their children? (ibid., p. 63)

And finally:

it is interesting to see how 'psychology' ... has always been on good terms with scientific discourse, but diffident about the *extraneous* nature of psychoanalysis.[10]

In the present-day context, legislative pressures seem to be accentuating these ties, as 'psychology' leans more and more in the direction of the 'object', and less and less towards the 'subject'. That is to say, psychology moves increasingly in the direction of certainties, of mediations and institutions; and is always less inclined towards the *irreducible*. (ibid., p. 68)

And so on. Already in the United States we have witnessed the deleterious effects of corporativism in the field of psychotherapy. Much of the field, in ideological if not *de facto* collusion with the licensing boards of the so-called mental health professions, has become an *industry* where the therapeutic relationship is subject to the intrusive management, oversight, and indeed the approval of HMO and insurance bureaucracies, interested more in diagnostic codes and per capita session revenue than anything like the experiential fruits of psychoanalysis. It is becoming increasingly apparent that Italy is headed in a similar direction – in part as a result of the perversions of Law #56, but equally as a result of the demise of a genuine lay psychoanalysis, perpetrated by law, but endorsed – albeit, perhaps, unwittingly – by a host of accomplices.

* * *

Afterthought. Is it a coincidence, I wonder, that the future of psycho-analysis everywhere may well depend on its reconfiguration along the lines of what Michel Foucault termed *anti-sciences*? On its redefinition, indeed, on the paradoxical recognition of its own modern-day status as a *subjugated knowledge*, of which Foucault – a staunch critic of psycho-analysis – invoked the insurrection?[11] Time, only time, will tell... But our fifty minutes are almost up.

NOTES

1. Since writing this chapter, the situation in the United Kingdom has changed dramatically. There too, a very strong bid for *statutory registration* of the coun-try's myriad psychotherapists has engulfed the professional community (including its psychoanalytic segments), and is being slowly but steadily pushed through Parliament.

2. I maintain here the distinction between 'academic' and clinical psychology since, for the most part, Italian university programmes do not provide an extensive clinical component as part of their training. Hence the strengthened ties – and the distinctly Italian 'arrangements' – between the university system and the government-recognized psychotherapy training institutes.

3.   Verdiglione was not selling God or karma or phony stocks or Florida swamps or any of the charlatan's classic offerings. He was a Cagliostro, selling a new kind of protection. Sometimes he called it 'psychoanalysis' and sometimes 'culture' and sometimes 'the word', and after he was arrested (*and sentenced – on charges ranging from extortion to fraud*) and decided that the state had coopted the word ... he called it 'the cipher'. What made him special was that nobody, not the analysts and their patients or the prosecutors and the judges or the French *philosophes* who wrote letters defending him to the Italian Presi-dent and sponsored an appeal on his behalf to the European Court of Human Rights – nobody, possibly not even Armando Verdiglione himself, could say for sure what he was talking about.
   This excerpt, from Jane Kramer's *Europeans* (New York: Farrar, Strauss & Giroux, 1988, pp. 58–77) is part of a marvellous portrait of Verdiglione, as well as of the background contexts of Italian psychoanalysis and of the Milanese social scene in which Verdiglione operated and thrived.

4. In its opposition to the law, the Italian Psychoanalytic Society did manage to have omitted from the legislation any use of the terms 'psychoanalysis' and 'psycho-analyst'. In this way, the discipline and the specificities of its training were arguably, and at least nominally, protected from any state appropriation. However, this left open the possibility that precisely because the title 'psychoanalyst' is not one regu-lated by the state, almost anybody – including people with no link whatsoever to the traditional and institutional forms of psychoanalysis represented by the Italian Psychoanalytic Society – can claim to be one. Derived from such a claim, of course, is also a presumed right to practise 'psychoanalysis'. To the best of my knowledge, however, to date the claim has been tested only sporadically and, needless to say,

unsuccessfully in a lower court. Such is the overarching grip of the psychology lobby and legislation that I too, five years after moving to Italy, had to find a lawful way to be registered as a psychologist and psychotherapist in order to practise.

5. I find it ironic that one of the founding fathers of Italian psychoanalysis, Cesare Musatti, was a mathematician by training.

6. For a balanced history of the American controversy, albeit one written from within its institutional confines, see Robert Wallerstein's *Lay Analysis: Life Inside the Controvery* (Hillsdale, NJ: Analytic Press, 1998). Paradoxically, while the American situation is such that trainings affiliated with the International Psychoanalytic Association (IPA) do occasionally admit candidates with backgrounds, say, in the humanities or social sciences (as also happens in the British Psycho-Analytic Society), this possibility is altogether and absolutely foreclosed in Italy. Indeed, as I hope to have made clear, *no psychotherapist whatsoever* – of any ilk or extraction – can come to the field except via psychology or psychiatry.

7. It should be said that in their forced compromises with the law, the training programmes of both the Italian Psychoanalytic Society and the Italian Psychoanalytic Association (a splinter group also affiliated with the IPA) have retained – in what has become a jungle of over 200 state-regulated trainings for psychotherapists – a characteristically demanding structure which at least doubles the basic four-year commitment required of trainees elsewhere.

8. I refer here, for example, to the efforts of free-standing, non-IPA training institutes (affiliated mostly with the New York-based National Association for the Advancement of Psychoanalysis, or NAAP) to have psychoanalysis recognized as an independent profession and their accrediting body recognized by the United States Council on Postsecondary Education and the Department of Education. The first of these efforts has met with some legislative success (i.e., in the States of Vermont and New Jersey, where psychoanalysts are now licensed as such), whereas attempts to be recognized by the Council on Postsecondary Education and the US Department of Education were defeated in the 1990s, mostly because of strong opposition to NAAP's application on the part of the American Psychological and the American Psychoanalytic Associations. I do realize, of course, that by their very nature such claims for state recognition invite the very risks of subjection and collusion that I otherwise denounce throughout this chapter.

9. Genoa: Costa & Nolan, 1989. In English the book's title would read: *The Dream of Interpretation: A Radical Critique of Psychoanalytic Ideology*. Note that Viviani's book was published in 1989, the year in which Law #56 was passed. The book was instead conceived and written amid the flurry of cultural and legislative debates leading up to the law's drafting and passage.

10. Consider the following words of Mario Bertini, former president of the Italian Psychological Society, at the time of the law's passage: 'The problem is the cultural and scientific safeguarding of (both psychology and) psychotherapy. *If the latter wants to stay glued to the perimeter of the sciences*, it will have to reroot itself in its own humus – which can only be that of psychology' (emphasis added). The assumption is, clearly, that only the ideological domain of the sciences – of which psychology is now a province – can validate the fringe fiefdom of psychotherapy. (Unless, that is, psychotherapists are so ridiculously 'naïve' as not to want the legitimation of science.) Incorporation, then, is, fundamentally, the only safeguard not merely against 'wild' practitioners, but against the uncodified knowledges that psychoanalysis invites. In Viviani's words: 'The fear of an indiscriminate psychoanalysis (no longer discriminated, it becomes available to all), is not tied to the "fate" of the patient, but to the spreading of a condition of autonomy.' (*Il sogno dell'interpretazione*, p. 63) See also Luigi Zoja's 'Analysis: Growth or Cure?' Chapter 6 in this volume.

11. 'What [a genealogical project] really does is to entertain the claims to attention of
    local, discontinuous, disqualified, illegitimate knowledges against the claims of a
    unitary body of theory which would filter, hierarchise and order them in the name
    of some true knowledge and some arbitrary idea of what constitues a science and its
    objects.' See Michel Foucault, *Power/Knowledge* (New York: Pantheon, 1977).

PART IV

Challenging Normalization in Psychoanalysis

17

The Possibilities of Pleasure
A Conversation with Adam Phillips

A 'pragmatic aesthete', as he calls himself, noted author Adam Phillips is one of the more provocative and engaging voices in contemporary psychoanalysis. A genuine descendant of the British Independent tradition, Phillips' dazzling essays and intriguing reflections on psycho-analysis have both returned it to its literary ancestry and confronted it, full-force, with the concerns and contradictions of contemporary society.

Anthony Molino: You open *Terrors and Experts*[1] with a quote from Andrew Marvell's 'The King's Speech',[2] where he writes: 'I am a changeling.' Yet the changeling that is the unconscious seems continually to provoke authoritarian, or *fixed*, understandings among the schools and 'experts' committed to its study. What do you make of this general picture, and what are its implications for the practice and politics of psychoanalysis?

Adam Phillips: This is a big question. I think that there is something inevitably, potentially authoritarian, or just authoritative, in formulation. I think that once we institutionalize psychoanalysis, there will invariably be people whom we trust as authoritative voices about this thing or practice called 'psychoanalysis'. But this is the place where Winnicott is very useful, because Winnicott's preoccupation, it seems to me, is not so much with the given thing but with what one can make of it ... not prioritizing the value of the analyst's interpretation so much as the use the patient can make of it. By the same token, I think the risk of an authoritative statement becoming authoritarian occurs when it's unusable, when people can't make something of their own of it, when they can't use it to dream something up. What we're really talking about, then, is the way people use and transmit so-called knowledge, or so-called information, or so-called technique. Both what their words invite, and what, by way of response, they can enjoy.

AM: Later in the book, you seem to speak to this same phenomenon
when you write: 'Psychoanalysts run the risk of believing there is a
King's English of the psyche and everybody is, or should be, speaking
it.' Is it accurate to suggest that there is something akin to a totalitarian
impulse that much of our profession is all-too-ready to accommodate?

AP: I wouldn't want to put it that extremely, but I think that the
anxiety, the self-doubt and the uncertainty that are integral to what
we're doing prompt people to extreme solutions. It's not surprising that
in something as uncertain as psychoanalysis, people are drawn to conversion experiences or to forms of idolatry, because there is a lot of anxiety
in this game. To call it *totalitarian*, however, ups the stakes too much,
and the risk is that if we start speaking like that we start creating
unnecessary antagonisms. I think that what we need to do in psychoanalysis is to see the points in theory, or the points in its institutionaliza-
tion, at which people become authoritarian, or become something that
makes us think of them as totalitarian. We need to see what it is at that
moment that makes people feel the need to be absolutely convinced of
something, or to have other people agree with them in some absolute
sense ... because in a way you could see the apparently totalitarian
moments as the most interesting ones. They're the moments when there
really is something profound and powerful and conflictual going on, that
create a pre-emptive strike called an authoritative statement.

AM: You ask in your preface to *Terrors and Experts*: 'If the unconscious is that which does not fit in, why has it been so difficult to sustain
non-compliant versions of psychoanalysis?' For me, this begs a prior
question: what are the forces that have exacted compliance? Compliance
with what? And why has it been so difficult for alternative versions and
visions to take root?

AP: I really feel inadequate to answer these questions, because I
haven't got an overriding view of the matter. If we take the situation in
Britain, which I know at least a little about, you will find a lot of prejudice about Kleinian psychoanalysts and Kleinian psychoanalysis. It
seems to me that one of the things the Kleinians represent – insofar as
there could be such a monolithic group – is the tyrannical parents.
There is a sense in which compliance starts at home, if you like ... and I
think what there is to comply with has to do with the fear of what will
happen if we don't comply. That is to say, there are fears of catastrophe

here, imaginings of some kind of catastrophic primal scene. The scenario is one in which, if I don't comply with somebody I need, I lose the relationship with them. So, at some fundamental level, if I want to become a psychoanalyst, I have to abide to some extent by the rules of the game, otherwise I don't know whether I'm a psychoanalyst or not. This poses an inevitable conflict, as the question becomes: at what point is something an innovation? Or at what point is it a change of the game? What do you have to do to stop being called a psychoanalyst, by the owners of psychoanalysis?

I think it's perfectly fair enough that psychoanalytic trainings should set out their game. That is to say, if you want to call yourself a psycho-analyst trained by our institution, then these are the things you have to abide by and believe in. The question then becomes how people deal with dissent. I don't want a situation in which dissent is dealt with in some absolute, dismissive way. But I do think it's inevitable for parameters to exist. Beyond a certain point you are no longer playing our game. It's suddenly turned from draughts to chess, but then you have to go somewhere else to play it. Ultimately, I think there's a lot of belly-aching and spurious rebellion that goes on in relation to psychoanalytic institutes, where adults are simply contracting into a specific game with specific parameters. At that point at which the game becomes unaccep-table, one should go and do something else.

Now it's not all that simple of course, because not only are there strong emotionally empowered beliefs and convictions about authority, or what it means to live a good life, and so on. There's also a very powerful economic factor. That is to say, if I want to practise as a psychoanalyst, I have to get this qualification. In this light people have to develop what we might politely call compromises, and what less politely we might call false selves. I think in order to do a psychoanalytic training, you have to have a repertoire of false-self solutions available to you.

AM: Your comments lead nicely to my next question. You conclude your preface to *Terrors and Experts* with the following words: 'The psychoanalyst and her so-called patient share a project. The psycho-analyst, that is to say, must ask herself not, Am I being a good analyst? . . . But, What kind of person do I want to be?' Is this project, then, concerned as much with ethics as with desire – which you yourself define as 'morally equivocal'? And how does the analyst's own answer to the question conse-quentially involve her patient in what you call a *shared* project?

AP: I think that desire is inextricable from questions of ethics. In a way, it is the ethical imagination that constructs the notion of desire ... that we can't separate what we want from people from our obligations to them. The very word *desire* has become a bit of a free-floating counter, since morality only seems to make sense if we have, as it were, a counter-force to it, something amoral, or that undermines our ethical positions. But this is only if we think of ethics as a monument, rather than as an ongoing process, in which we are continually coming to localized accommodations – within all our relationships – about what we want to do together and what we want to be for each other. I think it's both the worst kind of psychoanalytic theory that glamorizes a certain kind of ruthless unconcern, and the best kind of psychoanalysis. We're never going to be able to avoid, nor should we be trying to, the question of what kind of people we want to be. Our ideas about desire are integral or subsumed by that question. For example, you might say a lot of modern people ... the kind who might read a book such as this one ... will want to think of themselves as having or being involved in something they call desire. I think it's a very exciting, exhilarating notion. But it's not some kind of deep truth about the human condition: it's an historically and culturally located 'regulative fiction'.

AM: In contrast to the inherited, and still dominant figure, of an Enlightenment Freud committed to a project of self-mastery through knowledge, you play in *Terrors and Experts* with the idea of a 'post-Freudian Freud' intent on questioning 'the very idea of the self as an object of knowledge'. In your words: 'The post-Freudian Freud suggests that the project of self-knowledge is itself the problem, the symptom masquerading as the cure ... [P]sychoanalysis can now help us unlearn this modern religion of selfhood.' What is it that *now* enables psycho-analysis, and her patients, to forsake an idolatry of the self – especially within a culture that is ideologically invested in supporting that idolatry?

AP: Concerning the possibility that we might want to undo the idea of the self, I prefer to put the question pragmatically. What do we use the idea of a self to do? For example, we need a self to vote with, but selves are not always useful in love affairs or in writing. It seems to me that a lot of descriptions and formulations about pathology have to do with the creation of certain kinds of reified internal monuments. It is as though people become addicted to a version of themselves. They begin to have convictions that they are a certain kind of person. That's what a symptom is. I mean, if I'm agoraphobic, I'm the sort of person who can't go out. This is, so to speak, a *truth* about me – until I can see it as merely an aspect of who I am. For those of us daunted nowadays by all the people existing in a state of fanatical conviction about one thing or another, it might be quite important to think up or dream up alternative ways of being, alternative versions to fundamentalism, whether psycho-analytic or religious. It might be quite important to produce a counter-culture that questions states of conviction, and explores what we're using states of conviction to do, why we might want to be convinced of things, and what it is that we find in states of certainty. One thing you might say is that there is, potentially, a form of megalomania in such states. At best, of course, there's also a form of political commitment. This is to say, then, that to question states of conviction does not necessarily presume an absence of belief. The issue, rather, involves finding a way of believing that is not a form of domination, primarily of oneself. Belief is a form of cruelty.

AM: What has been the price, in your view, of the inherited Enlight-enment model of the psychoanalyst as scientist? At what cost have other models also present in Freudian theory – you yourself list the lover, the comedian and the mystic – been repressed, and how can they be recov-ered, not only theoretically, but in the practice of psychoanalysis?

AP: I'm not anti-science. What I am 'anti' is the idea that there is one dominant criterion of value which is, broadly speaking, scientific. I think science is for people who love science, and they should do it. The risk is that it does tend to occlude or make the other possible criteria look rather trivial or silly. I think it's very interesting how little mysticism there is in contemporary scientific theory, as well as in psychoanalytic theory. I think psychoanalysis is, in a way, intrinsically mystical or bordering on what would once have been called mystical experience ... I would much prefer a world of lovers, comedians and mystics to a world of scientists who find such people beside the point ...

My sense of the pleasures of science is that they are too much about the pleasure of consensus, and I suppose I'm more interested in the possibility of shareable private languages – which is obviously a contra-diction in terms. I'm more interested in the possibilities of pleasure: of sensual and erotic pleasures. It seems to me that what the comedian and the lover and the mystic all keep very close to is a notion of the erotic. I don't really know what that word means, but it conjures for me something that's to do with a certain kind of ease. It's not conflict-free, but is somehow akin to a joke ... a joke is the easiest pleasure in the world ... getting a joke, for me, would be the model of a good interpretation ...

What interests me about mysticism is that it is unavoidably preoccupied with certain kinds of intensity. That is to say, the project in mysticism is not to escape from or to cure the intensity; minimally, the project is to acknowledge that intensity, but it also involves finding representations for it and of it, to bring those intensities into the shared world. That, for me, is obviously something wonderful ... We can't help but be lovers in the broadest possible sense. But I would want erotic love to be our model of what it is to love things and people. I think the clichés about science, about its detachment, its domination and capacity for exploitation, are really very frightening: partly because they're true, partly because my guess is that they stop us from looking at the actual erotic components of scientific inquiry. And of course this is where Freud is quite interesting. When Freud talks about infantile curiosity, that's where we are as scientists. I would like scientists to give us accounts of the infantile nature of their curiosity and enjoyments, rather than to be producing apparently superordinate or transcendent accounts of the way the world is. I'm not at all interested in the way the world is. I'm very, very interested in what people make of the world. Psychoanalysis, unlike science and religion, does not offer us something to merely submit to.

AM: What do you see, then, as the pleasures or erotics that science brings to psychoanalysis? Or why does psychoanalysis remain so captivated by the erotic lure of the scientific paradigm?

AP: I think fantasies of prestige are erotically exciting. If one lives in a culture that is dominated by scientific prestige, where science defines what real knowledge is, and where scientists are the people who possess that knowledge, you can see the implications. But if we were to drop the idea of wanting to know the way the world is, we wouldn't be that interested in scientists. Personally, I'm more interested in local knowledge. It's much more interesting for me to know how to get to work in the morning than it is to know whether the sun goes around the earth or not. For example, I think that space travel is almost totally uninteresting. Sure, I enjoy the pictures of what it's like up there. It's absolutely astonishing that there are universes as big as ours, and that it's all infinite. But this, for me, is of the order of day-dream. It's like knowledge about evolution – very interesting, but about which we can do nothing. We're just going to evolve. Knowing about evolution, in a sense, is rather gratifying, because it shows us something absurd about knowing things ... because whether you know about evolution or not you are going to evolve. You can't start evolving differently. I also think we underestimate how much we take on trust. That is to say, there's a very interesting and widespread election of scientists as people who know things. And yet we're clearly not the ones going over their experiments. Most of us couldn't possibly do so. But there is a very powerful idealization of people whose knowledge we couldn't possibly possess, or of whose knowledge we couldn't possibly trace the process. They're like magical parents. We can't possibly imagine what it would be like to know what they know, or to get to what they've gotten to. I think that's very exciting.

AM: On the matter of science: given the entwined histories of psycho-analysis and its founder, the persistence of the Enlightenment Freud, and the invaluable contributions of studies in infant and child development, what do you see as the role of science in the configuration of a psychoanalysis amenable to the 'post-Freudian' Freud?

AP: I really think it's important for people to follow their curiosity. Some people, for all sorts of reasons, most of which they're not going to know about, will find scientific inquiry fascinating, and it will be preoccupying for them. It will engage them on some very deep level. Those are the people who should do science, and they should be part of a multiple conversation about what's going on in the culture at large. I want and like scientific stories when I can understand them, when they feed into the kind of conversation that I imagine for a culture. I don't at all envision a demise of science, nor would I want people to stop doing science. To the contrary. I would want people who love science to do it, and to feed their findings back into a public discourse. But I also would like people to feel free not to be impressed by it, or to submit so readily to it.

AM: To be more specific, can science co-exist with, and contribute to, a psychoanalysis no longer invested in the exhaltation of knowledge? Where traditional notions of *cure* are similarly called into question?

AP: I think so, because some of the most interesting theorizing is being done in the philosophy of science. One of the things that science brings in its wake is questions about its own project, so that it inevitably raises all sorts of issues about what we do when we're knowing, how we go about knowing, and what it is that knowledge is in the service of. When you read Roy Porter, or John Forrester, or Steven Shapin, science seems irresistibly intriguing. This, I think, is one of the values of science, which leads me to believe that those people who know about this form of knowing might be very good at telling us about the process itself and the motivations for engaging it. For this reason I wish there were more autobiographies by scientists, or even biographies of scientists. I am not of the opinion, however, that we should start believing that infant obser-vation is going to tell us about what people are really like. While some accounts are really lyrical and interesting and evocative, most of them, I think, are fantastically banal and boring. But of course, these are prejudi-cial tastes, and clearly there are lots of people who are ready to swear by it all.

AM: The issue of science and the kind of knowledge it fosters would seem to bear directly on the question of consensus. As you put it: 'It is the Enlightenment Freud that always pushes for consensus, that is willing a community of more or less shared knowledge ... The psychoanalyst is an expert on the ways in which the patient pretends to be an expert on himself; the ways, that is, in which he gravitates towards consensus, towards fitting in.' It's a short leap, it would seem, from consensus to what I call 'normalization'. Would you agree?

AP: Yes. In a way the purpose of consensus must be to create fantasies of normality. The use of fantasies, or standards, of normality is that it enables us to see difference. At its most coercive, it enables us to see deviation. I think we have to be very careful about what we're using our norms to do. That is to say, if they're coercive, if they demand our agreement, they seem to me to be dangerous. If they function as possible guidelines, then they can be useful.

We should be enabling people to tolerate disagreement. There's a terrific idealization of agreement, which I see as an idealization of togetherness and symbiosis. Instead, to tolerate difference means, poten-tially, tolerating other people's envy. One of the things consensus tries to do is create a group of people who, by agreeing with each other, need not be envious of or competitive with each other. I don't think that's a bad aim at all, but I do think it's never going to be the whole story ... There is a pressure on people to abide by the cultural consensus, because we all inevitably want to be part of the culture. Any cultural group is going to somehow be based on trust, or on fantasies of shared knowledge. It's not that I think there shouldn't be such fantasies; indeed, these are essential to any group. What's crucial, however, is the kind of difference a group allows, and what its relationship is to the people who speak that difference ...

Clearly, on one end of the spectrum, you've got scapegoating. Personally, I'd like to live in a world without scapegoats, but a world without scapegoats means a world with more conflict. We'd have to assume that eventuality, because we will get crosser with each other if we stop scapegoating people. Still, I think there are a lot of pleasures in conflict. It's underrated. One of the things we might be doing, then, is to enable people to tolerate fear.

AM: Similarly, do you see political implications deriving from the particular way in which the analyst deploys her *expertise*: i.e. whether she does so in an Enlightenment or post-Freudian scheme of things?

AP: Yes, I think the risk is that if the analyst needs to be believed or agreed with, the analysis recreates a certain kind of childhood trauma, of a relationship in which if you don't comply or agree then you're abandoned or rejected or punished. That, to me, seems a bad sadomasochistic model of a relationship. But, there is, of course, a problem here that psychoanalysis makes very vivid: if there are such things as resistances, and it seems to me that there are, then the analyst doesn't merely capitulate when the patient disagrees. That is to say, the analyst has to be tenacious without being authoritarian. And there might have to come a point, at times, where you as the analyst say, 'We disagree about this. I think this is what it means.' Or, 'I think it's about you and you think differently. I don't need you, however, to agree with me.' The analysis then continues despite the disagreement, but we do need to put the difference on the table, without having to decide now, or necessarily ever, which one of us is right. In fact, the question of right and wrong is exactly the problem. What we have to see is who can produce a story, or a version, that we can make something of that we want.

NOTES

1. A. Phillips, *Terrors and Experts*. London: Faber & Faber, 1995.
2. A. Marvell, 'The King's Speech'. In F. Kermode and K. Walker (eds) *Andrew Marvell*. Oxford: Oxford University Press, 1990.

18

Suffering from Biobabble
Searching for a Science of Subjectivity

Polly Young-Eisendrath

In the last two decades of the twentieth century, our popular and scientific accounts of human suffering have been inching their way towards a new form of scientific reductionism: a knee-jerk biological determinism that I call 'biobabble'. This is the widespread tendency to use terms (e.g. adaptation) from various aspects of the biological sciences to explain human actions and moods without even a reasonable understanding of the term, the science, the associated theory (or lack of it), and/or the target of explanation. Biobabble names biological, evolutionary and physical processes as the primary causes for human traits and behaviours from the undesirable (like alcoholism and schizophrenia) to the sublime (like altruism and happiness). In my view, biobabble confuses and harms us in our attempts to understand and alleviate human suffering, both on an individual and a communal level.

By the term 'suffering', I mean specifically the Buddhist notion of *dukkha* which is typically translated as suffering. *Dukkha* literally refers to a state of being off-centre or out-of-balance, like a bone slightly out of its socket or a wheel riding off its axle. I will use the word 'suffering' in this chapter to mean a state of being in which we are out of kilter because of a subjective disturbance that may be as mild as momentary frustration or as severe as a psychotic state.

Buddhist discourses on *dukkha* are wide-ranging and deal with both physical and mental suffering. I am referring here to the mental anguish that we create through our perseverations, distortions, evaluations and internal commentary. Much of this anguish is rooted in our conscious or unconscious desires to have things go our own way, and the resultant feelings of humiliation and despair when they do not. This suffering is distinct from the pain and adversity that are inescapable and out of our control. Differentiating suffering from pain allows us to address the aspect of human adversity that is potentially under the control of an individual and can be ameliorated through a change in awareness or consciousness.

Such suffering arises from desires and intentions expressed through emotional habit patterns that Western psychology calls 'unconscious' conflicts, deficits, complexes and defences, as well as through impulsive actions, addictions, cravings and demands. The arguments laid down by psychodynamic theories are similar to ancient Buddhist accounts of suffering. But the importance given to unconscious conflicts, desires and meanings in Western psychology has been rapidly shrinking, as biobabble has spread. The notion that people are responsible for their actions is disappearing from the popular imagination, along with the conviction that people can change their behaviour by changing their minds.

Twentieth-century scientific achievements have largely defeated the old metaphysics of Western Judaeo-Christian religions. Widely regarded as a sign that humanity has grown up from a childhood in which human powers (agency, rationality, creativity, etc.) were erroneously projected into an enchanted animistic world, enlightened secularism has had massive effects on our moral and ethical functioning. From a scientific perspective, we are now free to use the previously projected powers to understand ourselves and our accountability, responsibility and limitations as agents in our own lives in the world. And yet we can just as easily aggrandize ourselves and believe that *we* are now the gods and goddesses of the past, and should bring life and death under our control. And/or we can avoid all accountability for our own actions and simply continue to project these vitalizing powers into things that are largely outside our responsibility and control (e.g. genetic predispositions).

Science offers its own metaphysics that largely excludes human meaning. Indeed, we educated Westerners put our faith in almost every 'scientific' explanation whether or not we have any real knowledge of what is being explained or how it works. This in itself is not necessarily a problem; humans must employ a mythology, or bigger story, in order to know how to perceive 'reality'. And yet, if we are to make use of our powers of rationality and science, we must examine the social and cultural consequences of our current beliefs. Merely replacing the metaphysics of religion with the metaphysics of science does not bring us closer to truth or knowledge. And most people suspect that there *are* ethical consequences of our scientific metaphysics which have torn the social fabric supporting communities and families.

BIOBABBLE, BUDDHISM AND COMPASSION

As a clinical teacher in a department of psychiatry, I often feel overwhelmed by a *Zeitgeist* that promotes the mystique of the mighty gene, genetic 'predispositions', and biochemical explanations (not coherent theories) of mood and emotional disorders. As a psychoanalyst, psychologist and psychotherapist (and ordinary citizen), I have been shocked at the recent popular shift away from personal accountability for our actions and motives to vague organic explanations (e.g. I am depressed because of my genes) that eradicate the complexity of personal meaning and responsibility.

Whether or not individuals understand what they are saying, when they speak biobabble they eliminate the role of meaning and intentions in the development of societies and people. In this story the 'master molecule' of the gene, falsely endowed with an autonomous power, overrides the effects of personal desires, intentions and actions. The term 'gene' or 'adaptation' has replaced intention, purpose and morality in most popular psychological and psychiatric accounts of the ways in which people thrive or fail. All of our struggles, such as finding a mate or becoming a compassionate person, can be recast now in terms of their supposed advantages for our genes. Speaking biobabble, we sound like our genes are propagating themselves through us, and that *our* lives are meaningless without knowing what our genes are doing.

Many people who seek psychotherapy or analysis now come with such vague theories as 'I am depressed because I inherited depression from my mother's family' or 'I have an addiction because my genetic history is loaded for substance abuse'. These people continue to feel hopeless *after* they have taken the appropriate medications and comforted themselves with the company of their ancestors because they still suffer. This can be addressed through effective psychotherapy, but for those who never consider psychotherapy – and most people do not – these vague organic explanations block any desire to understand the personal motives and meanings that lead to their suffering.

A great deal of harm has already occurred as a result of our widespread biobabble. This is not to say that we should disregard the important advances that genetics and biochemistry have provided in helping us understand and medicate both physical illnesses and psychiatric conditions. It is to say that we need to be clear about the consequences of embracing an ideology that eliminates an account of our own intentions and actions in explaining our difficulties.

Unique among religions, Buddhism is rooted in empirical accounts and objective methods. Indeed, Buddhism is quite comfortable with scientific knowledge because many of its practices are grounded in dispassionate observation. In addition, the Buddhist psychology of *Abhidharma* has developed systematic empirical investigations of the roots of human suffering and the nature of human subjectivity. Buddhism offers a unique opportunity for those in the human services to become acquainted with methods of studying subjectivity in ways that respect science, but are not inclined towards physical reductionism.

Moreover, Buddhism offers many skilful means of increasing our experience of subjective freedom in everyday life, based on a theory of the interdependent, impermanent, finite and changing nature of reality which is remarkably consonant with Western post-modern philosophy of science. I believe that Buddhism and psychodynamic psychologies must, in the next decade or two, assist each other in diminishing the effects of biobabble by embracing a viable, scientific approach to the study of human suffering.

In a symposium, published as *Consciousness at the Crossroads* (Houshmand *et al.*, 1999), the Dalai Lama met with prominent Western proponents of contemporary neuroscience. In the Afterword, one of the editors reiterates a question posed to the neuroscientists by the Dalai Lama of whether strictly materialistic explanations of suffering will 'critically undermine love and compassion?' (ibid., p. 173). The neuroscientists claim that a person is *not* a brain (malfunctioning or not), and should not be treated as such. And yet their biological determinism, used to explain mood and emotional disorders, does not include any account of the 'whole person' that could become a focus of compassion. Such a materialist account in Western scientific language takes the unit of the individual (for example, one brain and one body) to be the focus of study, but necessarily eliminates the experience of subjective life so that the person is described as an animal or organism.

Buddhism agrees with Western science that the 'person' or 'self' cannot be found in the heart or brain; in fact, no self can be discovered in a detailed ontological investigation of our physical functioning. Buddhism adds that, although we cannot find a self in our physical being, we really *do* exist 'in profound interdependence'. When this is fully investigated and developed, it yields 'a far deeper sense of love and compassion than that' which is connected to a theory of humans as separate physical bodies or genetic programmes (Houshmand *et al.*, 1999, p. 173). The interdependent nature of reality yields an ontology of compassion in Buddhism, with ethical implications quite different from biological determinism, without any untenable 'old' metaphysics. Compassion – caring, kindness, affection – is considered to be a component of *reality* that is difficult for the individual to grasp because of the delusion of being separated from everything else through the experience of a separate self. Buddhism takes as its goal the direct experience and rational acceptance of this interdependence which demonstrates that our kindness benefits everyone, ourselves as much as others. In advance of having such a direct experience, practitioners are encouraged to imagine or learn about compassion and interdependence through stories, teachings and other practices.

THE STUDY OF INTENTION AND SUBJECTIVITY

Providers and teachers of human services now face a situation in which there is no viable dialogue between biological determinism and other scientific accounts of human subjectivity. Indeed, our clients and others appear to believe that proper medication or advice should alleviate suffering without any knowledge of how an individual or individuals create it. In the absence of such a dialogue, we may critically undermine love and compassion as the Dalai Lama suggests.

The epistemologies of the natural sciences (often called the 'hard' sciences), which undergird biological determinism, necessarily eliminate all questions and accounts of human subjectivity and intention. To put this another way, the systems of knowledge used to study organic processes must exclude the experiences of the human subject. All epistemologies are limited and constrained; those used in the natural sciences cannot ask or answer questions about human intention and its meanings.

By the term 'intention' I mean purpose, desire or aim: what one consciously or unconsciously *wants or wants to do*. Psychoanalysis and psychodynamic methods and theories constitute a nascent science of human intention and meaning. This science depends on the practice of psychodynamic therapies, and on related scientific studies of personality, therapeutic change and development. The psychodynamic science of intention comprises the following: a means to ameliorate human suffering through therapeutic treatment, a way of thinking about subjective life, and a set of testable hypotheses (contrary to Grunbaum, 1984) about such phenomena as defence mechanisms, attachment behaviours, motivations, core conflicts, therapeutic change, personality development, emotional memory, and more. By 'science' I mean systematized know-ledge – the product of agreed-upon objective methods of investigation – that become the basis for truth claims in a field of study.

Through clinical work and scientific studies in the psychodynamic therapies, we discover the complex, conflicted and often unknown inten-tions that are at the core of personal suffering. I agree with Strenger when he says about psychoanalysis:

> The assumption is that every aspect of human behavior is intelligible; i.e. behavior is seen as intentional action all the way down. Furthermore, it is assumed that by correctly understanding the meaning of actions, we help the patient to take full responsibility for who he is, and give him the freedom to change if he truly wants to. (1991, pp. 62–3)

In order fully to develop and make use of this science, we need to expand and articulate further our models of the human psyche, especially through research that does not import wholesale the epistemological categories of the natural sciences.

Human subjective responses must account for meaning and purpose and regard intentionality or free will as something other than adaptation to an environment. This goal is impossible to achieve through the natural sciences, even in such applications as systems theory and information theory which are constrained by the epistemology of process and reactivity. Only when we have achieved some solid foundation for understanding the complexity of human desire and intentions can we engage in a useful dialogue with biology, biochemistry and neuroscience to investigate such important topics as the nature and development of human consciousness.

As we have been increasingly encouraged to explain more and more of our personal difficulties in terms of organic and biological processes, and less and less in terms of our own desires and actions, we providers of mental health services now risk obscuring the complexity of subjective life. If we respond to questions about why we suffer, without any insight into human motivations, conflicts and desires, we may short-circuit a question of meaning. And if we explain human moods, emotional diffi-culties and other shortcomings mostly, or most adequately, in terms of biochemical or other organic processes, we will betray the thimbleful of social awareness of the role of unconscious intentions that has only recently become a part of Western culture.

In graduate school, I studied the complexity of human desires in a seminar on motivation. In this and other seminars, I learned that human agency and language demand a non-reductive method of study. We were taught that the human freedom to think *abstractly* – to theorize even about one's thoughts and moods – sets humans sufficiently apart from other organisms and animals to create a 'pathology of the person' that is rooted in meaning and intention rather than process or reactivity. I was taught that it is dangerous to believe that humans are biologically *or* psychologically determined because an adequate theory of human action must account for intentions that go beyond determining forces.

In the late 1970s, we psychodynamic types thought that cognitive behaviourism was *the* reductionism to oppose. We did not see what was coming around the biochemical corner. A mere twenty years later, most popular accounts of science would concur with English journalist Appleyard (1998), who states that 'Almost every aspect of human life has a large and frequently decisive genetic component' (ibid., p. 15). Although Appleyard is a critic of genetic programmes, he, like most other popularizers of biological science, is a true believer in the ideology. Human beings develop in inherently personal relationships that include intention, meaning and reflection from the very beginning. Although our biology may affect how sensitive we are to certain interactions with others, our relationships and their meanings also affect how relevant these biological factors may be.

Thus, there is a massive distortion using organic theories to explain human actions. Philosopher MacMurray says:

> We are not organisms, but persons. The nexus of relations which unites us in a human society is not organic but personal. Human behaviour cannot be understood, but only caricatured, if it is represented as an adaptation to environment; and there is no such process as social evolution but, instead, a history which reveals a precarious development and possibilities both of progress and retrogression. (1961, p. 46)

When the facts and methods of studying organic life are applied by analogy to the human field, they deny us the possibility of understanding ourselves in terms of intentions and actions. We transform our actions into organic processes which automatically erases the freedom to change through self-reflection (whether changing for better or worse). Biobabble makes unintelligible any explanation of human behaviour in terms of desire and intention, and transforms into gibberish the goal of subjective freedom through increased awareness, as found in psychodynamic and Buddhist practices.

For all these reasons, I passionately believe that we must articulate a multilevelled scientific study of the intentional and relational character of human subjectivity. Drawing on psychodynamic models and theories, and on the practices and methods of Buddhism, such a science would challenge the ideology of biological determinism. As the Dalai Lama says, we need to use the complexity of human intelligence in a constructive way:

> of all the various species of animal on the planet, human beings are the biggest troublemakers ... It is therefore important that human intelligence be utilized in a constructive way. That is the key. If we utilize its capacity properly, then not only human beings would become less harmful to each other, and to the planet, but also individual human beings would be happier in themselves. (Dalai Lama, 1997, p. 132)

The study of human intentions, motivations, desires and inner conflicts is the path to understanding how human intelligence can be used for constructive purposes in understanding its own powers and limitations. The methods of Buddhist practice encourage us to pay attention to the effects of our desires on our contentment, our intentions on our actions, and our fears and anxieties on our states of mind. Similarly, psychodynamic therapies encourage sober self-reflection on our destructive emotional habits and our repetitive omnipotent longings to have things under our own control. Only the human sciences can provide the backbone for expanding and studying these approaches.

THE HUMAN SCIENCES

When I first encountered the philosophy of science, through Kuhn's (1970) *The Structure of Scientific Revolutions*, I was impressed with the idea of scientific 'paradigms' or exemplary models that are used as if they were reality. Kuhn showed that the natural sciences have grown through revolutionary shifts in these paradigms, rather than through linear accumulation of new knowledge or information. From time to time, some scientists discover and investigate anomalies in the exemplary model, and these anomalies lead to a new worldview that topples the old paradigm and allows scientists to see data in a new way. Kuhn's theory appealed to psychological clinicians like myself because we believed that we were helping our clients shift their paradigms of reality by examining anomalies in their worldviews. But Kuhn strongly objected to applying his structural theory of the natural sciences to any understanding of the human sciences of psychology, anthropology, sociology, linguistics, economics or history. He believed that his theory belonged in the natural sciences, and was distorted in the applications to the human sciences.

The nineteenth-century German philosopher Dilthey drew the original line between the natural and human sciences. He claimed that the goal of the natural sciences is the discovery of causal principles and generalized physical laws, whereas the objective of the human sciences is to understand the purpose and meaning of human action. Because of this difference, Dilthey concluded that the natural sciences are inadequate for the study of human intentionality and experience at its most complex levels.

Philosophers of science have continued to debate the question of whether there are true differences between the natural and the human sciences and if there are, what they are. Is it the subject matter, the attitude of the scientists or the method of study that makes the two endeavours seem so different? There now appears to be some broad agreement among philosophers of science that all sciences are hermeneutical or interpretive at base. This means that all of the assumptions and methods of science occur in particular contexts of meaning that are not necessarily generalizable from one to another. As philosopher Putnam states:

> We can and should insist that some facts are there to be discovered and not legislated by us, but this is something to be said when one has adopted a way of speaking, a language, a 'conceptual scheme.' To talk of 'facts' without specifying the language to be used is to talk of nothing; the word 'fact' no more has its use fixed by the world itself than does the word 'exist' or the word 'object.' (1989, p. 114)

We can no longer claim that the simple facts of *reality* are discovered. Even by natural scientists, because no fact exists outside of some context of shared assumptions. Rather than discovering objective facts that are beyond interpretation, scientists are now understood to pursue their particular subject matter within a community of thinkers that share a worldview or a way of seeing something.

Is it still useful to maintain a distinction between the natural and human sciences? It is a necessity, in my view, from an epistemological perspective. The natural sciences are not capable of asking and answering questions of human meaning and desire. Nor are their methods designed to study the complexity of human intelligence, especially in its self-conscious and self-reflective aspects. This unique form of intelligence sets us apart from other animals and organisms, even those that have developed language. In adulthood, human self-reflective capacities give us, as a species, an unprecedented level of disengagement from our immediate experience and surroundings. This decentring of our awareness allows us to perform complex abstract processes, to meditate on our own subjective experience, to develop theories about ourselves and others, and to explore and dominate our environment in a radical way. Self-conscious, self-reflective intelligence depends neither exclusively on chance nor necessity for its development and use. With these kinds of unique powers at our disposal, we have become the biggest troublemakers on the planet, and may eventually find that our tendency to dominate other life forms will become our greatest downfall.

There are other philosophical reasons to maintain the boundary between the human and the natural sciences. In 1989, I heard Kuhn lecture on his own long-term conclusions about this issue. He claimed that the main difference between these two kinds of science is practical, in terms of what practitioners normally *do*, not how or what they study. What natural scientists do, given their hermeneutic base, 'is not ordinarily hermeneutic. Rather, they put to use the paradigm received from their teachers in an ... enterprise that attempts to solve puzzles like those of improving and extending the match between theory and experiment at the advancing forefront of the field.' Human scientists rarely work with such received knowledge. Their sciences 'appear to be hermeneutic, interpretive, through and through. Very little of what goes on in them at all resembles the normal puzzle-solving research of the natural sciences. Their aim is ... to understand behavior, not to discover the laws, if any, that govern it' (Hiley *et al.*, 1992, pp. 22–3). Asking himself whether the human sciences could eventually find paradigms that would support normal puzzle-solving research, Kuhn said he was 'totally uncertain', stating that some aspects of economics and psychology already seem to use models that could be generalized in developing a puzzle-solving science. On the other hand, he himself wondered if it would be constructive to move further in this direction. When the unit of study is a social or psychological system, Kuhn wondered if there would be any real gain in abstracting principles that might lead to puzzle-solving, rather than continuing to engage in a thoroughly herme-neutic enterprise.

Many psychological investigations that have emerged in dialogue with psychodynamic theories are already strong examples of a complex human science of subjectivity with strong records of reliability, validity and prediction. These include: (Loevinger's) ego development theory, affect theory and regulation, infant–mother observation, attachment theory, defence mechanisms research, psychodynamic psychotherapy outcome studies, some dream studies, and the core-conflict studies of psychotherapy. All have contributed important new understandings and expanded old ones, while they have used hermeneutical or qualitative research methods to investigate human emotions and intentions.

It is also fruitful to draw on certain findings in the natural sciences. Many of these are useful as heuristics and analogies. But if we ground our theories of subjectivity in natural science paradigms, we will distort our view of intentional life and also do very bad science. Taylor, another contemporary philosopher of science, states that the natural science expla-nations of our subjective experiences

> end up in wordy elaborations of the obvious, or they fail altogether to address the interesting questions, or their practitioners end up squandering their talents and ingenuity in the attempt to show that they can after all recapture the insights of ordinary life in their manifestly reductive explanatory languages. (1985, p. 1)

BIOBABBLE IN THE HUMAN SCIENCES

Biological determinism, as imported into the human services, is one such example of bad science. The typical way that this kind of thinking enters the fields of mental health services is through what geneticist Lewontin (1992) calls the 'empty bucket metaphor'. This metaphor depicts human beings as empty buckets of different sizes, waiting to be filled with the water of experience. If the environment provides all of the necessary resources, then every bucket is filled to its capacity. Still, the metaphor im-plies, there will be differences in our abilities, capacities and limitations because there are differences in how much water each bucket can hold. These differences are natural and inherent in the different sizes of the buckets from the start.

Lewontin claims that a major error is committed through the use of this metaphor because 'A change in environment ... can change abilities by many orders of magnitude ... [and] the differences between individuals are abolished by cultural and mechanical inventions.' For example:

> Although there may be biologically based average differences in physique and strength between a random group of men and random group of women (and these are less than usually supposed), these differences rapidly become irrelevant and disappear from practical view in a world of electrically driven hoists, power steering, and electronic controls. (Lewontin, 1992, pp. 29–30)

Environmental variation and genetic variation are not independent causal pathways; in fact, the interaction between the two is indissoluble.

Lewontin summarizes biological determinism as three main ideas: (1) that humans differ in fundamental abilities because of innate differences; (2) that those innate differences are biologically inherited; and (3) that human nature, therefore, guarantees the formation of a hierarchical society. He then reveals profound flaws in the largest twin and population studies that make claims for major genetic tendencies in human behaviour. These studies discover no causal laws (because their methods are correlational and statistical), but they claim to separate genetic and environmental influences for traits such as happiness and schizophrenia. In conclusion, Lewontin states that, '[T]here is at present simply no convincing measure of the role of genes in influencing human behavioral variation.' But we (scientists and public) have developed a problematic confusion 'between inherited and unchangeable' (ibid., p. 33) in our belief about these studies.

The complexity of human desire, both conscious and unconscious, has played a determining role in our current version of biobabble and the story of the mighty gene. But this is not the first time that a theory of inherited traits has played a powerful role in persuading people that the roots of human misery are 'in the blood' rather than in our intentions and actions. English journalist Appleyard (1998) traces the history of this notion from Plato who advocated an improved species as a necessary aspect of an ideal society, to the Christian Inquisition whose priests believed that faith and heresy were 'in the blood', and finally to the Nazi Final Solution: the extermination of those people considered to be

'genetically inferior'. Without a science of human intention that fundamentally and convincingly presents a systematic understanding of the
complexity of human desire, we risk repeating the most destructive
chapters of our history when the omnipotent longings of the few were
supported by the many.

AN ETHIC OF HUMAN SUFFERING

Those who practise psychodynamic therapies and those who practise
Buddhism share in an ethic about human suffering: that one is the
creator of oneself, and that whatever one does, one becomes heir to those
intentions. In psychoanalysis, this is a belief that we create our suffering
through the repetition of destructive emotional patterns that were, at
some time, an apparently suitable response to our emotional and interpersonal environment. All practitioners of psychodynamic therapies are
committed to understanding human beings as intentional persons, even
when they do not understand themselves in this way.

Practitioners of all forms of Buddhism would agree with the famous
words of the Buddha that open *The Dhammapada*:

> We are what we think.
> All that we are arises with our thoughts.
> With our thoughts we make the world.
> Speak or act with an impure mind
> And trouble will follow you
> As the wheel follows the ox that draws the cart.
> (Bryom, 1993, p. 1)

Buddhism teaches methods for observing the process through which our
thoughts and intentions become our *karma*, the consequences that arise
from our own actions and create patterns in our lives. To change this
karma, we must change our thoughts and actions; according to
Buddhism, our *karma* is fluid and emergent in our thoughts and actions;
it is neither wholly predetermined, as an adaptation to an environment,
nor completely unpredictable and random.

The Buddhist theory of *karma* is consonant with psychodynamic
theories and therapies about our tendencies to repeat the conflicts and
emotional habits that are outside our awareness. To free ourselves from
destructive emotional habits or change our irrational fears or reduce our

discontent, we must come to know our own motives, especially those that we repeatedly project into others. Schafer describes the course of a psychoanalysis as follows:

> The analysand progressively recognizes, accepts, revises, refines, and lives in terms of the idea of the self as agent. This is to say that, in one way or another and more and more, the analysand sees himself or herself as being the person who essentially has been doing the things from which he or she was apparently suffering upon entering analysis. (1978, p. 180)

Buddhist and psychoanalytic practices have developed theories and methods for understanding suffering. This way of thinking leads to a set of moral principles or values that holds people accountable for their actions. It should be sufficiently clear that this ethic stands in stark contrast to the ideology of biological determinism and the bad gene.

When the metaphysics of Western Judaeo-Christian religions was overtaken by the metaphysics of Western sciences, the ethics of Western religions were lost in the process. The ethic of suffering could just as easily have been formulated from an account of the Ten Commandments or the Golden Rule. Western religions advocate close attention to one's thoughts and actions in the practice of becoming an ethical human being. But the defeat of the metaphysics of religion by those of science in the West has also meant a loss of the ethical teachings of the religions in any form that might reach and influence large numbers of people.

Americans seem baffled by the senseless acts of violence carried out even by privileged young people benefiting from all of our advancements of the natural sciences. We have seemed unable to grasp the consequences of our loss of an ethic of suffering. When human traits, from the sublime to the undesirable, are explained in terms of adaptations and genes, how can anyone who has developed during these times take seriously a belief in personal responsibility for oneself, let alone for one's community and society?

Within a human science of subjectivity, ethics and morality become part of the contemporary metaphysics of science; the study of personhood would certainly be on a metaphysical par with the study of organic processes. Surely we deceive ourselves if we believe that the humanities and religion can carry the burden of impressing young people with the ethic of suffering. Science *is* the spiritual adventure of our age and we have to engage its methods in order to bring validity to our pursuits.

It is my hope that the early part of the twenty-first century will witness the convergence of the objective methods of Buddhism with the clinical methods of psychodynamic theories and practices in a systematic study of subjective life. This pursuit should apply especially the methods that have developed through Western psychology, rather than the exclusively physiological and biological methods already used to study aspects of meditational practice. Such psychological methods already exist and are used to investigate topics related to psychodynamic therapies. They include content analysis, narrative analysis, Q-sort, and other forms of self-report that produce predictable and reliable results.

Under the aegis of a human science of subjectivity, we could begin to organize our selves, our relationships and our communities towards an adequate account of the human development of responsibility, ethics and compassion. Until we have this kind of scientific model of the development of the human subject in relationship, we cannot hope to use our contemporary metaphysics of science to understand ourselves. Unless we develop such a model, we risk destroying the environment on which our species depends, as a consequence of our own disclaimed omnipotent longings.

BIBLIOGRAPHY

Appleyard, B. (1998) *Brave New Worlds: Staying Human in the Genetic Future*. New York: Viking.

Broyard, A. (1992) *Intoxicated by my Illness*. New York: Fawcett Columbine.

Bryom, T. (trans.) (1993) *Dhammapada: The Sayings of the Buddha*. Boston, MA: Shambala.

Dalai Lama, H.H. (1997) *The Four Noble Truths: Fundamentals of the Buddhist Teachings*. London: Thorsons.

Grunbaum, A. (1984) *The Foundations of Psychoanalysis*. Berkeley, CA: University of California Press.

Hiley, D., Bohman, J. and Shusterman, R. (eds) (1992) *The Interpretive Turn: Philosophy, Science, Culture*. Ithaca, NY: Cornell University Press.

Houshmand, Z., Livingston, R. and Wallace, A. (1999) *Consciousness at the Crossroads: Conversations with the Dalai Lama on Brain Science and Buddhism*. Ithaca, NY: Snow Lion.

Kuhn, T.S. (1970) *The Structure of Scientific Revolutions*. Chicago: University of Chicago Press.

Lewontin, R. (1992) *Biology as Ideology: The Doctrine of DNA*. New York: HarperPerennial.

MacMurray, J. (1961) *Persons in Relation*. Atlantic Highlands, NJ: Humanities Press.

Putnam, H. (1989) *Representation in Reality*. Cambridge, MA: MIT Press.

Schafer, R. (1978) *Language and Insight*. New Haven, CT: Yale University Press.

Strenger, C. (1991) *Between Hermeneutics and Science: An Essay on the Epistemology of Psychoanalysis*. Madison, CT: International Universities Press.

Taylor, C. (1985) *Human Agency and Language: Philosophical Papers*, Vol. I. Cambridge: Cambridge University Press.

19

Reflections on Values in Psychoanalysis

Jeffrey B. Rubin

The topic of psychoanalysis and morality refers to at least two different things: the unconscious moralities and value systems implicit in our psychoanalytic theories and practices, and how to deal with particular moral conflicts (reporting on cheating, contact with a 'deadbeat' Dad, having an abortion, and so forth). Moral philosophers, according to Jones (1998, p. 3), have distinguished two different approaches to understanding moral decision-making: a 'deontological' approach in which ethics entails developing a 'calculus of moral reasoning and refining and applying moral principles', and an 'ethics of character', involving becoming a certain sort of person. There are several ways that psychoanalysis can contribute to the latter type of moral decision-making. Psychoanalysis cannot offer a fixed moral calculus, but with its attention to the developmental nature of moral beliefs, the ubiquity of unconsciousness, and our inevitable embeddedness in various relational matrixes, psychoanalytic treatment does provide a unique atmosphere to explore moral conundrums, and aid individuals in detecting moral self-blindness and cultivating greater ethical sensitivity to the other. From this relational perspective, rather than functioning as a Platonist aiding the patient to get in touch with Reality or the Self, the analyst is a kind of Aristotelian engaged in a self-reflexive dialogue with the analysand about the developmental origins of one's morality and the contemporaneous consequences for oneself and others of one's moral beliefs and actions. Becoming moral, from this perspective, involves cultivating greater relational sensitivity and attunement, moral know-how and self-understanding in the patient.

Morality, like all facets of psychological life, is partially, although not completely, unconscious. Freud was not the first person to consider unconsciousness in the moral domain. Spinoza and Dewey, among many others, also recognized such unconsciousness (e.g., Fromm, 1947, p. 30).

But psychoanalytic treatment explores and reveals the unconscious ideals and values which undergird and are often opaque to ordinary introspection or even meditative contemplation. Psychoanalysis can, for example, pinpoint and reveal the costs of unconscious ideals, desires and fears that shape our values. Let me give an example. A deep Calvinist streak permeates Western civilization. There is, for example, what Fromm (1947, p. 119) terms a taboo on selfishness in modern culture. From this perspective, to be self-centred is to be sinful and to be selfless is to be virtuous. Conquering selfishness is one important purpose of spiritual ethics. It is assumed by many contemplative traditions that when human beings are left to their own devices they will be destructively egocentric, if not evil. Psychoanalysis deconstructs the self-betraying, and self-neglectful, propensities of renunciative spiritual viewpoints as well as the self-aggrandizing tendencies endemic to egocentric secular values. Each is an inadequate foundation for living a more moral life. When virtue entails renunciation of our humanness (for example, our self-centredness and our carnality, as in much contemplative thought), then self-care is deeply compromised. When self-inflation is the highest virtue, as in most secular thought, one falls prey to an alienating egocentricity, which precludes altruism and connectedness to others. Recognition of the other is then deeply neglected.

The dualist subject–object split underlying Western thought – particularly science and philosophy – undermines reflections on morality. It causes us to think of ourselves as self-encapsulated monads. Such a perspective is a problematic basis to think about ethics, for it inevitably polarizes the claims of the other and the needs of the self. Self-care and altruism are then erroneously treated as opposed rather than mutually interpenetrating. Psychoanalysis offers the potential of a more nondualistic, relational perspective about morality. In revealing our irreducible interconnectedness as human beings, contemporary relational psychoanalysts – whether object relational, self psychological, neo-Freudian, interpersonal or intersubjective – open up the potential of conceiving the other as a subject with its own unique values and needs, and not merely as an object-for-the-self's-use. An implicit (and perhaps not yet fully mined) implication of these disparate perspectives is that morality is a property of a relation between differently constituted persons, and not a possession of an isolated mind. A morality involving what Benjamin (1995, p. 30) terms 'mutual recognition' of the claims of self and other could thereby be fostered.

There is a plurality of ends that might be pursued in a particular treatment, ranging from the rationality and stoicism valued by Freud to the authenticity and aliveness cherished by Winnicott. The psychoanalyst's role in a psychoanalytic treatment attuned to the moral domain cannot, of course, be exhaustively delineated. Much depends on the particular therapeutic context, including the unique nature and needs of the analysand. Clarifying the analysand's existing values, pinpointing the developmental origins and contemporary meanings and functions of those values, and cultivating ethical attentiveness and know-how may all be operative in different ways at different times. The analyst's role is protean depending on the needs of a particular patient, which will obviously differ in each case. With some patients, the analyst might question or even challenge their moral code by asking unsettling questions about gaps or inconsistencies or tensions. The analyst might actively question the psychological impact of following a moral code that the patient has unquestioningly inherited from parents and/or the culture in which s/he lives. The analyst might also question the analysand's taken-for-granted narrative about his or her origins and moral relation to others and the world. The shaping influence of the analyst's active stance regarding the patient's relation to morality would, of course, need to be explored and understood. More inclusive moral perspectives about the patient's life might develop.

In other cases, the analyst may assist the patient in challenging self-nullifying familial values or oppressive cultural ambitions and ideals. With a disillusioned lawyer who felt unfulfilled and deprived in the adversarial world of his profession, I questioned the stifling materialistic values that he had internalized from his father, which defined him only in terms of how hard he worked, how much he earned and how much he owned. As I raised questions about his narrow image of male success we learned that he felt like a disappointment to his critical and high-achieving parents and endeavoured to justify his existence through professional success and personal acquisitions. As we began to understand the way achievements and products substituted for emotional hunger and deprivation, he initiated a critical examination of the values that had fuelled his one-dimensional pursuit of power and money. He began to feel that other ways of living might be possible. He eventually cut back his hours at work, reduced his compulsive conspicuous consumption, became more involved in raising his children, and took more time for sunsets, family picnics and relationships with friends.

For a depressed, divorced woman from a patriarchal foreign culture who had been abused in her arranged marriage, the treatment questioned her belief in her second-class status and validated her inchoate sense that she was entitled to a relationship of equality with a man. As I supported her challenging culturally sanctioned and internalized values about women's inferior status in relation to men, her depression began to lift and she sought equitable treatment from men.

With another person the analyst might participate in the creation, rather than the deconstruction, of a moral code. Here one facilitates the patient's development of a moral code and the capacity for moral reasoning.

In these cases, clarifying existing moral values, delineating the developmental origins and contemporary meanings and functions of the analysand's values, or refining the patient's ethical 'phronesis' or know-how, play a less central role – at least for a time. With a passive and detached young woman from an emotionally neglectful home, who felt that she was not entitled to a life – let alone a choice about her own values – the treatment provided a context in which she could engage in a non-coercive dialogue about her values, ideals, desires and needs. She had been profoundly silenced by her self-preoccupied parents. As we explored this theme and it became enacted within the therapeutic relationship, she gradually began to acknowledge and integrate what had been denied and whitewashed in her family. As the grip of her lifelong self-nullification was broken, she developed more self-trust in her own moral vision. She was eventually able to create a moral code based on personal values rather than on automatic and unconscious submission to and accommodation of others. She also developed greater empathy for the pain of other victimized women.

In closing, here are some of the questions psychoanalysts might ask in a psychoanalysis that was open to the moral dimension: What are the hidden moralities shaping the analyst's participation in analysis? Does the analyst or the patient avoid any moral issues? What are the multiple meanings, origins, psychological functions and relational consequences of the moralities that patient and analyst uphold? What are the costs of each? How does the analyst's moral stance effect treatment? How do we develop a relational morality? What is the impact of cultural context(s) and constraints on psychoanalytic reflections on morality? What are the moral costs of the 'new capitalism', in which job security is more tenuous, careers are shorter-lived, workers are eminently disposable, and vocational trust and loyalty towards work have eroded? What new moral dilemmas are raised by new communication technologies such as e-mail, virtual realities, and so on? What moral implications do synthetic forms of life – ranging from virtual realities to 'prosthetic' technologies (i.e., cosmetic breast enhancement) – have for analysts and patients? What moral conundrums are stirred up by new forms of family life/structure – such as same-sex unions, single parent homes, and families in which both parents are working outside of the home for extended periods of time?

Whatever our task in specific cases, psychoanalytic reflections on values and ethics will be invigorated and enriched when psychoanalysts and interested thinkers from allied fields make explicit and reflect upon the variety of values informing their stance towards treatment. I have tried to point out lacunas and raise questions about several dominant psychoanalytic stances towards living a moral life. Elsewhere (Rubin 1996, 1998), I have also articulated some of the values shaping my own consideration of ethics in treatment, as well as the partiality of my own perspective, in the hope that it will spur further dialogue on this important and neglected topic. Aware of the importance of the task and the incompleteness of my own vision, I take solace in a remark by Rabbi Tarphon in *Pirke Aboth: The Ethics of the Fathers*: 'The work is not yours to finish; but neither are you free to take no part in it.'

BIBLIOGRAPHY

Benjamin, J. (1995) *Like Subjects, Love Objects*. New Haven and London: Yale University Press.

Fromm, E. (1947) *Man for Himself: An Inquiry into the Psychology of Ethics*. New York: Holt, Rinehart & Winston.

Jones, J. (1998) *The Moral Implications of Psychoanalysis: Discussion of Papers by Jeffrey B. Rubin, Peter Carnochan, and Peter Shabad*. American Psychological Association Division 39 Meeting, August, San Francisco, CA.

Pirke Aboth: The Ethics of the Fathers (1945) Ed. and trans. J. Tepfer. New York: Schocken.

Rubin, J. B. (1996) *Psychotherapy and Buddhism: Toward an Integration*. New York: Plenum Press.

Rubin, J. B. (1998) *A Psychoanalysis for Our Time: Exploring the Blindness of the Seeing I*. New York: New York University Press.

20

Psychoanalysis
A Rendezvous with Disappointment

Chris Oakley

Since the early 1970s, both in Britain and throughout Europe, there has been a growing development of an insistent, and in most instances, an unquestioned wish to establish psychoanalysis (I am using the term generically to enlist all psychoanalytically informed psychotherapies) as a profession. While at one level it generates a set of somewhat parochial concerns, for who outside of Britain would have either the need or the desire to differentiate between the UKCP (United Kingdom Council for Psychotherapy) and the BCP (British Confederation of Psychotherapists), simultaneously the issue of registration, or licencing as it is called in the United States, is of enormous significance for the future of psycho-analysis. It is my thesis that psychoanalysis, always recognizing its multi-plicity, engages in a swerving away from the heart of the therapeutic tie to inaugurate a wearisome struggle with a relentless and ultimately fruit-less concern with regard to identity, persistently saturated with a battle over power and prestige. It was Foucault who in his attempts to do justice to Freud, and consequently to psychoanalysis, installed a double inscription: on the one hand, Freud takes his place in a privileged enclo-sure in addressing the question of madness. In this he is joined by, among others, Nietzsche, and it is a veritable site of possibility where madness might indeed speak. This is inevitably interwoven with an interrogation of transgression, with an emphasis on excess, the too much. But simultaneously and in contrast, Freud was also co-joined with, again among others, Pinel, in the history of Law, Order and Surveillance. It is this latter trajectory that psychoanalysis with its emphasis on standards, standardization, control and regulation so meekly and disappointingly collapses within.

Intriguingly, the etymological meaning of the word 'profession' is informed by declaration, admission and confession and it is this last term, indelibly linked to guilt, that may be critical in what drives this curious demand. Is the enjoyment of psychoanalysis too excessive, thus leading to structures of constraint and surveillance of precisely this very enjoyment? These are the themes that I seek to address.

Psychoanalysis is a storehouse of ideas superficially informed by a narrative with destination: a final rendezvous, a point of arrival at some ultimate truth, even if that truth which is laid bare is that there is no ultimate truth. The heart, the essence, the *sine qua non* of the psychoanalytical situation is, of course, the transference. Nothing can prevent us from saying that without transference there can be no psychoanalysis. It can also be said that the reason why anyone will enter a psychoanalytical situation is not so much to gain a particular knowledge: what is expected is an encounter. This is not to suggest that transference is not based on a fundamental misrecognition in which the issue of knowledge plays a crucial part. The analysand assumes that there is a subject: unconscious or repressed knowledge, which can so often and erroneously be assumed to lie behind what is said. For what may come to be recognized is not something that already exists somewhere; rather it is in the very act of naming desire that it is created ... It unfolds, is given conscious form, comes into being.

In all this there resides an assumption – and not, I hasten to add, only by the analysand – that by turning to an expert, by turning to a subject supposed to know, this knowledge will be revealed, and thus the analysand will come to see what it is that he wants. Right here there is bound to be a certain ambivalence, for what is at stake is not so much knowledge as an encounter with one's being, which is precisely what we seek to be 'cured' of ... However, it is this supposition of knowledge that gives rise to the love of the analyst. Lacan claimed that he or she whom I suppose knowing, I love. But, and one cannot overemphasize this, it is a function of the position and not of the analyst himself.

Now the encounter that is counted upon inevitably plays across a certain refusal – the refusal of the analyst to merely gratify the demands of the analysand: an initial brush with disappointment. Inevitably the analysis begins with suffering in one form or another – no one comes to sit at this particular table without that – and this suffering will be addressed to the place of the analysand; Lacan called this the place of the Other, a term that attracts and sustains a multiplicity of meanings, and is linked to a determining function in relation to our subjecthood. The analyst, standing in that symbolic place, is principally listening and will eventually be called upon to respond, and through this a potentiality in the situation can unfold ... a potentiality for coming up against the realization, again something of a disappointment, that this Other does not exist. What is meant by that, what comes to be revealed, is that there is no final authority, no ultimate truth. In other words, no meaning can come to rest at fullness, closure, completion, consummation or totalization. So the analyst, supposed to have the answers, is revealed as disappointingly lacking. But right at this threshold is the possibility of the analysand becoming the answer to the analyst's lack. It is here that we are at the site of a possible collapse – and that really would constitute a disappointment! – a collapse into a dual, imaginary relationship, with a primary objective of sustaining an avoidance of lack, propped up by the illusion of convergence. It is here that the analyst might become lured into a form of transaction, a perfectly balanced exchange, in other words a deal, and a great deal will hinge on the outcome of this.

Simply to engage in fulfilling another's desire (even if that were possible) is paradoxically to deprive the other, but equally as analysts we cannot refuse to have anything to do with it. This would be merely to cut off the other's desire. We are called upon to respond, to say something, which hopefully will proceed from the speech of the analysand, allowing him a place to put into words what hitherto has gone unsaid. This is psychoanalysis and the Heineken advertisement: it is a conversation that reaches parts that other conversations do not reach (Cooper *et al.*, 1989, p. 183). To allow oneself to be drawn into becoming merely the one who loves the analysand will give rise to inevitable consequences. First, there will have been an abdication from the position of the symbolic Other, to have become merely another among others. As Heidegger commented, to become preoccupied with particular beings may result in losing sight of the wider question of Being. Second, there will be a confusion in that the function of the position that I take up as analyst and my own person will have become horribly blurred, and however much that may be an inevitability, it is not I who occasions the desire of the analysand. It is hardly a function of the delightful nuances of the personality. Of course it can be shown as not being what is at stake precisely because the phenomenon has become a cliché, a truth worn out through repetition, this phenomenon of the love of the analysand in the context of the psychoanalytic tie. Freud himself, commenting on a patient who, on waking from hypnosis, threw her arms around him, said that he was modest enough not to attribute the event to his own irresistible personal attraction.

However, it is essentially right at this moment to emphasize that the analyst is most indubitably involved in the realities of a relationship of love. Again, Freud was most explicit about this: the reality of the passion of both love and hatred is a reality beyond contest. It is, after all, what is going on. Nor would Lacan, the variable-length session notwithstanding, wish to claim that the analyst is not involved. We pay with our very being, for if the activity goes to the very heart of the other's being, how could one remain entirely outside of this? The psychoanalytic enterprise was always already mistaken about its supposed destination. In lieu, we have this rendezvous with disappointment, an encounter with the excitations at the limits, the limitations, the impossibility of satisfying desire. Paradoxically, this realization becomes in itself a curious form of satisfaction. An unsatisfying yet satisfying dissatisfaction, which will always leave something (more) to be desired. The urge for an impossible satisfaction is at the heart of the demand for psychoanalysis, and is the desire for psychoanalysis itself: 'The desire for an impossible satisfaction, for the most intense enjoyment, is present within the logical, semantic and syntactic elements that are represented in that discourse' (David-Menard, 1989, p. xiii).

So right at the heart of the psychoanalytic tie resides not love but rather seduction and its crucial link with metamorphosis. Following Baudrillard, seduction is to be given the position of the world's most elementary dynamic, and what resides as fundamental to this is challenge (see Heidegger and his ideas regarding experience: 'When we talk of undergoing an experience we mean specifically that the experience is not of our own making ... to undergo means that we endure it, suffer it, receive it as it strikes us and submit to it' (Heidegger, 1971, p. 57)). Hegel saw that experience is not to be reduced merely to one's subjective awareness of an event; rather, that when I truly experience something I am affected by it, it comes as a shock, violates my familiar view, it unsettles, it challenges, it transforms. We could claim that the entire symbolic (otherwise known as the social) equilibrium of our world is founded on the relations of seduction and playfulness. This leads on to a crucial aspect of understanding psychosis and the psychotic drive to restore the guarantee of truth to the world. This assumed guarantee, which operates as the social glue, that which holds everything together, must be there, or we cannot make any sense of the world nor can the contribution of seduction play any part.

Now what seduces us? This is partly the contemporary problematic that saturates the issue of the registration of the 'profession' of psychoanalysis. In this very moment I am potentially engaging in one aspect of a critique of this issue of registration – psychoanalysis taken to be a configurable whole, a homogeneous body – rather than recognizing that it is always divided and multiple. But to return to the issue of seduction, it is imperative to realize that 'full' signs never seduce. Modernity insists that only the visible, the transparent, will have any value; so culturally there is a persistent inclination to submit to surveillance and the computerization of our world, the pernicious emphasis on identity, always entangled in a spelling it out. Seduction can only operate via the illegible, the indecipherable, the riddle, for the signs of seduction do not signify, or at least not straightforwardly. Rather, they are of the order of the shimmer, the ellipse, the flash (as in flash of wit). A trite example of this would be that linguistics always fails to recognize what seduces us in a poem, or that the delights of a rock song are never a function of the clarity of the lyrics.

Can we speak of the terrain of seduction? Should there be an emphasis on surface and appearance? Egoic law suggests that we take flight from the reign of appearances. Rather, we should jealously guard our meaning and so dismiss mere appearance. As Baudrillard says, 'Seduction is damned, not the least of its charms' (1988, p. 62). Inevitably it would be palpably absurd to suggest that the psychoanalytic encounter is unrelenting seduction. For much of the time we are to bide our time, forced to produce something under the yoke of meaning, allowing for the rare and so often accidental moments of seduction. This will so often operate through a letting be, allowing things to follow their own devices. Hopefully it will have become unequivocally manifest that this seduction has absolutely nothing whatsoever to do with the analyst being seductive. This would be to collapse into a caricature of seduction, an antithesis even, for there would be a fundamental confusion as seduction occurs quite naturally, so there is no call to coerce or blackmail. So we are not talking of any provocative fluttering of the eyelids, an inciteful leer. It is not something that can be worked at, nor strangely can it be taught, nor can it be staged as a strategy. Rather, what seduces us is none other than seduction itself. While there is to be an emphasis on the opacity of appearances, this is not to propose that something is to be kept secret for this would only serve to stimulate the will to knowledge. However, without becoming misty-eyed (sentimental) or mystical, there is this mystery which circulates as the rule of the game, as a symbolic pact, and yet there is nothing hidden, nothing to reveal. Seduction was always ever that which deviates. Two examples: in gambling it is money that is seduced, it deviates from the law of value, is transformed, is metamorphosed into that which one bids. In perversion it is the law that is seduced, it deviates *via* a transformation into a tactical element in a ritualized erotic space. Seduction will turn us away from the path, will lead us astray. Indeed, our very beginnings as speaking subjects involve our being led away from the world, the unmediated, immediate world of the natural, for we are all seduced by language, or 'the virus from outer space', as William Burroughs called it. So the discourse of truth with which psychoanalysis is entangled was always on course for disappointment. Always already impossible it always eludes itself, and we can only hurl ourselves fruitlessly at its point of disappearance. After all, psychoanalysis is merely another system of meaning and interpretation seeking to render the operations of the world intelligible, only to founder on the inability of any system to break open the secret, to unveil the mystery, to reveal whatever we might call it. Following Michel Henry (1993, p. x): life and nothing but life. We can witness an impotent fury to arrive at the naked truth, that which haunts all interpretative discourses. The more we approach this truth, always horizontal, the more the opacity and the drive to unveil simply bears witness to the eternal laws of seduction. Perhaps psychoanalysis was always fused about its destination – the fiction of being fully analysed. Rather the beautiful disappointment is none other than, *via* seduction, an encounter with the intoxication of sharing, a sharing of opacity of truth over and over again.

But what, one may well ask, of the role of sex in all of this? Surely it is very difficult to purify seduction entirely of sex, and indeed, why should one? Nevertheless, there is a very real possibility that psychoanalysis deceived both itself and others in this regard, both in the assumption that there is to be a final point to the story and that this final point, the secret to be revealed, is none other than sex and sexuality. But the secret is never the repressed, but rather is intimately linked to the grand fable of giddiness and its contagions (see Roger Caillois (1967) and his theory of play: the four categories of games, of expression, competition, chance and giddiness). It involves a subtle pleasure that resides precisely in the insistent opacity of appearances that challenge the grand narrative of truth and the relentless drive that all should be revealed. As Winnicott wrote, 'Only in a split-off intellect could one be 100% honest. As soon as there is life, living processes come in, then there must be self-deception, deception, compromise and ambivalence' (Rodman, 1987, p. 184). Of course we can never know in advance or predict the trance-formations (otherwise known as the trance state within the transference, which is the state particular to fascination and giddiness). Rather, the psychoanalytical situation is suffused with the contagions, the mesmerizing, the deceptive and indeed all that keeps one in suspense, holding one's breath, in other words, alive.

Earlier I mentioned that seduction was crucially linked to metamorphosis or transformation. Perhaps we only ever truly exist when seduced by whatever it is that moves us: a look, a face, an idea, a piece of music, a laugh, for however constrained, inhibited or suppressed we can all be at times, there is this urge to go beyond our pathetic rationality, our reality principle or, as Baudrillard would have it, 'to refract ourselves in another logic' (1988, p. 70). Psychoanalysis operates as a fable, a timeless fluidity of possibilities, although simultaneously bound by time, given over to the potentiality of seduction. This is underpinned by the model of amorous seduction where we pursue the strangeness of the other *via* an endless series of initiations. So psychoanalysis is in part an initiation ceremony, the analyst as founding other bringing one into the world, this world of seduction. We shroud the potentiality of this metamorphosis through the psychoanalytic ceremony, and because of its capacity certain renunciations such as sex and reproduction are called for; but through the beautiful disappointment there is the unfolding of a vertiginous succession where the subject may lose himself in ritual sequences.

I wish for a moment to turn to Adam Phillips and his collection of essays, *On Flirtation* (1994). Right at the beginning, almost as a flag statement, he asserts that the psychoanalyst and the patient are there for none other than enjoyment, which must never be conflated with pleasure. He quotes Ronnie Laing, who wrote of the psychoanalytic encounter: 'Let us try and enjoy ourselves ... I am really only interested in trying to entice people with all the skills at my disposal to live in that sort of way if they possibly can.' Phillips seeks to emphasize that psychoanalysis is not so much to do with understanding, an aggregation of self-knowledge, as with 'allowing the ceaseless freeing of a potentiality of inventiveness' (Phillips, 1994, p. xi), pathology being that which stifles or stultifies such possibilities. Here we come up against a site of reversibility, for how could this 'freeing' come into being if not *via*, however provisionally, certain understandings, certain glimpsed recognitions in relation to none other than oneself, i.e. self-knowledge? But what is underlined is that there is an essential value given to risk or an atmosphere of uncertainty, of evocation rather than information. This is not a claim for any virtue with regard to instability, but only a valorization of enjoyment: this mix of pleasure, frustration and relief, always propped up by there being something left to be desired, driving us on in further attempts, inevitably futile, to arrive at the implausible, the impossible, site of 'full enjoyment'. Phillips acknowledges – a form of covering his back – that any such statements of preference, in this instance for risk, will be implicated in a wider context of evaluations. So much of what I am saying is framed by the 'heroism of passion' (Phillips, 1994, p. xxii), and the enjoyment of the intrications of this, always in the service of the possibilities of potentiality. Ultimately this emphasis on seduction in the analytic encounter, the return of the repressed of psychoanalysis itself, gestures towards a different way of going about things. As Phillips says of flirtation (again not to conflate the two, despite a potentially fertile entanglement between the terms), it 'may not be a poor way of doing something better, but a different way of doing something else' (ibid., 1994, p. xxii). In other words, something other than the repair shop mentality of bad psychotherapy.

But let us move on to the final aspect of this interweave of psycho-analysis and disappointment, for, following Derrida, to do justice to psychoanalysis we must surely interrogate it. Is it possible that psycho-analysis has become hysterical? This is the story of a turning away from, an avoidance of, another scene. Indeed, this turning away occurs in the aetiology of hysteria, and is a latency in the discourse of psychoanalysis itself. Hysteria is inaugurated by an intense but improper pleasure, and this cannot, properly speaking, for propriety's sake, be admitted. To put it another way, the ego is so overwhelmed, so frightened, by this intense delight that it runs off in another direction. Indeed, Freud's theory of repression is based on hysterical repression, the hysterical defence against an overwhelming sensation of something being 'too much'. So what we glimpse is psychoanalysis being disgusted by this ineffable enjoyment and its retreat to a site of moral inadmissibility, of what is or is not allowed.

Possibly as an effect of dwelling in an age of uncertainty, an uncer-tainty regarding our very existence, we are subject to an imperative to prove this existence, so much so that it becomes an obsessive preoccupa-tion at the expense of any other desire. What we come to recognize is psychoanalysis allowing its enjoyment to be driven into this place where a principal concern is with shoring up its 'proper' identity, so that desire and the erotic – the risk factors – become displaced, secondary. Recently, at the Serpentine Gallery in London there was an exhibition organized by Damien Hirst, entitled 'Some went mad, some ran away'. Sitting outside the gallery was a dirty great purple box. It was utterly devoid of all illusion; there was nothing (more) to see; it said nothing, and in a literal sense was meaningless other than that it existed. What one witnessed, even engaged in oneself, was an extraordinary stupefaction – a forlorn peering, a touching, a looking round the corners as if to check the texture of the real, perhaps driven by a touching belief in magic, as if to verify to the point of giddiness the useless objectivity of things *via* a ritual of transparency. And this is precisely what psychoanalysis has become ensnared within: all attempts to define what the psychoanalytic tie is lamentably fail. As Bion claimed, it is ineffable, unrepresentable, unutterable, and it is crucial to maintain it as such. What has happened is that psychoanalysis gets caught up in a disembodied passion for transparency, and this can only lead to an insistent shallowness. Transparency is habitually linked to a fantasy of cleansing, a purification of the scene from 'swarms of healers', all entangled in a process of assumed contamination. Of course, so much of our culture is saturated by this voracious demand for representation, legibility, legitimacy and accountability, all of which congeal around this site where psychoanalysis meekly complies. Who desires this? Indubitably there is a collective collapse, an escape into this obscenity, this degradation of the enjoyment, this degeneration of psychoanalysis into a passionless conformity. Obscene because, like the close-up, the making transparent of the sexual act in the pornographic film, it is forced, exaggerated, rather than facilitating the secrecy of the private space.

Surely the very existence of a register of psychoanalytical psychotherapists, with the installation of potentially unending harassment – the question of insurance, ethics committees, standards and standardization: what was once 'free' by virtue of deregulated space is no longer so. Surely this must have effects, must transform our very habitat, so much so that the very survival of psychoanalysis may be brought into question. What is especially alarming is that this registration proceeds with a paucity of any thoughtfulness with regard to such potential effects. Can we not recognize a mutation of the psychoanalytic project *via* an irreversible tendency towards a formal homogenization into an imaginary single process, i.e. what is to be taken inside and outside psychoanalysis? The desacralization of the psychoanalytic situation occurs through this fantasy of regulation, an ecological ideal, informed by structures of control and management of an assumed whole. This computerized monitoring of the environment may culture out precisely what is valuable, that which constitutes the very site of psychoanalytic vitality: the play of seduction so crucially linked to the effacement of 'full signs'.

It may well become, *via* the immutable law of good intentions – this good will that, after all, only seeks to communicate, to enhance access but what it may become is a closed-off utility, a vast but ultimately diluted body wretchedly secured by this emphasis on omnipresent visibility. With these unquestioned virtues of communication assumed, surveillance prevails ... and surveillance of what? The risks of enjoyment? Aided and abetted by a dreadful focusing on consumption and efficacy, we rendez-vous with this grotesque and obscene disappointment. And this is destructive; it lays waste to the terrain, the stage that was previously preserved by a certain distance, by the maintenance of a secrecy of ritual known principally to the players. Naturally, one is called upon to acknowledge that something of this privacy elicits problems, particularly of elitism (even if it is open to all), and thereby engages in a form of alienation through separating one from another. However, at least it sustained otherness that could then be played out for better or for worse. But when all becomes transparent, all spectacle, all illusion is lost in the inexorable glare of an excess of information, by this pornographic insistence on legibility. Registration is informed by the fantasy of the close-up, and the idea of information as control. The body of psychoanalysis decomposes into a multiplicity of details, a register of numerical, synthetic images drained of vitality. This is the exact opposite of seduction; so rather than the richness of imagination, what we locate in such activities is only the allure of superficiality, and all potentiality for seduction recedes to the point of becoming lost altogether. Now it would be absurd to claim that the decline in the prestige and potentiality of psychoanalysis is simply an effect of registration. In fact, one might plausibly argue that registration, a concern for professionalization, is an effect of this decline. No doubt the reasons for this diminution and its continuation are multiple: the ending of the Cold War and a dissolution of boundaries *vis-à-vis* other disciplines have led to a blurring of the specificity of difference and a consequent activation of this preoccupation with identity – national, professional, or what-have-you. This is intimately entangled with a rise in fundamentalism and a wearisome immersion in nostalgic and ultimately self-perceptions. Now we may regard a disillusionment with psychoanalysis as not altogether a bad thing; perhaps it suggests that increasingly there is a realization that the capability of looking after one's own affairs resides principally in one's own hands. Perhaps.

But let us return to hysteria. The hysterogenic body, as distinct from the erotogenic, still has the power of thought and its will to enjoyment. We can speak of the body of *jouissance* and its entanglement with the addition of an artificial part to supply a defect, in this instance the sanitized space of the register. Their identity is inextricably caught up with 'hysterical desexualization', or as the psychoanalytical historian, Sonu Shamdasani, recently dubbed it, playing on the Foucauldian initiative, 'the great confinement'. A further characteristic of hysteria is to attribute to some unspecified others the responsibility for having 'spoiled' sexuality, as exemplified by an emphasis on the public need to be protected from sexual impropriety or other forms of exploitation. This is now installed as of paramount importance set within a context of a contagion of reproach, the dead hand of complaints procedures and a compulsive drive towards a setting up and a maintenance of a principality. It is as if psychoanalysis suffers in its own turn from the very disgust with the very body whose attempted cure had inaugurated the discourse in the first place. This particular form of suffering will inevitably have an array of symptoms, not merely the obscenity of registration, for it is also manifest in the theoretical difficulties with regard to the body (see Freud's uncertainty over the relationship between the psychical and the organic), the stagnant homophobia (see Noreen O'Connor and Joanna Ryan's *Wild Desires and Mistaken Identities*), its difficulty over the unrepresentability of the feminine drive (see Freud and penis envy and Lacan's unfortunate privileging of phallic *jouissance*), and finally the substantialization of unconscious process as if to make it a science, something proper, rather than allowing the possibility that it is constructed through another logic.

Some may seek to argue that in as much as one engages in a pathologization of psychoanalysis itself – and after all, why not? – allowing a bracketing of the problems congealing around the singularity of the name when the issue of the plural is so insistently at stake in this discussion. But let us once and for all do away with the myth of psychic health and any claim that psychoanalysis might have to be the sane authority ... but are not the structures of pathology more usually taken to be obsessional? Now both hysteria and obsessionality have difficulties with the construction of the erotogenic body, but for divergent reasons. In hysteria that which moves us is experienced as an inward movement, potentially an overwhelming dread of impossible desires. In contrast with obsessionality the dimension of movement is transposed outside the body and one is haunted by prohibitions rather than desire. Of course there are indelible traces of this with regard to contemporary psychoanalysis, ranging from a restaging of nineteenth-century attempts to outlaw itinerant hypnotic performers, through the concern of Freud and his followers about the proliferation of 'wild' psychoanalysis (see 1910 and the foundation of the

International Psychoanalytic Association) to the present-day configuration of anxieties. There are some people, and unequivocally I am among them, who might argue that what form of psychoanalysis other than 'wild' could one possibly want? Wild, not as in undisciplined – quite appropriately there are rules and rituals that inform the scene – but wild as in the wildness, the freedoms, of intimacy, sustained by the opacities of seduction. Indeed, let us give the last word to enjoyment, and to the old rogue himself, Lacan. He was addressing something quite other, feminine sexuality, yet it is so highly pertinent with regard to the repressed aspect of the psychoanalytic tie that the wretched issue of registration places in such jeopardy:

> There is an enjoyment that belongs to her and about which she doesn't know anything, apart from her experiencing it ... This she does know, she obviously knows about it when it happens. It does not happen to all. (Lacan, 1982, p. 145)

BIBLIOGRAPHY

Baudrillard, J. (1988) *The Ecstasy of Communication*. New York: Semiotexte.

Caillois, R. (1967) *Les Jeux et les Hommes*. Paris: Gallimard.

Cooper, R., Friedman, J., Gans, S., Heaton, J., Oakley, C., Oakley, H. and Zeal, P. (1989) *Thresholds between Philosophy and Psychoanalysis*. London: Free Association Books.

David-Menard, M. (1989) *Hysteria from Freud to Lacan*. Ithaca, NY: Cornell University Press.

Heidegger, M. (1971) *On the Way to Language*. New York: Harper & Row.

Henry, M. (1993) *The Genealogy of Psychoanalysis*. Stanford, CA: Stanford University Press.

Lacan, J. (1982) *Feminine Sexuality*. Ed. J. Mitchell and J. Rose, *Feminine Sexuality*. London: Macmillan.

O'Connor, N. and Ryan, J. (1993) *Wild Desires and Mistaken Identities*. London: Virago.

Phillips, A. (1994) *On Flirtation*. London: Faber.

Rodman, F. (1987) *The Spontaneous Gesture*. Cambridge, MA: Harvard University Press.

21

Dreaming Outside of Ourselves

James Hillman

A reply to the question, 'What will psychoanalysis be in the coming century?' depends on what we consider psychoanalysis to be, how it is defined. The sure solidity of its definition has been, especially in the past twenty years, seriously eroded. In fact, psychoanalysis can no longer define itself from within, since its own definitions – as a science of human nature, as a method of treatment, as a dialectical process of investigation and a theory of human development – have been thoroughly critiqued, refuted, and even held up as cultish shallow mysticism or worse, fraud.

Since I do not know what 'it' essentially is, I cannot speak about what 'it' will become. So rather than prediction, I would prefer to address the question of evaluation. What of its various virtues and strengths continue to prove fruitful and are worth maintaining?

Before we get to the fruitful, let's clear away what seems most barren. Let us ruthlessly ask psychoanalysis some questions, interrogate the field itself without denigrating its dedicated practitioners or its pioneering founders. First question: What value has psychoanalysis in this contemporary world of an endangered planet? Would the fish approve, the tropical forests? The undernourished, the jailed who do not deserve to be jailed? Does it bear in any way on the escalating technological networks of information? As a consciousness-raising societal force has it brought beauty anywhere? As a programme of self-reflection and sublimation has it internalized wasteful consumption; has it sophisticated entertainment, differentiated language, or heightened sensitivity to injustice?

Obviously, my inquisition intends a generalized 'No'. Psychoanalysis would have to bow its head in shame and admit its failure to address the major issues of our time. But then, maybe its defence rests on a simpler base. Psychoanalysis was never meant to carry responsibility for any of these large-scale dilemmas such as environmental distress and societal injustice. It is 'merely' a humanistic science aimed at relieving individual dysfunction by means of investigative insights leading to behavioural changes.

Yet even with this mildest definition of itself, it stands on wobbly legs. Individual dysfunction can be relieved promptly and effectively by pharmaceuticals; while the very idea of 'mind' is being radically challenged by evolutionary psychology, biogenetics and bioengineering. Moreover, the 'human' part of its humanistic science is narrowly western, white and young, and the 'science' part mainly an indoctrination of dogma by means of an orthodox systematic hermeneutics. So much for summing up in one paragraph what psychoanalysis has been accused of in the past twenty years.

What then remains? Where lies the residual good? I follow Ernest Jones in believing that Freud's formulation of repression and the unconscious were his most significant conceptual ideas. To me these two ideas recapitulate Plato's 'Myth of the Cave' (*Republic*): the human being is ignorant (unconscious) and ignores this ignorance (repression). This Socratic/ Platonic intuition of the human condition, translated by Freud into psychoanalytic language, is the main value of what his work brought into modern times from the Classical heritage (not Oedipus, Thanatos, Phallos, Libido, etc.). I would like to believe this value will be carried into the next century and any century thereafter!

This view states that the unconscious is neither a region of the mind, a system of dynamic impulses, nor a reservoir of images. Rather, it is a pragmatic idea that functions to tame the Promethean urges of human *hubris*. It says: you do not know what you know; all your truths are half-truths; all your life and its actions are shadowed by unknowing. Human life is situated in a profound invisibility that can never be mastered, and you, human being, keep this ignorance out of your awareness by means of repression.

Psychoanalysis acts as a critic of this ignorance, as violator of the innocence that is reinforced by repression. Therefore, its practice is a work of knowing in the midst of feeling the unknown and unknowable, a self-limiting, self-inhibiting ethical discipline, casting doubt on certitude, bringing hesitation to irrelevant desire and reflection to megalomania. Psychoanalysis: a last refuge of the moral reflex in a psychopathic civilization.

Because the discipline of psychoanalytic thinking tries to stay alert to the inevitable presence of the cave, psychoanalysis takes up positions outside the cave. Its thinking is that of the outsider, subverting and deconstructing the pervading innocence and persuasive delusions that inform society in general. It finds itself subversive, in essence revolutionary. In this way, as well as for its ethical concern, psychoanalysis remains in the Jewish tradition from which it originally sprang.

Finally, the dream. How shall we regard it now, a hundred years after Freud's extraordinary book? First, let us review just what Freud's accomplishment was in 1900. His *Traumdeutung* brilliantly solved the problem of the dream as it was then formulated. During the nineteenth century three dominating hypotheses held sway and conflicted with one another. The *Romantic* view regarded the dream as a personal message from the 'beyond' with personal significance for the dreamer. The *Rationalists* denied sense to dream content altogether. Romantics and Rationalists agreed that the dream — because it was nonsensical garbage produced by the mind/brain while resting (Rationalist) or it was poetic mystical inspiration from the deep soul or elsewhere (Romantic) — did not belong to the province of science. The *Materialist* view, in contrast, favoured scientific research, but only to prove the organic origin of the dream, its source in physiology. This research aimed to reduce dream events to body activities and sense-stimuli.

Freud's genius synthesized the three opposing views. By reasserting the ancient tradition that the dream has an immediate personal meaning for the dreamer, he absorbed the Romantic position. He also recognized the nonsense and irrationality of dream language, yet gave a rational account of the causality of this nonsense in what he called 'the dream work'. Thus his view was not only Romantic but Rational as well. Then, by means of the sexual theory of the libido, he could integrate the Materialist position that there was an organic basis for the dream. He thus brought together these contrasting strands of the nineteenth century and wove them into a coherent theory of dreams.

A hundred years later, what do we want to hold onto of this 'coherent theory of dreams'? Because of what has been so widely refuted and surpassed, we will no longer be captivated by Freud's 'science'. We will have to find new values in the dream other than revelations of infantile reminiscences and disguised sexuality. While holding onto the dream's importance, we will have to revise (why) it is important, no longer because it offers intra-subjective information, all about me. And, we will hesitate to interpret the dream by lifting repression from it with the selfish, empowering aim of gaining territory and energy so as to consolidate and strengthen the Promethean 'me'. Let's not forget, Prometheus was a Titan whose human-centred focus offended the Gods, cleaving us from them and disturbing the balance of the cosmos.

At this perilous point in the planet's history, we will have to go further out than even the Romantics, by drawing on archaic ideas of dreaming as a source of imaginal information from a psyche that is not merely mine, attached to my brain and within my skull. If the psyche is more than subjective, but has a collective, objective, transpersonal or archetypal aspect – which philosophical tradition calls the *anima mundi* – then the dream too must be referred beyond the person of the dreamer to the soul of the world.

This suggests that our dreams are dreamings of the 'other'. This other is not merely the other parts of myself ('my unconscious') or the other as the repressed, forgotten, distorted, disguised. Rather, the dream brings in the *fundamental* other – the 'not me' of the world and the specifics of how I am with it, in it. The world's soul echoes and moves its imagination in my dream.

The dream still remains 'mine'. It occurs in my part of the night. But as the night is not made by me, neither is the dream. In actuality, during the dreaming, I am in it, moving among its figures and scenes, held in its drama, which I did not write. I am in it until the moment of awakening, when I reverse the facts and take possession of the night by saying, 'I dreamt', asserting that the dream is in me. Yet, all night long I was in the dream.

Freud saw that the sickness of the other comes through the *via regia* of the dream. In his day, that sickness used young city women in centres of patriarchal empire (Paris and Vienna) to demonstrate its symptoms. Today, the symptoms are everywhere. The *anima mundi* is sick and the 'other' cannot be contained within the consulting room. After one hundred years, illness permeates the planet itself.

I am suggesting that we meditate dreams for a wider awareness of the cosmos that impinges upon us through the night-window of the soul. To refer the dream to the *anima mundi* implies that the dream be welcomed for its information regarding the state of the soul of the world. The *via regia* would now lead away from a human-centred psychology and into a world-focused cosmology – psychology deconstructing itself as it dissolves into cosmology.

We would still be following Freud's intentions and maintaining the deepest values of his thought because the unconscious would still be the concern of the work. However, the location of unconsciousness would now be out there rather than in us. We would still aim at lifting repression, though the content of the repressed would be different. For what is repressed today is the *soul* of the world, that the world of nature, of things, of technology and systems is not merely Cartesian dead matter, a barren objective *res extensa*, but also a *res cogitans* – layered with psychic potential once we shift our cosmology. That shift might end psychoanalysis as we now practise it, but it would provide a fresh vision for another century of Freud, his investigative intellect, his radical spirit, his therapeutic concerns for civilization, and his ideal of formulating a universally valid theory of psyche.

Afterword

Delirium, or the Sway of Desire

Anthony Molino

In a lovely chapter of his book *Einstein's Dreams,* Alan Lightman explores our all-too-human experiences and constructs of time. 'In this world', Lightman writes,

> 'there are two times. There is mechanical time and there is body time. The first is as rigid and metallic as a massive pendulum of iron that swings back and forth, back and forth, back and forth. The second squirms and wriggles like a bluefish in a bay. The first is unyielding, predetermined. The second makes up its mind as it goes along.[1]

It is the issue of time that I'd like to address. Of time and the times we inhabit, and about the peculiar relationship that psychoanalysts, in particular, have to time and history. A question arises immediately: mechanical time, or time of the body? In the writer's words: 'For miraculously, a barrister, a nurse, a baker can make a world in either time, but not in both times.' I'm sure that Einstein, who in the fertility of his delirium played with the concept as ruthlessly as anyone, would say the same holds true for a psychoanalyst. 'Each time is true, but the truths are not the same,' writes Lightman. Perhaps especially for a psychoanalyst. Another man, from another time and context but of equal stature to Einstein, put forth something of the same idea. His argument was that we ought not to serve two masters, indeed, that the very proposition is untenable. Which brings me to an incident that occurred several years ago, at the clinical facility of my psychoanalytic training institute.

I happened to walk in one afternoon on a group of trainees who were engaged, albeit in a kind of lazy and listless way, in a conversation whose overtones escaped me. I'd remained on the fringes of the conversation until a second-year student approached and drew me into the friendly fray. Apparently, the young man had been polling his peers on the attractiveness and feasibility of various graduate degree options, when, with the respect due a slightly senior colleague, he asked me what

I'd studied in college. 'Italian, and then anthropology,' I answered. I sensed what was coming.

A quizzical look lined his face when, in earnest confusion, he asked me the only logical question which, sadly and all-too-frequently, the times we inhabit generate in the minds of initiates. 'How do you bill?' he asked.[2] I say the question is a sad one, because it betrays the logic that has come to permeate psychoanalysis and, as Socrates might recognize, has come 'to corrupt the minds of our youth'. I realize fully, at this point, that to call on Socrates, Jesus, or Einstein – essential voices at odds with the oppressions of mechanical time – might well reflect some unanalysed sense of philosophical and moral superiority, derived from the most basic and primitive of sadistic urges or narcissistic wounds. But the verb *to corrupt*, at its root, means, quite simply, 'to break with'. And there is something being broken, if not already in need of serious repair, in the profession of psychoanalysis and, consequently, in the training of its candidates.

Once upon a time, the logic of psychoanalysis was the illogic of the unconscious. Amid contending and conflicted energies, which Freud himself was the first to suffer and embody, psychoanalysis struggled to define itself as art or science – where science loomed as the love child of Western positivism, conceived to dominate and slay the ill-begotten mysteries that for eons had riddled human existence. At its heart, even as the undying forces of ego psychology, medicalization, and now, the new economics of managed care systems tear away at an archetypal sense of what it means to be human, psychoanalysis struggles to retain the integrity of its origins. Born of myth, acknowledged by Freud to have been prefigured in the works of poets and philosophers, psychoanalysis was never elaborated principally as a treatment modality for colourful, reductionistic, and ever-changing and mystifying diagnostic categories. At its heart, in its conception, and for the men and women of later generations of analysts who fought, mind you, not to answer but simply to keep alive 'the *question* of lay analysis', psychoanalysis stirred a passion for the riddles of human existence and a genuine compassion for the pangs of human suffering that can never be encapsulated by any DSM III, IV, or 2004.[3] But it is the same logic that informs the medic-alization and dehumanization of our society that can filter down, on a lazy Friday afternoon, to the back rooms of a clinic and prompt, if not perversely legitimate, my young colleague's question. 'How do you bill?' In such a question – just in case psychoanalysts still do place any credence in the illogic of the unconscious and its storyed mechanisms of condensation, displacement, and symbolization – lie the rightful anxieties and apprehensions of a new generation of clinicians who, to a great extent, are already culturally estranged from the elements of passion and desire which are of essence to the psychoanalytic project.

'What is the analyst's desire?' I realize that the work of Jacques Lacan has found a great deal of America's psychoanalytic culture foreclosed to its articulation. There are several reasons for this phenomenon, not the least of which are the abstruseness of many of Lacan's writings and the iconoclasm of his person and technique. Moreover, rebels and marginals have always had a hard time of it on American soil, notwithstanding our culture's penchant for exalting individualism. At best, like a James Dean or Lenny Bruce, in accordance with some Oedipus myth whereby paranoid fathers plot the demise of their prodigal sons, such figures ascend to greatness, and sometimes godhood, only after they are slain or dead (of course, from the standpoint of myth, there are the occasional lucky sons, like Zeus and Isaac – but let's leave them aside). Happily, except in some cult-like circles, this process of deification did not happen with Lacan, notwithstanding his expulsion in the 1950s from the International Psychoanalytic Association – nominally, for his heretical practice of the short session, for tinkering with the question of time. But what I find most disturbing about the resistance Lacan encounters in American circles is the absolute repression of the question that marks the cornerstone of his inquiry, and his attempted revolution of psycho-analytic training.

'What is the analyst's desire?' Admittedly, a fundamentally Puritan culture such as the American one is at best ill at ease with the notion of desire. It's no coincidence that in the United States, where processes of infantilization are everywhere hypostatized, from the supreme idiocy of much contemporary television to the pre-Oedipal logic that informs that other favourite question of mine (take a guess: 'How do you bill?'), even psychoanalysis has managed to insulate and reify Freud's concept of the infantile wish, and to keep it uncontaminated from the insidious-ness of desire. How so?

Desire is something infinitely more complex than the wish, something vital and fluidly compelling, that only gels at the crossroads of Freud's radical dualistic vision of 1922, of the competing life-and-death instincts. Would it not follow that the repression of the very notion of desire has as its symptomatic correlate our culture's obsession with and denial of death? But that's all grist for the mill of another paper. What I want to stress here is that a psychoanalytic culture that cannot move beyond the

gropings of the wish is fated *not* to be able to ask its candidates: 'What is
your desire?' Not that the question needs a ready answer; it is simply
that the question demands being asked. For if it is not, psychoanalysis
risks staying stuck in the realm of the pre-Oedipal (or what Lacan calls
the Imaginary), wherein practitioners will invariably continue to value
therapeutic success along the lines prescribed by the dominant culture:
relationship, job, a semblance of 'happiness', etc. The analysts among us
need look no further than our own curricula: nowadays, where is the
father in our work, in our theories? Indeed, in this age of Freud-bashing,
the old man has come upon hard times even among certain psychoanalysts, as his genius cannot redeem his blind spots, his own human frailty
and history, and the realities of the patriarchal culture that formed him.
Lacan, the last father, has been all but barred from American training
programmes, which in many instances have gone so far as to deny visita-
tion rights even to the ghost of Hamlet's father ... And what is psychoanalysis left with? At best, only the corpse of desire and the skeletons of
passion. These, and a sterile sphinx whose empty question now
resounds: 'How do you bill?'

Mechanical time, or time of the body? There is a third time too, the
time of the unconscious, which is what Lacan dared to toy with in his
now notorious short sessions. A time which is closer, in all likelihood, to
the time of the body, but which the evolution of the profession has by
necessity compromised with mechanical time, the time of the clock. The
50-minute hour. Just enough 'time' to allow patients to prepare for ritual
submersions into the pitch-black waters of regression, to explore what
the liquid depths may have to offer, and to re-emerge, retooled, for the
light, at times unbearable, of day. The ritual has long been established.
And rituals, we all know, have their place – and not only in the lives of
obsessionals. But what Lacan did was to challenge not only the psychoanalytic establishment but the established, preponderant notion of
mechanical time, in a radical attempt to resituate psychoanalysis in the
very dimension of its own time: in the suspended timelessness of the
unconscious, where yes and no, past, present and future co-exist,
somewhere between the quiescence of Eden and the infernal throes of
Hades.

What I'd like to emphasize here is not the the feasibility or advis-
ability of applying anything like the short session. In fact, ideally, if one
were to remain consistent with Lacan's lesson, his example remains
inimitable: for to even attempt to duplicate the practice of the short
session, or anything else that pertains and is born of the Other, would by

necessity involve the adoption of Lacan's desire, and thus to remain estranged from one's own. Such a choice would cheapen our own own writhing, lifelong quests for oneness and unity: quests whose illusory quality is our common human heritage, mandated by the very lack that structures desire and that everywhere intimates our deaths in time. Such a choice would mean, as a result, to privilege the Imaginary, to assume the image of the Other's desire and to remain in an inherently narcissistic relation with Lacan or any other 'master'. But it would also mean to ignore – at our own risk and peril – desire's stubborn, capricious, ennobling capacity to inspire our creativity.

What I do want to emphasize, then, through the example of the short session, is the creative leap, outside of all mechanical time, that characterized one of the most controversial moments and innovations in the relatively recent history of psychoanalysis. In this way, what I aim to do is make a plea for the preservation of a creative spirit throughout the profession. This means to continually question the status quo, in both its maternal and paternal dimensions; it means to fight to preserve a sense of the unique history of psychoanalysis, and to reject the compromises imposed by ideological and economic superstructures which gnaw, like termites, at the core of its professional identity and mission; it means to cultivate, in the best Freudian tradition, a sense of integrity that is irreconcilable with a philosophy of 'How do you bill?'; and, for the analysts and would-be psychoanalysts among us, it means to question and plumb the depths of our desire so as to recognize, at some level of the layered sediments of our unconscious, that *to be* an analyst is to be engaged, passionately, in one's every fibre, with the radical otherness of our theories and derived techniques, indeed, with the radical otherness of the very idea of the unconscious. For the unconscious cannot be legislated, nor can it be usurped by insurance companies, HMOs and every other sort of corporate body that would flood our inner space – that free-floating dimension of the psyche reserved for the quasi-mystical movements of *reverie* – with forms and codes and sundry other pernicious infiltrations of a culture intent, not on questions, but on quick fixes and *prêt-à-porter* answers.

Caught in the cross-currents of a social and political history that was and continues to be adverse to the autonomy, if not to the very claims, of our profession – lest we, as psychoanalysts, forget that the very word has to do with what we *profess* – let us be clear about what makes us who we are, about what we do profess, and let us to try to be just as clear about what we purport to do and why we do it. In a posthumous book entitled *Meshugah,* Isaac Bashevis Singer speaks in semi-autobiographical tones through the voice of the main character, Aaron Greidinger, a 47-year-old narrator who, like the author, is a writer of fiction. Like his creator, Greidinger vigorously defends writing in Yiddish, a dying language. He says:

> Becoming extinct is not a shortcoming in my eyes ... Ancient Greek became extinct, and so did Latin. Hebrew was a dead language for two thousand years. All of us who are alive today will sooner or later become extinct ... [But] if Yiddish was good enough for the Baal Shem Tov, for the Gaon of Vilna, for Rabbi Nachman of Bratzlav, for the millions of Jews who perished at the hands of the Nazis, then it is good enough for me.[4]

In a similar vein, if it is the extinction of psychoanalysis that we are trying to thwart, in ways ranging from compromises with bureaucrats and approving agencies to the search for attractive, feasible, and 'licensable' degrees, let us seriously consider. extinction as a possibility. As Singer suggests, it is certainly no disgrace, and for people who ought to be comfortable with myths, the one about the phoenix is as good as any ...

Earlier I had dared speak of Einstein's genius as a form of delirium. Well, psychoanalysis, we all know, has to do with words. And the word *delirium* has a marvellous etymology. It derives from the Latin, from a time when the Roman empire was at its apex and archaic agrarian communities collaborated harmoniously in preparation for the planting season. Peasants would gather in the fields and set out together to plough the arable land. Well, what a plough leaves in its wake is a furrow, and *lira,* besides designating the pre-Euro currency of modern-day Italy, in Latin meant 'furrow'. And when one of the peasants in the group slipped, as would sometimes happen, into the mindless lulls of a daydream, he or she would invariably deviate from the straight and narrow furrow. This would concern the rest of the fraternity, who would immediately shout out to their deviant member: *'De lira, de lira'*: this, in short, to alert the daydreamer to get back on track, and straighten things out in a hurry.[5]

What I am saying is that we all need to be a little more delirious, more attuned to the sways of desire, to resist the processes of normalization, adjustment and accommodation that are today engulfing psychoanalysis. To this end, I want to cite a book that, to the best of my knowledge, has yet to be translated into English. *Une saison chez Lacan* is an autobiographical account of the analysis of a well-known French journalist and novelist named Pierre Rey. In the best French autobiographical tradition, with the models and inspirations of Montaigne, Rousseau and Pascal at his back, Rey weaves into the account of his analysis with Lacan a series of philosophical reflections on creativity and desire that sparkle like aphoristic gems, a few of which I would like to offer here:

Culture is the cumulative memory of the intelligence of other people. Culture is continuity.

Creation, on the other hand, is the opposite of culture. Creation is rupture.

The real creator will under all circumstances continue to create, but in new and different ways, pushing towards and beyond the limits imposed by language on his field of endeavour ... Like the peasant of Roman times, he will break into new fields, onto new openings, because in his delirium he has become fertile.[6]

If in the throes of desire I were allowed one wish, it would be for delirium to again pervade psychoanalysis, so that the latter might revisit the fertile rhythms of rupture, and not be seduced by the trappings of corruption. Would that psychoanalysts might hang on the walls of their consulting rooms clocks like Dali's, melting ....

NOTES

1. Alan Lightman, *Einstein's Dreams*. New York: Pantheon, 1993.
2. At least in the United States, billing practices in psychotherapy increasingly involve so-called 'third party payments' to 'approved' therapists by insurance companies and managed health care systems of whom the patient is a 'subscriber'. See Christopher Bollas and David Sundelson's *The New Informants: The Betrayal of Confidentiality in Psychoanalysis and Psychotherapy*, Northvale: Jason Aronson, 1995, for an incisive critique of such reimbursement practices and the dehumanizing market-economy logic that they reflect.
3. Here is what Bollas and Sundelson have to say on the influence of the psychiatric professions's *Diagnostic and Statistical Manual* (DSM): 'the DSM-ing of America is an unfortunate extension of the labelling of persons in a culture that seems blindly resistant to individual idiom. That such a mass assignment of selves into pigeon-holes should take place in a country that every hand-on-the heart day reminds itself of its freedoms is surprising only to those who are not psychoanalysts; this is a

country that too often talks about freedom but enacts restriction.' See *The New Informants*, pp. 133–4.

4. Isaac Bashevis Singer, *Meshugah*. New York: Farrar, Strauss and Giroux, 1994. Translated by the author and Nili Wachtel.

5. My source for the etymology of the word *delirium* is a chapter in Pierre Rey's *Sul lettino di Lacan: Il Romanzo di un'Analisi*, Milan: Arnoldo Mondadori Editore, 1991. Translated from the French by Doretta Chioatto. See note 6, below.

6. These passages are from the above-cited Italian translation of Rey's *Une saison chez Lacan*. The English translation of the excerpts, from the Italian, is my own.